This Thing Called Reason

This Thing Called Reason

Its Subjectivity and Dependence on Faith

By
BENJAMIN K. AKIH

WIPF & STOCK · Eugene, Oregon

THIS THING CALLED REASON
Its Subjectivity and Dependence on Faith

Copyright © 2025 Benjamin K. Akih. All rights reserved. Except for brief quotations in critical publications or reviews, no part of this book may be reproduced in any manner without prior written permission from the publisher. Write: Permissions, Wipf and Stock Publishers, 199 W. 8th Ave., Suite 3, Eugene, OR 97401.

Wipf & Stock
An Imprint of Wipf and Stock Publishers
199 W. 8th Ave., Suite 3
Eugene, OR 97401

www.wipfandstock.com

PAPERBACK ISBN: 979-8-3852-2546-0
HARDCOVER ISBN: 979-8-3852-2547-7
EBOOK ISBN: 979-8-3852-2548-4

VERSION NUMBER 050225

Unless otherwise indicated, cited Biblical passages are taken from the Holy Bible, New King James Version® (NKJV). Copyright © 1982 by Thomas Nelson. Used by permission. All rights reserved.

Scripture quotations marked RSV are from the Revised Standard Version of the Bible, copyright © 1946, 1952, and 1971 National Council of the Churches of Christ in the United States of America. Used by permission. All rights reserved worldwide.

Dedicated to the memory of my mother,
Anthusa Beh Geh Akih

Contents

Preface | XI

PART I

CHAPTER 1
The Concept of Reason, Though Widely Used, Is Vague | 3
   A. Pythagoras: Philosophy as Natural Philosophy and Theology | 6
   B. Plato and Aristotle: Idealism Versus Realism | 7
   C. Zeno and Epicurus: Theistic Monism Versus Atomistic Materialism | 10
   D. Augustine of Hippo and Thomas Aquinas: Faith Superior to Reason Versus Compatible Faith and Reason | 13
   E. Locke and Leibniz: Empiricism Versus Rationalism | 15
   F. Hume and Kant: Ethics Based on Passions Versus Reason | 18
   G. Hegel and Kierkegaard: Absolute Idealism Versus Subjective Truth | 22

CHAPTER 2
Reason Is a Goal-Oriented and Contingent Motion of Thought | 28

CHAPTER 3
Natural Science Can Be Pursued Without Invoking the Vague Concept of Reason | 44
   A. Causation | 49
     Laws of Nature | 53
   B. Logic | 54
   C. Probability | 56
   D. Coherence as a Test of Truth | 56
   E. Problem of Reference and Conceptualization in Science | 58
   F. Placebo and Nocebo Effects | 59

PART II

CHAPTER 4

Compositional and Causal Analyses Can Enhance Reasoning | 63
  A. Thoughts | 64
  B. Propositions | 64
  C. Assertions | 65
  D. The Nature of a Question | 66
  E. Thinking About Substance | 70
  F. Developing Part-Whole Intuitions | 73
  G. Developing Intuitions About the Principle of Sufficient Reason | 76

CHAPTER 5

Reason's Contingent Truths Can Come from the Knowledge of Natural, Social, and Human Sciences | 79
  A. Knowledge of Contingent Truths Through Physics as the Most Fundamental Natural Science | 81
  B. Knowledge of Contingent Truths Through Sociology—The Study of Human Beings in Society | 87
  C. Knowledge of Contingent Truths Through History | 92

CHAPTER 6

Memory and Imagination, Though Fallible, Are Necessary for Reasoning | 96
  A. Memory: Between Doubt and Certainty About Remembered Facts | 98
  B. Imagination: New Things from Connection of Units of the Familiar | 106
  C. Embracing Uncertainty in Reasoning | 110

PART III

CHAPTER 7

On the Universal Minimum Religion of Conscience as the Source of Reason's Goals or the Impossibility of True Atheism | 115
  A. Sense of the Divine (*Sensus Divinitatis*) and Conscience as the Seed of Faith | 117
  B. Protestant Theology and Ethics | 121
  C. Impossibility of True Atheism from a Moral Perspective | 126
  D. The Universal Minimum Religion Cannot Be Successfully Challenged by the Argument from Divine Hiddenness | 133
  E. The Yearning for Something More than the Universal Minimum Religion | 136

CHAPTER 8
The Universal Minimum Religion Develops Toward a Systematic Revealed or More Critical Minimum Religion | 139
   A. Philosophical Religion | 142
      Hesiod's Theogony and the Gods of the Greeks | 144
      Orphism, Personal Religion, and Orphic Philosophers | 145
      Stoicism and Epicureanism: Summit of Religion or Dead End? | 148
   B. Systematic Revealed Religion | 152
      Abrahamic Commandments as Extension of Minimum Religion | 156
      Systematic Theologies of the Abrahamic Religions | 158
   C. Reason Is Rooted in Faith, Not Folly | 159

CHAPTER 9
Rituals and Doctrines of Afterlife Are Central to Systematic Religion | 161
   A. Rituals as Indispensable Part of Systematic Religion | 163
      Membership Through Conversion | 164
      Prayer and the Forgiveness of Sins | 166
      Religion and Art | 171
      Atheists' Regret: Rituals to Rescue | 175
   B. Soteriology or Doctrines of Salvation and Funeral Rituals | 178
      Inhumation and the Linearity of Life | 182
      Cremation and the Cycle of Rebirth | 183
   C. Tolerant Religions in a Metaphysical Marketplace | 188

PART IV

CHAPTER 10
Ethics, Based on Sentiments or Reason, Rests on the Religious Conscience | 193
   A. Ethics Based on Reason or Emotions? | 195
      Hume, Moral Sense, and Emotions in Morality | 195
      Kant's Moral Philosophy: From Reason or Moral-Sense Theory? | 200
      Kant and Moral-Sense Philosophers | 200
      Conscience, More than Reason, Grounds the Categorical Imperative | 202
      Kant's Religious Faith as Source of His Moral Theory | 205]
   B. Pointing to Common Grounds in Ethics: Sidgwick's Methods | 206
   C. Against Utilitarianism: G. E. Moore on the Naturalistic Fallacy and the Open Question Argument | 210

CHAPTER 11

Ethics Is Based on a Religious Conscience: A Divinely Commanded Duty to Love God, Neighbor, and Self | 214
   A. Basic Elements of Religion for Religiously Grounded Ethics | 216
   B. Ethics Based on the Triangle of Divinely Commanded Love | 222
      How Much Love to Each of the Three Persons? | 223
      What Does It Mean to Love? | 225
      Imperfect Love that Tends Toward Perfect Love | 228
   C. Guilt, Injustice, and Evil as Opposition to Ethical Duty | 230
   D. Relation of This Religion-Based Ethical View to Others | 232

CHAPTER 12

Religion-Based Ethics and Reason Affect Politics, Economics, and Law | 234
   A. The State of Nature and the Primacy of Law | 236
   B. The Plausibility of Liberal Socialism | 241
   C. The Reasonableness of Multiparty Constitutional Democracy | 244
   D. Punishment | 248

Bibliography | 255
Index | 263

Preface

Although the concept of reason is widely used in philosophy and ordinary discourse, it is rather vague. This vagueness obscures significant debates wherein reason is contrasted with other concepts, such as reason and faith, with respect to the foundation of a general worldview; reason and experience, with respect to the source of human knowledge; and reason and emotions, as in the foundation of ethics. These debates proceed by presupposing that the meaning of the concept of reason is self-evident. But such presupposition renders it rather difficult to evaluate arguments advanced in support of one side of the debate or the other. Progress beyond this confusion ought to begin by recognizing the conceptual vagueness, and then proceeding to a search for a plausible theory of reason.

This book is a step in that direction. I have attempted a scrutiny of the concept of reason, leading to the idea that the concept is fundamentally subjective and dependent on noninferential matters of faith. It offers a theory of reason as an integrative motion of thought that connects a given circumstance to a desired goal by means of intermediate contingent truths. If this view is correct, then methodological conduct of reason depends on the size of one's inventory of knowledge of contingent truths. That is, it requires knowledge of various causes and their effects, properties of composite things and visions of goodness, beauty, truth, and justice. This implies that targeted improvement of rational thought can benefit from the study of causal and compositional relations as pursued in natural, social, and human sciences as can be represented by physics, history, sociology, and religion, among others. In assembling these knowledge elements, memory and imagination play a central role, but they are limited by their own inherent fallibility and subjectivity.

Despite the inherent subjectivity in reason and the tools used for reasoning, we can arrive at a practical consensus in reasoning exercises because we all participate in a universal minimum religion that grounds all human reasoning. Our conscience is the seed of this universal minimum religion. This implies that the nature and operation of our conscience lead to the realization that true atheism is impossible. The existence of a wide variety of religions can strike us as evidence against the impossibility of any such universal minimum religion. But this analysis argues that the variety of religions in the world arises from an unquenchable desire to further develop the innate universal minimum religion toward a richer systematic religion that features practical ethical teachings, useful rituals, and a doctrine of human salvation.

This analysis of reason and its associated universal minimum religion has far-reaching implications. It bears on debates about the relation between faith and reason as well as on the relation between ethics based on reason and ethics based on sentiments or emotions. The debates can be resolved by a synthesis that recognizes the centrality of faith in reason and the role of emotions in reflective ethical judgments. This new and original view of religiously constrained reason ought to also inform our thinking about law, politics, and economics.

This work further argues that the relation of reason to conscience, as the seed of a universal minimum religion, and the implication of conscience in emotions about right and wrong conduct, allow for a rapprochement between ethical theories based on reason and those based on emotions. A sketch is provided on how fundamental ethics can be grounded on a religious conscience that is minimally enriched by elements of systematic religion. Beyond this reformulated fundamental ethics, we can speculate on practical applications of the proposed theory of reason and its attendant religious conscience to law, politics, and economics.

I have written this work from the perspective of broad Protestant Christianity, where faith plays a more fundamental role and reason is generally considered suspect or auxiliary. This is a broad generalization but nonetheless true. I have tried to show that the fundamental suspicion arises from the fact that reason is vague and pretentious. Kant's critique sought to set limits to grandiose pretensions of reason with respect to human understanding. It left the vagueness of the concept intact. I have tried to show that this vagueness can be addressed by anchoring reason in the more dependable noninferential matters of religious faith, with human conscience playing the role of an innate universal minimum religion.

In terms of organization, the book is in four parts, each consisting of three chapters. Part I establishes the vagueness of the concept being analyzed and proposes a plausible theory of reason. Part II deals with the source of the contingent truths implicated in reason and shows their fallibility. Part III establishes the fact that the goals implicated in reason can be traced to a universal minimum religion of conscience that renders true atheism implausible. The extension of this minimum religion toward a richer systematic religion is then explored. The final part deals with pure and applied ethics emerging from the universal minimum religion of conscience, enriched by a generally acceptable result from systematic Abrahamic religions.

PART I

CHAPTER 1

The Concept of Reason, Though Widely Used, Is Vague

WHAT IS THIS THING called reason? Reason is generally contrasted with other concepts in various debates about reality. For instance, it is contrasted with faith as a superior source of a dependable worldview that guides human actions. Further, with respect to the source of our knowledge about the world, reason is contrasted with experience. Furthermore, when it comes to ethics, reason is contrasted with passions or emotions as a more dependable ground for moral actions. Given the significant role that reason plays in these debates and other general conversation topics, it is surprising that we do not have a clear theory of reason.

Some may say that we all know what reason is, or they may simply dismiss the question about its nature as having no practical use. But the various significant debates that implicate reason should prompt us to go beyond these dismissive attitudes.

We may hope that a conceptual analysis of reason will magnify the gap between reason and its contraries, but what if I told you that rather than clear differences, there is a fundamental relation between faith and reason, or between reason and passions? What if a critical analysis of the concept of reason revealed that it fundamentally depends on faith? This is the objective of this book.

I would like to first show that without a sound theory of reason—that is, an account of the nature of this thing called reason—the concept remains vague. In that vague form, it introduces many vexing problems into discussions implicating reason. The confusion worsens in debates where reason is contrasted with another concept such as faith or passions. It is largely due to this vagueness that some scholars have boldly suggested that faith has run its course in our society, and now is the time for reason to reign supreme. Sam Harris, for instance, asserts that

> it is time that we admitted that faith is nothing more than the license religious people give one another to keep believing when reasons fail.[1]

If two concepts are brought into such strong opposition, then we need to critically analyze their nature to judge for ourselves whether one side makes more sense than the other or whether the debate is ill-conceived. It would be ill-conceived if it can be shown that the two concepts contrasted do, in fact, stand in relation to each other, even to the extent that one depends on the other.

I would like us to analyze reason and explore the view that reason fundamentally depends on faith. If this idea is tenable, then the debate about reason and faith as contraries is ill-posed. One must then pay attention to the various degrees of reason and the nature of the faith that lies at its basis. By *faith* here we may tentatively refer to the religious notion of human beings standing in relation to a Supreme Being in their conception of reality and their grounds for moral actions.

Ironically, the relation of reason to faith is even hinted at during the French Revolution, when reason was elevated over faith as the guide to social and political life. Reason was fashioned after Greek religious myths, unleashing a heterogeneous cult. The revolutionaries destroyed Christian symbols at the Notre Dame Cathedral in Paris and set up the statue of Athena, the Greek goddess of reason. Later, influenced by Rousseau's idea of civic religion, Robespierre replaced this cult of reason with the nonspecific cult of the Supreme Being. Even in these tumultuous times, the historical intuition that reason is anchored in a religious idea asserted itself.

The debate about reason and faith is only one dimension of the discourse. We cannot help but contemplate the nature of reason when we take stock of other current public debates about social problems. Political debates on the relation of scientific knowledge to human actions sometimes appear irresolvable, with people often accusing one another of being unreasonable. Surely, if we have a clear understanding of reason and if we consider it to be objective, there must be a way to adjudicate conflicting views on issues of common interest by means of that reason. But if we don't have a clear understanding of reason, and it turns out after a conceptual analysis that reason is fundamentally subjective, then we cannot expect to agree on issues about which people from different cultural backgrounds are passionate. The

---

1. Harris, *End of Faith*, 232.

search for cultural intersection must be our first task before we return to the more controversial social problems that impact us all.

How can we analyze reason, a concept of both general and technical interest? It seems that we must choose a discipline that is most likely to reward our effort with clarity and historical context of the use of this concept.

Despite the unfortunate tendency for the mere mention of philosophy to turn people off, it is precisely this sphere of human knowledge that can be of most help in our situation. Unlike in ancient times, modern philosophy distinguishes between academic philosophy practiced by a few experts and general philosophy that deals with relatable daily problems. It was in this relatable sense that the ancients intended philosophy to be used: the examination and improvement of the lives of all human beings, not just the wisdom of a few experts.

With this ancient view of philosophy as a way of life, we will focus on the big picture of the way thinkers have used reason in their works. It would be good to do so with an eye on contrasting views and the evolution of the surrounding context. This concession does not diminish the strength of the arguments in support of a new theory of reason or the implications of this theory on religion and ethics.

This is how I intend to survey philosophical currents and their relation to reason. I take the relation involving God or gods, the natural world, and human beings as indicative of the main difficulty clouding the concept of reason. From this perspective, therefore, I will begin with Pythagoras and the philosophy he initiated. I will then look at pairs of philosophers in relation to their views of God-world, God-human, and human-world interactions. These are Plato and Aristotle; Zeno and Epicurus (with Epictetus representing the views of Zeno's Stoicism and Lucretius representing Epicureanism); Augustine of Hippo and Aquinas on reason and faith; Locke and Leibniz in relation to the reason-experience debate about knowledge; Kant and Hume in relation to their reason-passions foundation of ethics; and Hegel and Kierkegaard with respect to the contrast between objectivity and subjectivity of reason.

The suggested division is by no means exhaustive, and it is also not too long to establish the general idea that the concept of reason is vague. The proposed classification is intended to bring out the seed of the distinction between reason as subjective and reason as objective.

In general, we shall find that to thinkers who believe in the existence of God or gods, and that this existence affects the world and human lives, the contrast between objective and subjective reason does not arise. But if they were to be pushed to take sides, they would likely say that reason is subjective, and it is connected to the divine or to religion in a fundamental way. The opposite view would be shared by those who either question the existence of God or gods or those who acknowledge the existence of gods but deny their influence on the present world, its principles, and human affairs. That is, this camp would consider reason to be objective, that it is tied to the causal interactions of the material world, deterministically or occasionally admitting elements of chance.

A. PYTHAGORAS: PHILOSOPHY AS NATURAL PHILOSOPHY AND THEOLOGY

As the thinker who is alleged to have given the name *philosophy* or "love of wisdom" to the field, Pythagoras (570–495 BCE) presents philosophy as an inquiry into religion, human nature, and nature itself. He is said to have been a student of Thales, who is considered to be the first philosopher. The philosophy of Pythagoras encompassed mathematics, music, astronomy, and theology. It is said of Pythagoras that he considered the work of a philosopher as that of one among three types of people who go to a festival. The first type goes there to buy and sell goods; the second goes to compete in the games, hoping to win a prize and fame; but the third goes there to observe, to study, and to make sense of all the activities and make sense of the world. This third group of people are the philosophers, or lovers of wisdom.[2]

If one considers Pythagoras's view of the philosopher, and the fact that he held mathematics in high regard, it will first appear that he recommends a life of purely abstract contemplation of the nature of the world in mathematical terms. But quite the contrary, because most of what is known about him is derived from his descendants who seem to have been more attracted to the view of philosophy as a way of life that combines the intellectual study of nature and a religious life full of rituals.

In addition to the many rituals that characterized Pythagoras's religious school, there were distinct theological teachings that influenced later Pythagoreans and early Christians. Among these are the immortality of the soul, which soul Pythagoras believed to be transmigrated upon death into another body and returned until perfection was attained. Contemplation of the beauty of the universe allows one to understand the underlying essence—namely, the nature of number and reasons or what Iamblichus calls productive principles—which pervades all things. Bertrand Russell attributes the distinctive style of Christian theology in the Western world to the direct influence of this intellectual orientation of Pythagoras's theology.[3]

2. Iamblichus, *Life of Pythagoras*, chap. 12.
3. Russell, *History*, 71.

The practical import of this intellectual theology was to be found in the moral training of Pythagoreans toward frugality, friendship, and humble piety.

What has all this got to do with reason? By giving the name *philosopher* or "lover of wisdom" to someone who observes, contemplates, and tries to understand how everything hangs together, though fuzzy, we see elements of what may be rightly guessed to belong to reason. But philosophy is not purely for the understanding, it is intended to bring one's soul into harmony with the gods and with fellow human beings. Reason in Pythagoras appears then to deal with refining thoughts to better inform one's action, with rightness being viewed as that which aligns with the harmony of the gods. The triangle of God-world-human nature is tightly knit together in Pythagoreanism. Reason appears therein as human thought that apprehends this harmony, with the mystical role played by number and musical harmony.

Followers of Pythagoras see him as more than just a man, hence the fact that his life account is a blend of legends and facts. Iamblichus relates of mythologies linking Pythagoras to Apollo: either Pythagoras was sent by Apollo, or he is a son of Apollo, on account of the depth of Pythagoras's wisdom. This wisdom is viewed as a revelation from the gods rather than just empirical study of nature. He was influenced by Orphism, a set of beliefs and customs of the Greeks. Orphism features many prominent Greek figures who were thought to have contact with both the transcendental world and the physical world. Pythagoras's combined theoretical and theological orientation is crucial for his account of the physical world and mathematics. Reason in Pythagoras therefore does not easily side with our modern concepts of objectivism or subjectivism. It would be difficult for Pythagoras to take a stand in a debate about faith versus reason because reason, as the main business of philosophy, considers religion as the central point, including revelation and mythical aspects.

B. PLATO AND ARISTOTLE: IDEALISM VERSUS REALISM

The philosophy of Plato (ca. 429–347 BCE) can be viewed as Pythagorean while in Aristotle (384–322 BCE) we find signs of divergence from the Pythagorean emphasis on abstract ideas as being more accessible to us than the sensible world. In his introduction on Pythagoras, Iamblichus views Plato as the best of all the disciples of Pythagoras while Bertrand Russell opines that Platonism is essentially Pythagoreanism.[4] Although Aristotle

---
4. Russell, *History*, 37.

was a student of Plato, his views on religion and the role of mathematics in philosophy are different.

In a very general sense, differences between Plato and Aristotle can be seen in the orientation of their available works. Whereas Plato writes mostly on moral philosophy and its applications, Aristotle develops treatises on physics, metaphysics, ethics, and politics. Where their subject matter overlaps, Aristotle contrasts his views with Plato. As a result of these differences, we should expect the concept of reason in Plato to be closely related to moral philosophy, even if it also applies to the theory of knowledge. Although Aristotle's work includes ethics and politics, he engages with the study of the physical world empirically, and even his ethics takes on an empirical approach where virtue, as the observed mean in behavior, is the recommended principle.

We can understand Plato to be concerned with the key question that Socrates poses: How should one live? In pursuing this question, Plato offers a theory of the soul, according to which the soul consists of three parts—the appetitive, the spirited (*thymous*), and the rational (*logistikon*) or reasoning part.[5] A good life is one lived in accordance with reason, and that reason regulates the appetitive and spirited parts of the soul; these two, the appetitive and the spirited, must not be allowed to dominate a rational person's life. The theory of the soul is the building block from which the features of a just city are to be identified. Analogous to the soul, the city has guardians who excel in their use of reason, auxiliaries who are spirited, and producers who are like the appetitive parts of the soul. A city governed by philosopher kings—that is, guardians specially trained in reason—would be just, and it would lead to the flourishing of its citizens.

But what is reason according to Plato? Although he analyzes various concepts in many of his dialogues, reason is not directly subjected to analysis. Concepts such as knowledge, courage, piety, and the beautiful, among others, are analyzed. Although these analyses do not often lead to a conclusive theory of the targeted concept, they highlight the importance of conceptual analysis in philosophy. It is through clear understanding of the nature of a concept that we can then identify a particular thing as belonging to the class that is universalized by the concept. We can then also properly relate it to other things.

The inconclusive analyses of concepts do set the stage for Plato's more involved analyses. For instance, after the groundwork in the smaller dialogues on virtues, Plato analyzes justice in his major dialogue, *The Republic*. Here, the tripartite theory of the soul is expounded. Plato's justice emerges

---

5. Plato, *Republic* 4.

as the quality of the soul in which reason is the harmonizing principle; reason brings into concord other virtues that may otherwise be in opposition.

We can say that reason is used in ancient Greek philosophy as if it were self-explanatory; but it is by looking at how it is embedded in the triangle of God-world-human nature that we can surmise its meaning. For Plato, such insight is to be found in his theory of Forms and in the *Timaeus*, where he gives an account of the creation of the world.[6] The theory of Forms mediates the interaction between human beings and the world as well as between human beings and God. The world must have been created by God (Intellect, Craftsman, or Demiurge) after an unchanging pattern. He desired that the world be good, as far as possible. The Form of the Good is unchanging. What is unchanging can be apprehended by intelligence and reason, whereas the apprehension of physical and changing things amounts only to opinions. The unchanging includes Forms of virtues and Forms of things in the physical world. The soul, of which reason is part, is partly indivisible-unchangeable and partly divisible-changeable. Thus, we see that although reason is not separately analyzed, it is embedded in a theological framework and regulates human behavior as well as human understanding of the world.

As a student of Plato, Aristotle shares some of the views of his master, disagrees with him on other matters, and advances new ideas on a range of other issues. It is not easy to distinguish, coherently and consistently, the views of the two on some questions. But there are certain clear differences. For instance, Aristotle believes in an eternal universe and views God as an unmoved mover in a universe where things are eternally in motion.[7] He does not believe in the theory of Forms and his theory of the soul differs from Plato's in some respects. In the *Nicomachean Ethics*, for example, the soul is made of rational and irrational parts, with the irrational further divided into the appetitive and vegetative part.[8] These latter distinctions differ from Plato's classification; the vegetative part in Aristotle's theory does not participate in reason, whereas the appetitive part is responsible for desires and can be brought under the control of reason.

In discussing knowledge of the physical world in his *Physics* and *Metaphysics*, Aristotle extensively uses the concepts of causes, motion, and change. In his ethics, however, the rational soul is further divided into the scientific and the deliberative, with the deliberative being linked to practical wisdom (i.e., *phronesis*, which some refer to as "practical reason").[9]

---

6. Plato, *Timaeus*.
7. Aristotle, *Physics* 8.6.
8. Aristotle, *Nicomachean Ethics* 1.13.
9. Aristotle, *Nicomachean Ethics* 6.2.

A closer look at this practical reason can show how the ethics of Aristotle becomes less theistic than Plato's. Aristotle's ethics is oriented toward empiricism and reasoning about the real world, as opposed to transcendentally guided principles. Christopher Taylor[10] summarizes his discussion of practical reason in a useful way. Practical reason has to do with the true conception of a goal to be achieved and a deliberation of how to achieve this goal. The true conception of the goal to be achieved can be obtained: (1) by virtue of character, (2) by dialectic (that is, critical reasoning concerning authoritative beliefs), and (3) by induction from data of experience. What we see from these three sources of ends or goals of practical reasoning is that the sources are not directly linked to a theology or a transcendental idea, although the first can be developed toward theology. In the famous painting of Plato and Aristotle by Raphael, Plato is holding the *Timaeus* and pointing to the heavens, indicative of his rationalistic and theological orientation, whereas Aristotle is holding his *Ethics* and pointing out to the physical world. To Aristotle, man is a political animal and has a rational soul. This sets up his system in which scientific knowledge and practical reason (ethics) are derived from empirical study and reflection thereupon, either of the physical world or the political system in which human beings are embedded. His ethics seeks to achieve the average in the virtues already expressed within a culture. A transcendental source is not privileged.

If we are looking for a clear account of reason in Plato, and a refutation or endorsement from Aristotle, we won't come to a definitive statement. But we do see that in the theory of the soul and the relation of the whole to theology, Plato leans more toward theology, theory of Forms, and rationalism, whereas in Aristotle, we see more of empiricism and a simplification of the soul into rational and irrational parts, with the rational further divided into scientific and practical reason.

C. ZENO AND EPICURUS: THEISTIC MONISM VERSUS ATOMISTIC MATERIALISM

We want to look at Stoicism and Epicureanism, the former being a school of philosophy started by Zeno of Citium (334–262 BCE) and the latter by Epicurus (341–270 BCE). These schools emerged in the period of Greek philosophy after Aristotle, the Hellenistic period.

The difference in the conception of reason between Stoics and Epicureans is to be found in the degree of human dependence on the gods for their ethics and knowledge of the world.

10. Taylor, "Aristotle on Practical Reason," Abstract.

For the Stoics, the world is like an organism, essentially good. This organism is governed by divine reason and from this fact derives all principles that undergird the interactions of the various parts of the world. As a Stoic, Epictetus declares in his *Discourses*:

> If we could completely subscribe, as we should, to the view that we are all primary creatures of God, and that God is father of both gods and men, I don't believe that we would ever think mean or lowly thoughts about ourselves.[11]

Belief in God is thus a proper grounding of self-knowledge and actions based on that knowledge. In addition to this view, he asserts that human beings have bodies like animals, but they also have reason and good judgment, which they share with the gods. Our sense of the self is influenced by our understanding that we are part of the divine order. The ultimate end of life is to live virtuously, in accordance with the will of God as suggested by the concluding prayer in Epictetus's *Enchiridion*:

> Lead me Zeus, lead me, Destiny, to the goal I was long ago assigned, and I will follow without hesitation. Even should I resist, in a spirit of perversity, I will have to follow, nonetheless. Whoever yields to necessity graciously, we count wise in God's ways.[12]

Reason, to Epictetus, is the faculty that analyses itself as well as the other faculties; reason can evaluate itself with respect to what it is, what it is capable of, and how valuable it is. In addition to this analysis, reason can judge other faculties.[13] The use of the term *faculty* in reference to reason points to some ambiguity, since in some cases reason can be spoken of as a process or relation of things and in other cases as a thing, a capacity.

If Zeus (king of the gods) and the gods (intermediate between humans and Zeus) play a central role in the Stoic worldview, their role in Epicureanism is minimized. Epicureans seek a tranquil lifestyle, free from fear. Whereas human flourishing for the Stoic means living a virtuous life, seeking pleasure is the goal of a good life for the Epicurean. Pain, and not vice as in Stoicism, is to be avoided. The existence of the gods is acknowledged, but they are thought not to meddle with the affairs of human beings in the world. Politics is shunned, but the social pleasure of friendship is encouraged. The physical world is atomistic, where particles are in motion, and, occasionally, some particles suffer a collision caused by an unpredictable

---

11. Epictetus, *Discourses* 1.3.1.
12. Epictetus, *Enchiridion* 53.
13. Epictetus, *Discourses* 1.1.4.

swerve of a few particles. The soul is mortal, in contrast to the varying positions on immortality in Stoicism. From these elements of their worldview, the Epicurean use of reason can be contrasted with the religious worldview of the Stoics.

Most of the teachings of Epicureans have come down to us through the poem of Lucretius (99–55 BCE). The atomistic worldview leads them to mechanistic and causal explanations of phenomena. The concept of reason is therefore not a prominent feature of their philosophy. In place of reason, we find the concept of mind, which is also explained mechanistically in book 3:

> The mind is thoughtful by itself, rejoices on its own
> When nothing agitates the flesh and spirit.[14]

He continues:

> Nothing is speedier than the mind. We see that nothing acts
> As fast as the mind imagines and initiates. We find,
> Therefore, that nothing rouses itself as quickly as the mind,
> And what moves very easily must be composed of such
> Rounded, very tiny particles, the slightest nudge
> Sets it in motion.[15]

This mind grows in strength when combined with flesh and sensations of phenomena, but it is reduced to its basic elements at death. If one sets out to avoid pain and maximize pleasure, then knowledge of the nature of things, through experience and with the help of the versatile mind, can help to attain that goal. The gods and religion in general are a source of fear, though we are not told how this is the case.

Clearly, these two schools leave us with different views about the nature of reason, with the Stoic laying emphasis on harmony with divine reason, and the Epicureans seeking refuge in a mechanistic understanding of the universe to guide their quest for a tranquil life of pleasure and minimal pain. The path taken by Epicureans has a significant impact on natural science, where the study of stable causes and the nature of things can be conducted without direct reference to theology and ethics. We can show that in such study of stable nature, the concept of reason is not very useful. But how one relates the nature of physical things to how one should live remains a question because Epicureans presuppose knowledge of what they want (that is, pleasure) and what they want to avoid (namely, pain and fear of the gods).

14. Lucretius, *Nature of Things* 3.145–46.
15. Lucretius, *Nature of Things* 3.182–87.

Whereas Stoicism had a strong appeal among subsequent philosophers and the Christian religion, Epicureanism did not gain a strong following. Its significance lies in the transmission of atomism to renaissance science. Its weakness lies in its shallow moral theory, devoid of religion, that is an important aspect of human life throughout the ages. In this context, reason is not a very widely used concept in purely natural philosophy as can be seen in Lucretius's poem.

D. AUGUSTINE OF HIPPO AND THOMAS AQUINAS: FAITH SUPERIOR TO REASON VERSUS COMPATIBLE FAITH AND REASON

Augustine (354–430 CE) was a Christian philosopher with Neoplatonist influences. Aquinas (1225–1274 CE), on the other hand, also a Christian philosopher, was more influenced by Aristotle, though traces of Plato's philosophy are also found in his thought. Although philosophy in the pagan understanding included theology, in the Christian context, a distinction is made between philosophy and Christian theology. The latter, though developed with the influence of pagan philosophy, distinguishes itself in its subject matter and method. The revealed religion of Christians has the Holy Scripture as the main source for the study of God and his relation to human beings. Pagan philosophy, then, is not considered to contain dependable revealed religious truths, although useful ideas may be borrowed from Pythagoreanism and Platonism. Because of this clear divide, reason and philosophy are sometimes used synonymously among Christian theologians. In philosophy, the human quest to understand God, the world, and human nature is approached through speculation, reflection, and experience of the natural world.

For Augustine, faith is a more dependable path than reason to the knowledge of God and the self. In his *Confessions* he declares:

> For where I found Truth, there I found my God, the Truth Itself; which since I learnt, I have not forgotten.[16]

In his *Christian Doctrine* he declares revelation as the true source of the wisdom of God among human beings. Reason is severely limited, given that human beings, though endowed with an inner eye to know God, fail to do so because of weak inner sight.[17]

---

16. Augustine, *Confessions* 10.35.
17. Augustine, *On Christian Doctrine* 1.12.

Augustine views Christian philosophical theology as faith in the quest of understanding, an idea shared by later thinkers such as Anselm of Canterbury. In this process of seeking understanding, he recommends the use of tools developed by pagans, such as philosophy. The study of nature, history, and rhetoric are encouraged for the Christian teacher. Although these tools can help in developing a systematic understanding of Holy Scripture, Augustine advises that "it is safer to explain a doubtful passage by other passages of Scripture than by reason."[18]

For Aquinas, on the other hand, the relation of faith to reason is that of compatibility. Reason is mostly understood to be philosophy, which at the time encompassed all areas of knowledge. But the compatibility of faith and reason can only be concretely understood with respect to questions of interest. A useful summary of his views is provided by John Wippel.[19] Reason can prove the existence of God: from our understanding of motion to the need for a first mover; from cause and effect to the first cause; from the transition from not-being to being to the possibility of an Eternal Being; from our knowledge of degrees of perfection to maximum perfection in a Supreme Being; and from the ordinary causal patterns in things to the need for a Supreme Being who confers causality on nonthinking things. In addition to the existence question, the attributes of God can also be investigated using reason. These questions of existence and attributes of God are the subject matter of what is called natural theology.

Since not all human beings are capable of such rational enquiry into the existence and nature of God or the implication of that existence on human life, the grace of God's revelation is necessary. Aquinas thus recognizes the importance of Christian faith derived from revelation, notwithstanding his favorable view of reason.

The contrast between Augustine and Aquinas on reason and faith is partly based on the consideration of reason as philosophy and on the focus areas of their theologies. To Augustine and his followers, the proof of the existence of God is not of central concern; the existence of God is properly basic. Among later theologians with this view are William of Ockham, Martin Luther, and John Calvin. Luther is famous for having said that reason is the devil's whore,[20] a hyperbolic way of expressing the view that faith is superior to reason. In modern days, this position is defended by Alvin Plantinga of the Reformed Protestant tradition (Reformed epistemology). Aquinas and his followers would agree on the inaccessibility of certain revealed truth to

---

18. Augustine, *On Christian Doctrine* 3.28.
19. Wippel, "Aquinas, Saint Thomas," 38.
20. Blanshard, *Reason and Belief*, 130.

reason, but recognize the compatibility of reason and faith, especially in questions about God's existence. Followers of Aquinas accordingly devote more attention to questions of God's existence.

It can be said that Plato's and Augustine's philosophy constitute a set of methods with occasional insight that their followers can apply to questions of interest. This method-focused philosophy is visible in Plato's dialogues, some of which do not resolve the debate at hand but illuminate it. It can also be seen in Augustine's *Confessions*, full of unanswered questions that propel his thoughts forward. On the other hand, Aquinas synthesized Christian doctrines and Aristotle's philosophical system into the Thomism that is the main system of Roman Catholic teachings. This method-focused and system-focused contrast in philosophy played a role during and after the Protestant Reformation.

What is missed in the distinction between faith and reason in Christian debates is the fact that reason among the Greeks is rooted in faith and nature. The Greeks critically analyzed their customs and religion, expanding the analysis to the study of new questions and nature. This fact is obscured by the lack of a clear conceptual analysis of reason. If Greek reason comes with pagan faith, then Christian philosophy can be said to be cautiously protecting the purity of Christian faith from what they view as errors in the pagan faith.

E. LOCKE AND LEIBNIZ: EMPIRICISM VERSUS RATIONALISM

Let us turn our attention away from questions about philosophy and religion to knowledge in general, especially knowledge of the physical world. Where does our knowledge of the world come from? Two views stand in opposition, empiricism and rationalism, but their distinguishing features turn on the meaning of reason and the role played by the mind in the acquisition of knowledge.

John Locke (1632–1704 CE) is one of the British philosophers who defended the view that our knowledge comes from experience. In his famous essay he writes:

> Let us then suppose the mind to be, as we say, white paper, void of all characters, without any Ideas; How comes it to be furnished? Whence comes it by that vast store, which the busy and boundless fancy of man has painted on it, with an almost endless variety? Whence has it all the materials of reason and knowledge? To this I answer in one word, from Experience. In

that, all our knowledge is founded; and from that it ultimately derives itself.[21]

From this passage, we get the idea of the mind at birth being a tabula rasa, a blank slate. Our knowledge comes from sensation from without or reflection on ideas acquired from sensation. Locke uses reason interchangeably with understanding as faculties but defines reason when he refutes the possibility of using reason to discover supposedly innate ideas. He asks how can reason be used to discover innate principles

> when reason ... is nothing else but the faculty of deducing unknown truths from principles or propositions, that are already known?[22]

According to this definition, reason is a capacity used to obtain, by deduction, new propositions from generalizations or other propositions. Defined this way, reason to Locke is the same as logic, concerned solely with deductive inference; it does not seem to include induction (inference from particulars to the universal) and abduction (inference to the best explanation).

Locke does not tell us exactly the mechanism by which reason and knowledge arise from his experience. This point is picked up by Leibniz in his reaction to Locke:

> Although the senses are *necessary* for all our actual knowledge, they aren't *sufficient* to provide it all, because "The senses never give us anything but *instances*, i.e. particular or singular truths. But however many instances confirm a general truth, they aren't enough to establish its universal necessity; for it needn't be the case that what *has* happened always *will*—let alone that it *must*—happen in the same way."[23]

The deductive and inductive principles used to anticipate new situations based on past experience must arise from something that is not given by experience—something that already exists in the mind. According to Leibniz, logic, metaphysics, ethics, and natural philosophy rely on principles that are innate.

Leibniz sheds light on his innate ideas by offering some principles. To these belong the principles of noncontradiction, sufficient reason, and identity of indiscernibles. Noncontradiction is a fundamental principle of

---

21. Locke, *Essay* 2.1.2.
22. Locke, *Essay* 1.2.9.
23. Leibniz, *New Essay*, 2.

logic; the mind knows innately that a thing cannot both exist and not exist at the same time. The principle of sufficient reason is a fundamental law for phenomena; it is innately grasped that all things happen for a reason or cause—that is, events are effects of earlier causes. This innate principle is not concerned with the obvious difficulty that in most cases we do not know the causes. From the principle of identity of indiscernibles, many units of the same type of thing can be grasped and pulled into inferences about their relations to other things. Further, Leibniz identifies two truths: truths of reasoning that are necessary by logic and truths of facts that are contingent and knowable by experience.

Although Locke and Leibniz differ, they are closer than generally appreciated. Although an empiricist, Locke displays some awareness of the rationalist's preoccupation about how sensed experience becomes knowledge, though he tries to address these by appealing to repeated exposure to the same experiences. Leibniz, though a rationalist, understands the participation of sense experience in the acquisition of knowledge of facts.

These two thinkers are from the early modern era of philosophy initiated by Descartes. A general feature of this period is that they take seriously the assertion of Protagoras that man is the measure of all things; that is, man is the measuring instrument by which knowledge of the world is acquired. We may use a barometer to measure the pressure of the atmosphere; in the study of the world, including the place of humans in it, we are using the human being as an investigative instrument. Descartes initiates the tradition of first critically examining this instrument to ensure its proper functioning and preclude our ultimate deception about the world we experience. This is subjectivity in a very broad sense; it places the enquirer, the human being, on the examination stand to ascertain how they gain knowledge of the external world, and how they keep track of their knowledge from one point in time to a later time.

The views of Locke and Leibniz on knowledge of the outside world find their synthesis in Kant's epistemology. In a sense, it can be said that Kant further develops the ideas of Leibniz on the cooperation of the mind with sense data in forming ideas about things as they appear, and speculatively, linking them to the inaccessible nature of things-in-themselves. Contrasting Lockean empiricism with Leibnizian rationalism shows how problematic the dichotomy is, since the two are rather close and differ only on how simple ideas are connected and generalized. This problem is caused by the lack of a detailed account of reason. We don't know how reason is related to innate ideas and perceived sense data. We can therefore conclude that the rationalist-empiricist debate owes its significance to the vagueness of reason.

F. HUME AND KANT: ETHICS BASED ON PASSIONS VERSUS REASON

Two opposing views on the foundation of ethics can be represented by David Hume (1711–1776 CE) and Immanuel Kant (1724–1804 CE), the former claiming that ethics is based on passions, and the latter defending reason as the proper basis for ethics. This is an important question since ethics concerns us all, much more than other branches of knowledge. Hume's position is a departure from a historical trend, where it was generally acknowledged by the ancients that a life lived in accordance with reason is to be preferred as virtuous over one lived according to the passions. Even in Plato's theory of the soul, passions must come under the regulating authority of reason for there to be virtue in human behavior.

Hume rejects reason as a determinant of the human will to act:

> Reason is, and ought only to be the slave of the passions, and can never pretend to any other office than to serve and obey them.[24]

But what is reason to Hume? In his treatise, he says:

> Reason is the discovery of truth or falsehood. Truth or falsehood consists in an agreement or disagreement either to the real relations of ideas, or real existence and matter of facts.[25]

Reason therefore obtains from juxtaposing and comparing ideas, a process that Hume considers to be incapable of determining the will. Since this reason is concerned with ideas in a human mind, operated without direct reference to God or the world without, reason is therefore associated with the subject—in a sense, it is subjective—in line with modern philosophy's focus on the human as an instrument for knowing the world.

But how are passions the determining forces for moral actions? According to Hume, "morals excite passions, and produce or prevent actions."[26] This seems to be circular because it is not clear what morals consist in since they could refer to reflections on a situation or impressions produced by a situation. The sense in which he uses passions derives from his classification of perceptions. These are divided into impressions and ideas, with the impressions consisting of sensations, passions, and emotions. Here, sensations are primary impressions whereas passions and emotions are secondary or reflective impressions.

---

24. Hume, *Treatise of Human Nature*, 318.
25. Hume, *Treatise of Human Nature*, 355.
26. Hume, *Treatise of Human Nature*, 355.

If passions arise reflectively from primary impressions which lead to ideas, and if the process of reasoning involves juxtaposing and comparing ideas, it seems then that a region of intersection escapes Hume's thinking. Had he not defined his reason in terms of discovery of truth and falsehood (absolutes), it would have dawned on him that passions may be a degree of reason.

On the face of it, Hume's position on the source of morality can be viewed as a statement against reason. A similar position is taken by Rousseau in his moral thought, emphasizing compassion, closer to Hume's passions. Reason, to Rousseau, has a corrupting role in society, where earlier societies that were guided by conscience and compassion are portrayed in a more positive light. Thus, there is a relation among conscience, passions, and compassion. What has not been given serious consideration in the literature is that, despite his agnostic position, Hume is a Calvinist, just like Rousseau. Calvinist moral thought in Hume can perhaps be traced to Francis Hutcheson, deemed to be the father of the Scottish Enlightenment. Their skepticism about reason traces back to Augustinianism in Protestantism. We shall return to this point in parts III and IV, where we consider the implication of the account of reason in chapter 2 on religion and ethics. Let us first consider Kant's position on ethics.

Kant is closely associated with the view that reason is the source of ethical principles. Thinkers before him, in the Platonic and Stoic traditions, also identify reason as a guide to right actions but they do so with emphasis on the role of the soul. Kant offers a path that can appeal to those hesitant to invoke theological concepts in ethics.

Three questions, according to Kant, ought to interest philosophy as a system of inquiry: What can I know? What ought I to do? What may I hope? The first is obviously epistemological. The second question is concerned with ethics and already demonstrates his view of ethics as having to do with one's duty or obligation. This deontological presumption can be discerned from Protestant ethics, drawing from Augustine and Plato. It is contrasted with virtue ethics in the Catholic tradition, traceable to Aquinas and Aristotle. Having posed the problem of ethics as that of duty, the search for a principle is then a search for an imperative, a command. In revealed religion, this principle of duty is supplied as a divine command. We will explore in parts III and IV the view that Kant's ethical and theological systems are mostly based on the logic of a revealed religion—that is, Christianity in its Protestant interpretation.

The imperative, Kant maintains, must be categorical; it must not deal with any specific or hypothetical goal but must be general. This categorical imperative is then the supreme principle of morality ascertained by reason.

It reads, "Act only in accordance with that maxim through which you can at the same time will that it became a universal law."[27] The moral agent must see themselves as a legislating authority and take the course of action that could be a universal law without unethical consequences.

If the categorical imperative is the dictate of reason, what is reason to Kant? In the preface to the second edition of the *Critique of Pure Reason*, Kant speaks of reason in terms of a coherent whole of related ideas or principles:

> Pure speculative reason is an organic structure in which there is nothing isolated or independent, but every single part is essential to all the rest; and hence, the slightest imperfection, whether defect or positive error, could not fail to betray itself in use.[28]

In the introduction to *Groundwork*, Kant distinguishes between directing a will to its object and producing a will that is good in itself. It is the duty of practical reason to influence the will so that it becomes good in itself; it is not the role of reason to direct the will to its object of moral action.

It is difficult to nail down Kant's meaning of reason because it is shifting and, when defined as above or used in relation to the will, it fails to give us a mechanistic view of how reason operates and what its constituent elements are. This difficulty is evident when Kant uses pure reason, by which he is referring to scientific knowledge as acquired with the help of experience and a priori principles. Practical reason, as used by other philosophers before him, is supposed to be reason that is related to moral action. But elsewhere, Kant speaks of pure practical reason, by which is meant a certain metaphysics only concerned with moral principles and not moral actions themselves.

In Kant's *Religion Within the Bounds of Bare Reason*, an argument is made for belief in God from the existence of the moral law. Kant goes on to defend Christian dogmas, especially the two commandments to love God and neighbor, showing their relation to the moral law. Kant answers the third question, what may I hope, with reference to a teleology that is basically Christian in its outlook. These Christian sources, it seems, are the true sources of Kant's main moral principle, with reason being applied as a way of making the imperative coherent through universalization.

After establishing the proper relation of metaphysical speculation to experience that is required to produce knowledge, Kant points out the difficulty in using pure reason in the study of God and the soul. Here he admits

---

27. Kant, *Groundwork*, 37.
28. Kant, *Critique of Pure Reason*, xxxvii.

that he cannot even use the concepts of God, freedom, and immortality because they are not accessible through experience. This leads him to the statement: "I must, therefore, abolish knowledge, to make room for belief."[29] Here is a hint of Kant's dependence on his religious faith. Brought up as a Pietist Christian, he is closer to the Calvinist branch of Protestantism, and so, by upbringing, is closer to Rousseau and Hume on the supremacy of conscience, including religious conscience, on the crucial questions of our duty toward others. About this moral duty, the sensible world cannot tell us much.

If this sounds as if we are misinterpreting Kant or reading too much into his biography, consider his first statement in the conclusion of *Critique of Practical Reason*, the beginning of which is on his tombstone:

> Two things fill the mind with ever new and increasing admiration and awe, the oftener and more steadily we reflect on them: the starry heavens above and the moral law within me. I do not merely conjecture them and seek them as though obscured in darkness or in the transcendent region beyond my horizon: I see them before me, and I associate them directly with the consciousness of my own existence.[30]

The immediacy with which Kant apprehends these two objects of wonder appears much closer to his third critique, *Critique of Judgment*, where aesthetics and teleology are brought together. It is by combining Kant's aesthetics, philosophy of religion, and the vagueness of reason in his system that we gain insight into the true source of his categorical imperative. The religious source, not the cloudy concept of reason, may be justifiably advanced as the foundation of Kant's ethics. Closely examined, that source turns out to be linked to conscience. If this is the case, Kant may be far from Hume in the vagueness of his rationalistic theory but closer to him in practice through his appeal to a religious conscience. In fact, one can agree with Onora O'Neill when she charges Kant with antirationalism and characterizes his practical philosophy as ultimately saying "the categorical imperative is the supreme principle of reason."[31] As to the source of the categorical imperative, she rightly points to Kant's theology, which leans more toward revealed religion than purely rational theology, as Kant claims.

Hume's account of morality seems to capture the way things are in society. If we combine the vagueness of reason with the popular notion that most people are unreasonable, we can see why we tend to point to passions

29. Kant, *Critique of Practical Reason*, xxxiv.
30. Kant, *Critique of Practical Reason*, 166.
31. O'Neill, *Constructions of Reason*, 3–4.

that are supposedly opposed to reason to be the motivation for human actions. People seem to wish for a society where people are more reasonable. Kant's moral theory offers a desirable vision of that society and how reason can take us there. The only problem is what we mean by reason; if we cannot universalize the tool for determining the good will, we can't hope for a society where the categorical imperative determines morality. What really is reason? Does everyone have it to the same degree? If not, how does one develop it? These are questions which demand answers, considering the conflicting positions and shifting use of the concept.

G. HEGEL AND KIERKEGAARD: ABSOLUTE IDEALISM VERSUS SUBJECTIVE TRUTH

Of all the contrasts based on the use of reason so far, none is as far apart as the absolute idealism of Georg W. F. Hegel (1770–1831 CE), which is a rationalistic and holistic system, and the subjective truth of Søren Kierkegaard (1813–1855 CE), which is a passionate defense of Christian faith as subjective truth. Despite this clear difference related to emphasis on the objective and the subjective, some scholars think the influence of Hegel on Kierkegaard and their similarities have not been given due consideration.[32]

Hegel's philosophy is very speculative and challenging to readers. Bertrand Russell considers him to be one of the most difficult philosophers to understand. Perhaps we should ask the question what reason means to Hegel. In his words, reason is related to God and is a complex union of substance and power:

> Through its speculative reflection, philosophy has demonstrated that Reason—and this term may be accepted here without closer examination of its relation to God—is both substance and infinite power, in itself the infinite material of all natural and spiritual life as well as the infinite form, the actualization of itself as content. It is substance, that is to say, that by which and in which all reality has its being and subsistence. It is infinite power, for Reason is not so impotent as to bring about only the ideal, the ought, and to remain in an existence outside of reality—who knows where—as something peculiar in the heads of a few people.[33]

---

32. McLaughlin, "Relation Between," 338–39.
33. Hegel, *Reason in History*, 11.

A variant of this also appears in his larger *Philosophy of History*. The difficulty this definition presents to the reader is attacked in the opening paragraph of Hans Reichenbach's *Rise of Scientific Philosophy*. As a positivist bent on clarity and verificationism, Reichenbach finds no justification for such convoluted statements. The truth is that one cannot understand Hegel's view of reason without understanding the springboard of his philosophy. It is helpful to see two key influences on Hegel's metaphysics—namely, Kant's writings on history and politics on the one hand, and Lutheran doctrine on Holy Communion or the Eucharist on the other.

In Hegel, universal history unfolds according to reason, evolving toward a goal. This teleological approach and the role of conflict or contradiction are anticipated in Kant's "Idea for a Universal History," "The End of All Things," and the "Speculative Beginning of Human History." It is easy to see some of these influences once the relevant works of Kant are identified, but what is more difficult to understand is the source of his absolute idealism, a system in which the rational alone is real.

Hegel's background as a Lutheran theologian is often missed in the interpretation of his metaphysics. It is in the Lutheran view of Christ's presence at Holy Communion that we find inspiration for his idealism. An indication of this is in his *Philosophy of History* where he discusses the Protestant Reformation. Protestantism rejected the Catholic doctrine of transubstantiation, according to which Christ is bodily present in the Eucharist. In contrast to the Calvinist view of Holy Communion as a commemorative act, the Lutheran view, which Hegel enthusiastically expounds on, is that Christ is an actual presence, but his presence is only in faith and Spirit. That is, the body of Christ, a real object, is present at the sacrament, not as a physical object but as Spirit, which the believer immediately grasps in faith and contemplation. This is the seed of Hegel's idealism: a real body of Christ is present as an idea, a spirit. To this, one can add his characterization of the Reformation as essentially announcing that man is destined to be free.

To go from the subjective relation to Christ to the objective, Hegel draws from the idea that "God was in Christ reconciling the world to Himself"[34] to develop his idea of the Absolute Spirit—that is, God, in Christ Jesus, with man and the world reconciled to himself. It is hard to miss the Protestant bias toward the end of his *Philosophy of History*. According to Hegel, a unity between private and public life is achieved in Protestantism and the Church and State have reached a degree of harmony, even if formally separated. This leads him to point to Protestant Europe and Protestant North America as evolving in the direction of realizing the Absolute Spirit.

---

34. 2 Cor 5:19.

Logic to Hegel seems to be more related to the Logos or the Word of God that became flesh in John's Gospel. Christ existed as the Word before and during the creation of the world. But in his incarnation, that Word became flesh; that is, spirit became an object. In Holy Communion, the physical becomes spiritual and is apprehended by faith, while in incarnation, the Spirit becomes physical in the person of Jesus Christ. The interchangeability of an idea with physical reality is thus hinted at. The consequence of Hegel's system built on these theological premises is that in the ethical life, the objective and the subjective are present and are alike. The state plays a far greater role in his system, since the state is closer to the whole, the absolute, than the individual.

In contrast to Hegel's dissolution of the individual into the overwhelming political theatre of the state, Kierkegaard is concerned with the individual, especially the subjective faith of the individual as truth. His position is not only an attack against Hegel's speculative philosophy, it is also an attack against the Enlightenment's project of reason grounded in empirical knowledge. The Enlightenment's position directly leads to the flourishing of Deism, the view that acknowledges God as creator but declares that God does not interfere in the affairs of the world. To understand Kierkegaard's faith-based subjectivity, his religious background is also relevant. Kierkegaard is, like Kant, a Pietist Lutheran—that is, he belongs to a movement in Lutheranism which adopted elements of personal piety from Calvinism. The individual and their personal relation to God are central to religious practice. From this perspective, the disagreement between Kierkegaard and Hegel is quite expected.

Kierkegaard draws from Socrates's relation to reason to point out a paradox he perceives:

> The supreme paradox of all thought is the attempt to discover something that thought cannot think.[35]

In thinking, the individual participates in something that transcends themselves and cannot therefore grasp truth and falsehood based solely on thinking about the transcendent.

To Kierkegaard, the truth that is worthy to die for is subjective. One must seek to understand oneself and what is true for that oneself:

> What I really need is to be clear about what I am to do, not what I must know, except in the way knowledge must precede all action. It is a question of understanding my own destiny, of seeing what the Deity really wants me to do; the thing is to find a truth

---

35. Kierkegaard, *Philosophical Fragments*, chap. 3, para. 1.

which is truth for me, to find the idea for which I am willing to live and die.[36]

But what is that truth for which one can live and die? It is faith, the highest of all passions. Kierkegaard famously uses the story of Abraham being asked by God to sacrifice his only son. Abraham's behavior distinguishes him as a knight of faith. Faith requires a double movement: first, an infinite resignation to God; and second, a regain of that which was lost in the first movement. To see how this applies generally to those who embrace faith, one must appreciate that God presents himself to Abraham with a task that requires resignation, but the resignation ends in a regain of what was lost. Reason cannot grasp this paradox and cannot be the ground for one's faith. With this picture of faith, it cannot be related to reason as in Hegel's system. A decision is involved, a resignation, on the part of the individual.

Kierkegaard's philosophy questions some presuppositions in Hegel's system that seem compatible with the Christian faith. Hegel's system assumes the truth of Christianity, especially in the Protestant expression of it. This makes Protestant Christianity a higher stage in the evolution of the Spirit. Hegel also assumes that everyone living in the Christian state is a Christian and then focuses on investigating the nature of the state and its institutions. A Pietist Christian such as Kierkegaard is apt to see this as absurd and a disregard of the individual's place in Christianity. Coming to faith is a personal decision, an inward experience, Kierkegaard would say. One must make the required leap of faith as an individual, not be presumed to have done so simply because one lives in Christendom. In his development of the state as if the secular world has become the spiritual, Hegel suggests that there is no distinction between the visible and the invisible church, the latter being the realm of the subjective and spiritual.

Kierkegaard is viewed as the first existentialist philosopher since the modern era of philosophy from Descartes. He deals with problems of the heart in a way that returns philosophy to the ancient view as a subject dealing with how one should live. By the time of Kierkegaard, empirical science had clearly defined its territory and Kierkegaard's philosophy is not in dispute with that body of knowledge in natural philosophy. In the realm of ethics and faith, he is persuasive about the failings of Hegel's philosophy to address the anxiety of the single individual. Also, if one observed the earth from a distant planet such as Jupiter, the grandiose movements of the Spirit speculated by Hegel would be hardly observable; yet his absolute idealism concerns the universe and the minds of feeble rational beings. It is only in the subjective realm of human beings that the religious development of the

---

36. Kierkegaard, *Journals AA–DD*, 19.

world can be appreciated against the backdrop of a planet that seems to spin and revolve in indifference from a cosmological standpoint.

This brings us to the end of our selective survey of reason in philosophy, especially as it applies to the theory of knowledge, foundations of ethics, and religious knowledge. We have seen that reason is either presupposed or each philosopher gives an inconsistent account. This vagueness is not limited to the distant past. In developing the reason-based ethical theory called contractualism, T. M. Scanlon opens *What We Owe to Each Other* with the declaration "I will take the idea of a reason as primitive."[37] This may be true for *a reason* for something being one way and not the other. We understand this as a cause or a warrant for something to be in a certain way. But when we refer strictly to reason, the vagueness so far discussed beckons for analysis.

The debates arising from the largely unnoticed vagueness are of great social value. The opposition of rationalism to empiricism seems to have found its resolution in the practice of science where hypotheses sometimes arise from speculation and are later verified in experience. Kant's contribution to that resolution is important. The hypothetico-deductive method in science already suggests that, although empiricism is at the center of science, its quality differs, with the result that a more efficient scientific procedure is one that benefits from the hypothetico-deductive method.

In ethics, the gulf between ethics founded on reason and that founded on passions is beginning to be questioned by research in neuroscience. Based on studies of the brain, Antonio Damasio finds a closer link between reason and feelings than is admitted in current discourse. He says:

> Reason does seem to depend on specific brain systems, some of which happen to process feelings. Thus there may be a connecting trail, in anatomical and functional terms, from reason to feelings to body. It is as if we are possessed by a passion for reason.[38]

Conceptual analysis of reason can help scientific research that seeks to unravel the secrets of human feelings and human understanding. The narrowing of the gap between rationalism versus empiricism and reason versus passions suggests that once we gain insight into the meaning or the mechanism of the contrasted concepts, we begin to see a synthesis that resolves the contradictions of the past. The general feature of fideism in Protestantism, combined with the use of philosophy and logic in Protestantism, can also

---

37. Scanlon, *What We Owe*, 1.
38. Damasio, *Descartes' Error*, 245.

lead to a narrowing of the gap between faith and reason, not in the sense of compatibility but more in the sense of dependence. For example, this could lead to the discovery that faith is an axiom of reason, and passions are axiomatic to a system of theistic ethics that makes further inferences based on logic. This is the direction of progress: conceptual analysis of reason, followed by examination of the relation of such a theory of reason to religious faith, passions as basis of ethics, and empiricism. This is the objective of this book.

CHAPTER 2

Reason Is a Goal-Oriented and Contingent Motion of Thought

WE HAVE SURVEYED THE use of reason in philosophy and found it to be vague. The situation needs to be addressed. In doing so, one must recognize that there are elements in past views of reason that may be constitutive of reason itself, but a more robust theory is needed that displays the interrelation of those apparently contradictory views.

To investigate the nature of reason, one must distinguish between reason itself and the propensity of human beings to reason. This propensity can be extended to other sentient beings, such as dogs, cats, and others. The propensity to reason may be linked to the more general principle of sufficient reason. This principle can be stated as the view that everything that exists must have a reason or a cause. This principle is often stated with credit to Leibniz as discussed in chapter 1.[1] To understand why this separation is important, we can draw from the analogy between the innate desire of human beings to know and the concept of knowledge. Aristotle opens his *Metaphysics* with the insightful observation that all human beings, by nature, desire to know.[2] We can pursue the matter further by seeking to understand the nature of this desire to know. But there is a different question that has occupied philosophers more: it is the desire to understand the nature of this thing we call knowledge. Understanding the nature of knowledge seems more useful to us than understanding why we, by nature, desire to know. As all human beings by nature desire to know, so too are they endowed with

---

1. Leibniz, *Monadology*, paras. 32–33. Although this view is closely associated with Leibniz, it predated him and featured prominently in the arguments for the existence of God by Anselm and others.

2. Aristotle, *Metaphysics* 1.1.

the sense that every event that occurs does so for a reason, or is caused by something else.

A second analogy to strengthen this distinction comes from ethics. It appears to us as a general observation that human beings, by nature, tend to seek pleasure and avoid pain. On the one hand, we can enquire into the nature of this tendency to seek pleasure and avoid pain. That is, we may want to know why people tend to aim for pleasure or shun pain. On the other hand, we may be interested in understanding the nature of pleasure and pain as well as the mechanism by which people seek pleasure or avoid pain. In ethics, why people do, or should desire, pleasure and shun pain has been more interesting than understanding the nature of pleasure and pain. Only recently has the question about the nature of pleasure and pain become a key issue in the philosophy of psychology.

Thus, we see two different philosophical problems that do not tend to be confused in epistemology and ethics, but they unfortunately remain obscure in the discussion of the natural tendency to reason and the nature of reason itself. From these two analogies in epistemology and ethics, we should recognize that the investigation of reason is not the same as the investigation of our innate disposition to reason. The former, and not the latter, is the focus of this essay.

Once we disentangle reason from the natural disposition of human beings to reason, we have removed one of the stumbling blocks to the analysis of reason. The next step is for us to see reason as related directly to a human subject. To do so, we must consider once more Aristotle's suggestion that to give a reason for something is to identify its cause. Here, reason appears to be synonymous with a cause, but it is not entirely the case. The cause of changes in the external world can reside entirely in the external world. When one gives a reason for those external causes which we perceive, it is the operation of thought that is internal to the subject. In discussing about nonsentient things and the changes they undergo, it is more efficient to use the language of causes, making these independent of the sentient beings who observe such changes. With this perspective, reason then becomes closely associated with a reasoning thing, a sentient being that is bound by the principle of sufficient reason and who seeks to uncover causes or reasons associated with various actions.

Two things distinguish reason more generally from the concept of causes. The first is mental—that is, the involvement of thoughts about the world. The second is the operation of the human will. These two elements are responsible for the variety we may encounter in reasoning about events in the world. With these preliminary observations, we can then propose the following as elements of a theory of reason:

1. Reason is a motion of thought.
2. This motion precedes, accompanies, or antecedes actions or events in the external world.
3. The motion follows rules adopted from experience—that is, it is contingent or culturally sensitive.
4. The goal of the motion of thought from a situation to a consequence is established based on a sense of values—that is, a telos, or a goal, or an end.

Taken together, we may say that reason is a goal-oriented, contingent motion of thought that precedes, accompanies, or explains actions in the external world. In other words, reason is an integrative train of thought from a given circumstance to a desired goal, considering the feasibility of the intermediate steps and competing pathways between the circumstance and the desired consequence. The feasibility of the intermediate steps and pathways depends on experience; it is judged based on contingent truths about the natural world and human nature. The goals are determined by ethical or religious judgments and intuitions.

What does it mean for a given action or explanation to be reasonable? Where do we derive the judgment to stamp the action or explanation as reasonable? If someone carries out an action, we are led by the principle of sufficient reason to assume that they did so for a reason. We may try to guess what their reason is, and if we enquire of the reason from the person, we may turn out to be right or wrong. But the action may also be in the future, and we are furnished with an explanation of the circumstances, the desired goal, and the intermediate steps that will lead to the goal. We can make two judgments about this plan. First, we can examine how the intermediate steps from the circumstances are likely to lead to the desired goal. Second, we may directly judge the desirability of the goal itself. We could choose to be indifferent to the goal, accepting it as presented by the agent and only examining the rightness of the contingency connecting the circumstance to the goal. In this case, a judgment can be offered, presupposing the givenness of the goal. If the intention of the agent is to go from this given circumstance to that stated goal, the proposed intermediate steps and pathways can be judged as reasonable. But does this mean there is always a unique pathway connecting a given circumstance and a given goal? This cannot be automatically answered in the affirmative. It is possible that different combinations of intermediate steps may link the circumstance with the desired goal.

We therefore see the first sign of imprecision in the judgment of what is reasonable emerging from the theoretical possibility of different empirically established pathways that link a circumstance with a desired goal. The second indication of imprecision is the variety of goals that can be desired by the subject based on their beliefs. This implies a fundamental subjectivity in our conduct and judgment of reason. To move from this subjectivity to an objective view of reason, a separate argument is needed. Such an argument may also not gain universal affirmation. Recognizing the fundamental subjectivity provides society with a useful tool in debates about rationality. Unless one asserts a common culture, a sense of community, and a shared library of contingencies, only the gradient of power can lead to confident or arrogant declarations of what is, and what is not, rational.

Perhaps we should expand on the elements of the theory of reason that we are proposing. The first element is the idea that reason is a motion or train of thought. More generally, philosophy is regarded as the examination of thoughts and the way they relate to the experienced world. In this sense, reason is central to the practice of philosophy as a goal-directed and contingent integrative train of thoughts about the world. We have said this train of thoughts could precede, accompany, or explain actions on the world as well as experiences of the world. Can it be objected that reason is concerned with a train of thought? In other words, do we need a reasoning agent to talk about reason? The answer is yes, but the fact that the seed of subjectivity is sown by such an admission can be a cause for denying that reason involves a train of thought.

Those who would like to uphold a view of reason that is not subject centered would like to consider reason as having to do with the intelligibility of the entire universe, independent from a human mind. It seems to me that this is a rather grandiose presentation of a problem which could be more tractable by considering the concrete exercise of reason by a thinking subject. Even in rationalistic systems such as Hegel's philosophy, the entire universe as an object is transformed into mind, thought, or reason. As we noted in chapter 1, the other planets of the solar system do not really share the optimism about the evolution of Hegel's Spirit. In the next chapter, we defend the view that in discussions about the natural world, excluding the operation of the free will of human beings, it is more useful to adopt the concepts of causes, logic, laws of nature, science, and coherence. The fundamental role of the motion of human thoughts in the analysis of reason seems hardly disputable. We have taken the concept of thought as a primitive notion to start our analysis. Thought is a unit of cognition, an idea that occurs in the human mind, from memory, from imagination, or from direct contact with impressions from the external world. External world here includes the physical frame of the human being, insofar as it is separate from mind as the psychological part of a human being.

The second element in our analysis of reason is that it is concerned with human action on the world and/or their understanding of the external world. The integrative motion of thought therefore precedes, accompanies, or follows an action by the reasoning agent. It can also relate to the understanding of phenomena or actions carried out by other human beings. This point strikes us as defensible, since in our analysis of the rationality of an agent, we are generally either concerned with their actions or their understanding of the world around them. When we consider whether an action is reasonable from the perspective of an agent, we are both considering whether the agent should do that action or whether that agent would approve as reasonable that action if it were done by another person. With regards to their view of the universe, we want to know whether their thoughts about the nature of a phenomenon cohere with the way things are in the world. When we judge the reasonableness of an action or someone's understanding of a phenomenon, we are therefore interested in the quality of the train of thought linking the initial circumstance to the goal or the new state of knowledge or belief about the external world. Thus, the motion of thought we describe as reason has as a constituent part, a relation to action on the world or understanding of the world.

The third aspect of the integrative train of thought that rises to reason is contingency. This needs careful explanation. By *contingency* here we are simply referring to facts we know from experience and from our community, not from any form of necessity. Perceived necessities abstracted from contingent events are still generalized contingencies, not necessities per se. We couldn't have come to knowledge of these facts by the sheer power of pure thought alone. That is, reason makes use of experience and the norms of a community to link thoughts from a given circumstance to a desired goal. The reasoning agent needs acquaintance with causal relations, properties of things, and rules of behavior that are permissible within a given community. The immediate implication of this point is that reason without experience is impossible.

We should perhaps note here that even before birth a baby is engaged in learning by sense experience. This cuts into the debate about rationalism and empiricism, and the manner of connecting reason to experience as done here highlights the plausibility of Kant's epistemology. The proper account of human understanding is a synthesis of empiricism and rationalism, whereby rationalism, according to the position being presented here, feeds off earlier seeds of empiricism. If we describe an agent's understanding of the universe as rationalistic, we are in fact denoting that person as an efficient or parsimonious empiricist; one who, by a special integrative train of thought, links experience to produce a coherent picture of things. When it comes to actions, the train of thought that rises to reason seeks to respect the principles of right and wrong. These principles are imposed by the self or by a community. To make sure this view includes theistic religion, the union of an agent and a Supreme Being who reveals to the agent a command or rule of right and wrong can also be considered as a community consisting of two persons, that is a relation between human and a Supreme Being. This point is intended to provide generality, not yet as an argument for or against such personal revelation.

Even if the principles of right and wrong linking a circumstance to a desired goal are imposed by the agent, it can be argued that this is done in consideration of a community or in total defiance of humanity. The first case is like one who considers Kant's categorical imperative, acting in such a way as they would be willing to elevate their guiding principle to a universal law, whereas in the second case, we may be dealing with Bernard Williams's amoralist[3] who can find no reasons why their actions should take into account their effects on others.

The contingency of the train of thought that has the quality of reason is easier to grasp once we remind ourselves about the distinction between the natural tendency of human beings to reason and reason itself. The defense of the principle of sufficient reason may dispense with experience and community, dwelling on innate properties of an agent, but the actual conduct of reason by a thinking thing cannot easily dispense with experience and community. By bringing out the role of contingency in reason, we do more than a simple analysis of reason. We also point to the way reasoning works and how it can be improved. In part II of this essay, we shall consider the implication of this on the methodological conduct of reasoning. The identification of the role of community in reasoning also offers helpful suggestions on how seemingly irreconcilable debates can be made more tractable by analyzing them down to the communal dispositions that enter the reasoning of those who strongly disagree about an experience or a given action.

The final constitutive element of the integrative motion of thought that rises to reason is that it is goal oriented. There are alternate names to be given to this goal. It can be referred to as an *end*, an *aim*, or a *telos*. Thus, reason is a teleological motion of thought. This telos has a certain value to the reasoning agent. But if we are called upon to judge the reasonableness of the motion of thought associated with an action, we may consider the value of the telos from a universal perspective or from the subjective perspective of the reasoning agent. The motion of thought links an unsatisfactory circumstance to a more satisfactory consequence or goal. The goal that a

---

3. Williams, *Morality*, chap. 1.

reasoning agent sets for themselves can take the form of visions of the good, the beautiful, the true, and the just. These different goals can all be classed under the good in the Platonic sense.

The appearance of teleology in this analysis can be viewed as problematic; it smells of a theological commitment and a defense of objective moral goals. At least we can admit the ethical twist introduced by this goal-oriented aspect in reason and we can hold off on the theological argument for now.

An objection can be raised regarding the necessity of a goal in the analysis of reason. This objection would likely be inspired by subjective instincts or a desire to avoid introducing religious language into the analysis of reason, since teleology tends to be linked to religion. The objection from the perspective of subjectivism would aim to establish that people set different goals for themselves and act according to those goals. If the course of actions taken by a subject coheres with their stated goal, who are we to judge the validity of their goals but to applaud them as having acted reasonably within their own constraints of circumstances and goals? This objection ought to be embraced as an outcome of the proposed analysis. We are not yet concerned with judgment of the universal goodness of the goals set by reasoning agents for themselves. We have so far sought to lay out the elements that are constitutive of reason, and our intention is to show that reason is fundamentally subjective. For reason to rise to objectivity, an extra theoretical consideration is needed.

With the subjectivity inherent in the process of how a reasoning agent sets their own goal, end, aim, or telos, we still must address an important concern. How can we share common rationality? What if the actions of the reasoning agent are such that they bear on the lives of other people? How are we to assess one's subjective vision of goodness? Can we grant a train of thought as subjectively reasonable while also being universally unreasonable? What makes an action universally good and reasonable? These questions push us to consider the social dimensions of subjective reason and, therefore, look at ethics, religion or, broadly speaking, culture.

Before embarking on the ethical and religious dimensions of the goals of a rational being during the reasoning process, it is important to consider the relation of teleology to contingency. What is intended is an exposition of the central but problematic role of causation in the analysis of reason.

We have said that the intermediate states linking a circumstance to a goal are contingent; they come from experience and within a community of norms. Could the goals set by an agent have any structural relation to the contingencies that link a circumstance and a goal? If we consider the contingencies to consist of cause-effect relations, compositional relations, rules of right and wrong actions, it seems that contingencies are just micro arrangements of intermediate circumstances and intermediate goals. The contingencies describe a mechanism of the much broader relation between the circumstance and the desired goal.

The question we need to get out of the way is whether what we understand by contingencies is not something other than cause-effect relations, compositional relations, rules of right and wrong that are internal to a community, etc. What we can agree on is that contingencies are not necessities; we cannot lay hold of the content of these without connection to the way things are in the world. In this respect, we are led by the intuitions of the hardcore empiricist to whom it is obvious that our knowledge of facts comes from experience. This knowledge arises through impressions from without that we then rearrange, taking advantage of our various inbuilt dispositional traits to make sense of things. For instance, the principle of sufficient reason participates in our conceptualization and organization of our experience. Locke attempts an explanation of this disposition to causal thinking when he says:

> Having thus, from what our senses are able to discover, in the operation of bodies against one another, got the notion of cause and effect, viz. that a cause is that which makes any other thing, either a simple idea, substance, or mode begin to be; and an effect is that, which had its beginning from some other thing.[4]

This connection of the cause-and-effect thinking to experience is to be expected from an empiricist such as Locke. We do not want to investigate the reasonableness of the principle of sufficient reason in this work. It would require going beyond the empiricist's position, but what Locke's statement indicates is the fact that contingencies efficiently present themselves as collections of cause-effect relations. To these, we can add compositional relations and rules of right and wrong conduct as considered normative in a society. The collection of contingencies linking a given circumstance to a desired goal of a reasoning exercise can be said to be a mechanism, a sort of arrangement of intermediate circumstances and intermediate goals.

When we view contingencies as a mechanism consisting of causal and compositional relations that display the network underlying a more opaque relation of things, we make it easier to grasp the relation between goals and contingencies in a train of thought that attains the status of reasoning. It is by examining causation that we find the needed elements of similarities and differences.

---

4. Locke, *Essay* 2.26.2.

The relation of cause and effect is a challenging one that has led to different views among philosophers. For our purpose here, only two views are useful. One is Hume's and the other is an Aristotelian view of causation. A similar contrasting picture has been adopted by Koons and Pickavance in describing causation as either neo-Humean or powerist.[5] Hume's view can be considered an empirical view of causation, which he expresses in *An Enquiry*:

> We may define a cause as an object, followed by another, and where all the objects similar to the first, are followed by objects similar to the second. Or in other words, where, if the first object had not been, the second never had existed.[6]

The view is empirical because it offers practical ways of investigating causal relations by observing the constant conjunction in space and time of causes and their effects, all other things being equal. It leaves the metaphysical nature of causation obscure, a weakness duly noted by Koons and Pickavance.[7] The powerist view of causation is closely related to Aristotle and it deviates from the more well-known taxonomy of four causes. In his *Physics* and *Metaphysics*, Aristotle delineates material, formal, efficient, and final causes.[8] The material cause of a thing is the material from which that thing is made, whereas the formal cause is the definition of the essential nature of the thing being made. The efficient cause is that from which the process of change begins, and the final cause is the end, purpose, or goal for which something is being made.

Without going into a detailed analysis of these causes, we can see that what is offered is a mechanistic description of complex change, composite change that involves intermediate processes for which various means and ends can be separately defined. At the end of the day, the efficient and final causes give us an overarching view of a circumstance beginning with the efficient cause, and a goal, which is the final cause.

But the powerist account of causation that properly contrasts with the empirical Humean view is one that considers potentiality and actuality. It comes out more clearly in Aristotle's *Physics* where he discusses motion. Indeed, it is in the discussion of motion and change that the features of causation are sometimes clarified and freed from the trappings of the principle of sufficient reason.

---

5. Koons and Pickavance, *Metaphysics*, chap. 3.
6. Hume, *Enquiry*, 51.
7. Koons and Pickavance, *Metaphysics*, 74.
8. Aristotle, *Physics* 2.3; *Metaphysics* 5.2.

According to the powerist account of causation, change occurs because of the actualization of potentials in things. There is a difference between what exists potentially and what exists actually. What exists potentially can exist actually when the right conditions obtain. If two things are involved, we can view one to have a capacity to cause change or move and the other to have the passion for the change or the passion to be moved. The words *power, capacity, disposition,* and *potential* tend to be used interchangeably to describe the ability to cause change or motion. While this view may not appear to provide immediate clarity, its metaphysical value rests in directing our attention to the existence of certain properties of things which in their right pairing can bring about change without creating new bodies or annihilating old ones. This is our preferred view of causation in this work.

The powerist view of causation is closer to the scientific rationalization and investigation of causes. This point will be taken up again in the next chapter when it will be emphasized that reason ought not to be employed heavily in the discussion of natural sciences since causation is far more effective. But briefly, the general view of causation in the sciences is that change or motion results from the existence of differences of certain dispositions or capacities in things, and such motion proceeds until such differences are annihilated.

Take the example of a hot block and a cold block, both made of the same material but only differing in their hotness and coldness. The so-called hotness is an expression of an excess potential called thermal energy relative to the coldness in the other block, by which we perceive a deficiency in thermal energy. This thermal energy we consider to be the mechanical disposition of constituent particles to agitate in the block. If the two blocks are brought into contact, experience shows that heat will flow from the hotter block to the colder one until such a time when both shall attain the same temperature. Beyond that point, we no longer observe motion or change—that is, a condition of equilibrium that particle scientists insist is really a dynamic exchange of motion but with no net observable differences.

If we approach the problem of the hot and cold blocks from the two perspectives of causations, we find ourselves struggling, in the Humean sense, to state which is the cause of the subsequent heat transfer, but in the powerist perspective, we grasp the existence of potentiality that can become actuality. It is the pairing of a hot and a cold bock that induces the transfer of thermal energy from the one with excess thermal energy to the one with less thermal energy until the disposition is equally spread in the two bodies. The end or the goal of change is to remove the original cause of change.

We are thus led by the powerist account of causation to see a relation between causation and teleology. An actualized cause is a condition of differences in disposition or potential and the effect is a new situation in which the difference in potential is less, if not annihilated. In the science of mechanics, bodies are set in motion by unbalanced forces, and they remain at rest in the absence of unbalanced forces. This is the essence of Newton's three axioms of mechanics. In analytic mechanics, a more overt teleological condition of stability of a mechanical system is advocated. A system is at equilibrium when its energy is minimized; it has no energy gradients.

This is as far as we want to drag out the relation between causation in the natural sciences and causation in principles of moral actions. We have first said that what we call contingencies in the conduct of reasoning are indeed collections of cause-and-effect relations, compositional relations, and rules of right and wrong actions in a society. We have then said that these contingencies connect a given circumstance to an overarching desired goal, that is the goal of the reasoning exercise. But after looking at the nature of causation, we discover that it consists of the pairing of a circumstance with differences in potentiality that ebbs into an intermediate goal with less differences in potentiality. It is therefore reasonable to see that cause-and-effect relations permeate the analysis of reason but in such a way that when one considers a given circumstance, an integrative train of thought seeks out a mechanistic network of cause-and-effect relations that ultimately connect the circumstance to a desire end, goal, purpose, or telos.

The richness and extent of the network of contingent considerations used in a reasoning exercise can distinguish one rational agent from the other, while both may still be credited with some degree of reasonableness. If we desire to make more obvious the differences in the quality of the reasoning exercise, we can define a *radius of rationality*. A *radius of rationality* would be a measure of the extensiveness of a network of contingent and normatively ordered steps from a given circumstance to a desired goal. The larger the radius, the richer and more reasonable one's connection of circumstances to desired goals.

So far, we have concentrated on the four aspects that we consider to be constitutive of the integrative train of thought called reason. We wanted to establish the structure of that motion of thought without focusing on the content of the reasoning and its determining principles. What we consider to be obvious is the absence of necessity on matters of the content of the specific contingencies and the nature of the goals that the reasoning subject sets for themselves. The possibilities open to the reasoning subject are therefore not limited beforehand. We have shown that this account of reason is defensible. It is impossible, without further arguments and development, to introduce objectivity into this picture. It follows that the defensible account of reason thus offered is fundamentally subjective and its elevation to generality requires further discussions on a warrant to do so.

Before we address the possibility of obtaining objective reason from the fundamentally subjective nature of reason, let us strengthen the view of reason we have now obtained with some plausible cases of reasoning exercises. These should lead us to the point where we may be willing to consider the agents to be reasonable while still withholding our assent on the desirability of their goal or the means by which they seek to attain their stated goals.

Case 1: An old Kantian problem on lying to a potential murderer. Let's consider that Peter is about to be approached by an angry murderer. Peter lays out his plan of action and demands to know if that plan is reasonable. The angry murderer is pursuing Peter's friend who has just entered Peter's house. It is clear from the pursuer's intention that if the pursued friend is caught, he will likely be mortally beaten. The circumstance is one of insecurity, but hope is sustained by ignorance of the pursuer regarding the whereabouts of Peter's friend. Peter intends to lie to save his friend. He sees no danger in violating Kant's admonition about sticking to the truth, irrespective of the consequences. The idea is to tell the angry pursuer, tremblingly, that the pursued is indeed in the basement. In reality, his friend is upstairs, and his hope is that if the pursuer goes downstairs, he will encounter a fierce dog and the basement entrance will be blocked from above, giving the pursued enough time to escape further to safety. We are asked to say whether such a plan is reasonable. Without judging about the morality of lying, we can evaluate the potential of the outlined steps to lead to the goal of securing the temporary safety of the friend being pursued. Possibly there are other ways, potentially more effective, to guarantee the safety of the pursued friend, but the one presented so far seems reasonable to us. Were more of these options presented, their relative merits would be examined to see if each of them rises to a certain level of reasonableness, or which one has the larger radius of rationality.

Case 2: Suppose we are approached by a Robin Hood character, a heroic outlaw, whose intention is to rob a bank known for benefitting from legislation against the poor in society. Our outlaw has a clear plan to take advantage of security lapses and the hosting of an important political event in town to successfully carry out a bank robbery. The robbery is not the goal of his whole operation. He intends to use all the money to anonymously donate to a food bank in town that has run out of funding. We are presented with a plan of action that paints the current situation—the bad state of society's poor, especially a certain food bank. The goal is a future state in which a bank loses money, the food bank receives an anonymous donation to meet their needs, and nobody is held accountable for the bank robbery.

The reasoning exercise we are called upon to judge is an integrative train of thought that maps out the movements of our Robin Hood from his home, selecting routes to the bank that are less likely to raise suspicion, an elaborate scheme of operations in the bank based on prior hours of study of the bank's internal operations, and even nudging actions for reduced security in the bank in the form of medical- and personal-day absences.

When we examine the plan for reasonableness, we would be interested in spotting any move or loophole that can lead to foiling the robbery. If we do not find any such loopholes or high probability of surprises that can foil the plan, we would say the plan is reasonable. But if we are fundamentally concerned about the morality of the goal of robbing a bank, we may find the plan unreasonable and argue against the charitable end as a good justification for a crime. We can also argue that the plan can never be reasonable on grounds that this raises the prospect of the ultimate revelation of the robber's identity.

Case 3: Suppose a friend suffers from chronic depression, a widespread medical condition in the modern world. They conclude that it is best for them to take their life, and their reasoning exercise is to find the most convenient way and day to carry out that desired goal. Suppose this friend comes up with what they consider as the most appropriate plan to achieve their stated goal; it is hard to imagine a plan that will easily earn our approval as reasonable. The first two cases have involved stated goals that purport to consider the welfare of other people. We were dealing with ethical problems and plausible solutions. The reasoning exercise in this third case can comprise many reasonable intermediate steps but the nature of the final goal is unsettling, and even granting a right to selfish consideration does not seem to shake away the feeling that there must be other ways of aiming for a goal that preserves the life of the friend. The Hamlet soliloquy raises questions on the goodness of the goal and despite the Epicurean consolation about death, we feel that each life is embedded in a network of other lives such that any reasoning exercise about one life cannot be completely indifferent to potential pain that can be brought onto other lives. We cannot judge the reasonableness of this project based only on the contingent steps; the goal strikes us as a disqualifying element in the rational project.

Many more cases than the three above could be presented to bring out the nuances introduced by the fundamentally subjective nature of reason. In each case, we could also consider a multitude of options linking a circumstance to a desired goal. From this multitude, further comparative choices can be made. Some of these plans would involve aspects of the future which remain probabilistic or involve aspects that are not fully known to us. Thus, we see elements of subjectivity as well as elements of probabilism, which make the judgments on rationality imprecise, uncertain. The goals set by reasoning agents are based on beliefs and values, prompting ethical and religious reflections in their judgment.

From the above, this species of reason is subjective, but is objective reason possible? Are reason and passion not distinct, because subjectivity seems to be more connected with individual passions?

Before we end this chapter on the exposition of this theory of reason, we need to consider two implications which will be taken up again in parts III and IV, where we consider the religious and ethical ramifications of the new theory. One is the possibility of objectivity from this fundamental subjective nature of reason. We need to consider how this is possible since it does seem to us that a certain objectivity can be attributed to that which truly rises to attain the quality of reason. The other is the impact of this theory on Plato's theory of the soul, where reason is distinguished from the spirited and appetitive parts of the soul as discussed in chapter 1. These latter two parts of the soul are less related to reason but would appear to be equally operative in reasoning according to the proposed account of reason.

If reason is fundamentally subjective, the hope for objectivity in our tendency to compare the reasonableness of people seems to be lost. But since we have argued that contingency includes norms of a given community, we can at least see that the reasoning subject, being embedded in a community, can be expected to share certain instincts about desirable goals with other members of the community. If we follow this path, it is not without its challenges. We would encounter questions about the source of the norms in that community. How do things get to be right and wrong and how does moral change, or moral progress, become possible in a community where it seems that we act in accordance with the prevailing norms?

An empiricist account of culture and ethics maybe attempted, whereby the rules of right and wrong are viewed as generalizations of centuries of experimental actions conducing to good effects or pain. The very possibility of moral progress in such a system may also be tentatively explained by reference to curious experimental actions. Questions would remain on the faculty of judgment which elevates experimental actions to right or wrong actions.

But we must admit the puzzling feeling: the analysis of reason reveals its fundamentally subjective nature, yet we have a strong feeling that objective reason is not only possible, it appears to form the basis of society and language. It seems that a community is not even possible without objective reason. A speculative closure of the problem seems to be the most appropriate step in addressing this puzzle. We must see the reasonableness of the existence of a Supreme Being who is the original source of the faculties and intuitions of the reasoning subject. If this Supreme Being is perfectly good and perfectly wise, it is reasonable for the Being to equip subjects with capacities of judgment and instincts that seek causal relations in a manner that their proper functioning can produce similar results in very different subjects. This is not a proof of God's existence; it is a natural consequence of our intuition about the existence of other minds, the existence of common language, and the individual innate sense of the divine.

There are two levels of this objectivity from subjective reason: aesthetic and the religious. The aesthetic has to do with raw feelings, passion, emotions, and conscience in the narrow sense that they are attended by limited reflection on the matters at hand. The Supreme Being has infused every subject with this aesthetic capacity of discerning certain values of goodness, truth, justice, and beauty. Drawing from this primitive capacity of a universal nature, the fundamentally subjective reasoning of many different subjects can rise to a generalizable product of reasoning. If the aesthetic capacity can account for general feelings of perceiving beauty, for example, in good art music, then it can also ground the emergence of a general sense of reasonableness from subjective judgments of reason.

The religious or cultured level of elevating subjective reason to objective reason involves deliberative attempts to understand the nature of the Supreme Being and the purposes he has for his created order. It also involves a deliberate effort to understand, through learning from the extensive library of past lives, those things that have led to pleasant and unpleasant results.

Thus, objective reason from its fundamentally subjective nature is possible if we understand the relation of each subjective being to a Supreme Being and a culture of learning from past lives, personal past experiences, but above all, with a sensitivity to the existence of the Supreme Being who teleologically directs reasonable actions toward good purposes. These issues will be taken up again when we consider the full implication of the theory of reason on religion.

As we discussed in chapter 1, Plato's theory of the soul stipulates three distinct parts: the reasoning, spirited, and appetitive parts. He is careful to acknowledge that, with proper education, the spirited part of the soul can be enlisted in the service of reason. The unbridled spirit in the form of anger, however, can act at variance with reason. The relation of the three parts of the soul to the proposed view that reason is fundamentally subjective will be complete if we find the appetitive part to also be operative in subjective reason. An example is in order.

An interesting study of extraneous factors in judicial decisions was conducted by Danziger, Levav, and Avnaim-Pesso.[9] They found that the percentage of favorable court rulings drop from 65 percent to 0 percent and return to 65 percent after a food break. This means that the practice of reason in a profession deemed to be committed to objective reason is indeed affected by the craving for food. The authors, perhaps jokingly, observe that this seems to support the view that justice is what the judge had at breakfast.

That the passionate and appetitive faculties of a person can bear on the reasoning of that person is not difficult to see in the context of the proposed theory of reason. Passion and appetite highlight subjectivity. Anything that affects the subject can bear on the quality of their reasoning exercise. The claim that there is a clear separation between a rational part of a person and an irrational part (emotional, passionate, angry, hungry, vindictive, etc.) is an unhealthy prejudice; it should be dispensed with. In exchange, we must embrace a more complex view of reason as a blend of emotions and an integrative train of thought that differs by the degree of equilibrated internal reflection and value judgments.

Indeed, it is the degree of reflection, the extent of the library of contingencies from which a person draws, and the desirability of the goals that can differentiate higher quality reason from lower quality reason. The lower quality reason is closer to the spirited manifestation of a person's soul in the Platonic sense. Plato's theory of the tripartite soul helps us to conceive of a mechanism of improving reason, but we must never forget the elements of the soul that make reasoning a fundamentally subjective exercise. This revised view will allow us in part IV to delve into the basis of ethics, where we bring sentimental and rational principles of ethics into a synthesis.

---

9. Danziger et al., "Extraneous Factors."

CHAPTER 3

Natural Science Can Be Pursued Without Invoking the Vague Concept of Reason

IN DISCUSSING NATURAL PHENOMENA, the concepts of science, causation, laws of nature, logic, probability, and coherence are better suited than the concept of reason.

Through our survey of the historical use of reason in philosophy, we first established that reason is vague. To remedy the situation, we then developed a theory of reason, essential to which reason is a goal-directed integrative motion of thought that depends on experience and culture in linking a given circumstance to an end. This view carries with it a fundamentally subjective character. In this chapter, we are going to argue that in discussing phenomena of the natural world, greater precision is to be found in adhering to a different set of concepts other than reason. These natural phenomena are those that are not directly linked to free will in a way that can falsify regular causal patterns.

If the natural phenomena can be satisfactorily described using the concepts of science, causation, laws of nature, logic, probability, and coherence, then the concept of reason can be restricted to the discussion of such issues as those that involve the operation of human will or will of sentient beings. The involvement of free will raises questions of value. We are then in the domain of ethics.

There are two practical advantages in favor of adopting the proposed strategy. The first advantage is a revisit of the peculiar view of philosophy advanced by the logical positivists in the twentieth century. Theirs is a view that focuses on redefining philosophy as a subject that is solely devoted to the logical analysis of experience; it only admits of conjectures as a way of propelling science toward answering questions of a positive nature. The aspects of philosophy most criticized by the positivists are those concerned with questions of ethics, religion, and, in short, those questions of human psychology that do not seem to be directly addressed by the deterministic system of science. The distinction proposed here recognizes the clarity gained by adopting the positivists' emphasis on using more precise language and staying as close as possible to experience whenever we discuss natural phenomena. By *natural phenomena* here we mean all those phenomena which proceed without free will and reflection. Whereas a person may drop a ball consciously, the motion of the ball proceeds according to the laws of nature. The goal of dropping the ball is, however, not part of the natural phenomenon; it is the product of a free will.

The second advantage afforded by avoiding the use of reason in discussing natural phenomena is its bearing on the debate between rationalism and empiricism. The rationalists hold that knowledge of the external world is possible using reason alone. To some rationalists, their vague concept of reason boils down to a world-independent motion of thought that is capable of latching onto the essential features of the world without experiential contact. The empiricists, among whom one should also count Kant, hold that our knowledge of the external world comes from impressions on our senses from natural phenomena. As Leibniz, the rationalist, concedes, our intuitions are generally in favor of the view that our knowledge has its origin in experience. Just by being alive, one is embedded in a stream of experience.

If we can see the advantage afforded by avoiding the use of rationalistic terms (reason, reasonable, rational, etc.) in discussing natural phenomena, we will be more attuned to the empirical origin of our knowledge about the external world. The consequence of this is to affirm a commitment to the empiricist side of the debate, or a realization that such a debate is ill-posed, or both. The debate can be viewed as ill-posed in the light of the theory of reason presented in chapter 2. This is the case because that which is referred to as *reason* or *rationalism* is founded on experience in a way that can be expressed coherently using other less ambiguous words than *reason*. Empiricism is the basis of human understanding. When empirical acquisition of knowledge is conducted in an efficient, reflective, and coherent manner, one may be justified in calling such an exercise *rational empiricism*. We admit the use of *rational* here to describe a kind of empiricism because it carries with it the human agency of seeking a certain goal or set of goals: namely, parsimony, efficiency, and internal coherence. Goal-oriented search for knowledge is an ethical act, such that one's procedure in search of knowledge, not the knowledge content itself, can be judged as reasonable or not.

Perhaps it is not quite clear where we are going with this distinction. We have said that the debate between rationalism and empiricism will be affected by the suggestion here to avoid reason in discussing natural phenomena. One often hears about the tension between faith and reason. By this, it is implied that the debate is indeed a debate between faith and science. Others may disagree and say that at issue is a debate between faith and philosophy. They'd say reason is synonymous with philosophy, not science. Such a view would not be welcomed by one devoted to the radical view of scientism. Those who hold the view that true philosophy is a logical analysis of science would not see any distinction between philosophy and science. But the essence of this chapter is to disentangle the debate between faith and science from the debate between faith and philosophy, where we understand the second debate to be synonymous with the debate between faith and reason. We also intend to expose this reason-versus-faith debate as ill-posed because we will see that reason is not possible without faith.

Let us examine the advantage of using the proposed sets of concepts in talking about natural phenomena. We will end this discussion by looking at two problems that can arise within the study of nature, leading to the subjectivity that natural science seeks to avoid. We embrace reason and subjectivity in discussing the operation of human will. This operation of the will governs the spheres of ethics, religion, politics, law, economics, and so on. These are the spheres of human practice.

One of the two problems leading to subjectivity in the study of nature is the use of language to conceptualize our experience of natural phenomena in a very general, communicable manner. There is room here for subjectivity among scientists and their audience. The second problem has to do with the so-called placebo and nocebo effects. These are supposed to be deviations from the general principles of causal relations. Here we find that a substance acquires causal power purely based on misguided psychology. This creates challenging questions for the ethicist and the empiricist of causation.

Natural science is the preferred way to refer to the study of nature today. Historically, such a human endeavor was part of philosophy and with the distinction between the study of human free will and nature, natural philosophy became the precursor to modern science. Natural science, as understood today, is the systematic study of natural phenomena with the aim of understanding their causes and predictive patterns. Although the nineteenth century saw increased separation of science from the term *natural philosophy*, one can also find extensive use of the term *science* in the eighteenth-century writings of philosophers. Kant refers extensively to science when he speaks of knowledge in general.

The relation of science to philosophy can be seen in three stages. The first is when *science* is indeed another name for *natural philosophy*. It highlights its subject of study as being the natural world; it is less about the thoughts and behavior of thinking things, humans and the Supreme Being included.

The second stage is the post-Enlightenment break from natural philosophy, preferring the distinct name of *science*. As many other disciplines broke from philosophy, they also adopted the status of a science. In the French and Germanic world, many academic disciplines are still described as different kinds of sciences that are distinct from the natural sciences. Thus, one speaks of historical and juridical sciences. In the Anglophone world, *science* tends to be used to refer exclusively to natural sciences, while the other social sciences are distinguished by their various prefaces.

The third stage of the intersection of science and philosophy is in the logical positivist's attempt to redefine the sphere of philosophy. In this bold attempt, science and philosophy, not just natural philosophy, must be addressing the same reality which is, according to some extreme views, nothing but the physical world.

The logical positivist speaks with great passion about the mission of making philosophy the logical analysis of science; it does produce an impressive philosophy of science. The dogmatism notwithstanding, it is therefore possible to use science in discussing problems of the natural world without confusing it with subjective reason that introduces imprecision. This strategy can work well in the natural sciences. In the social sciences, one must carefully treat the appearance of subjectivity, whose presence justifies the use of reason as a judgment of thought.

The attempt by some analytic philosophers to restrict philosophy to logical analysis of experience can be discerned from Bertrand Russell and from A. J. Ayer's exposition of the doctrine of logical positivism.[1] They acknowledge the importance of ethics but declare the impossibility of solving the problems posed by ethics using logical analysis.

Russell blames the lack of progress in philosophy on mistaken moral considerations, such as attempts to prove the existence of God. About these metaphysical attempts, he says:

> All this is rejected by the philosophers who make logical analysis the main business of philosophy. They confess frankly that the human intellect is unable to find conclusive answers to many questions of profound importance to mankind, but they refuse to believe that there is some "higher" way of knowing, by which we can discover truths hidden from science and the intellect. For this renunciation, they have been rewarded by the discovery that many questions, formerly obscured by the fog of

---

1. Ayer, *Language, Truth and Logic*, 134–37.

metaphysics, can be answered with precision, and by objective methods which introduce nothing of the philosopher's temperament except the desire to understand.[2]

In essence, logical positivists hold that the analysis of experience using logic seems to be the only truly rewarding philosophy to be pursued by those who seek truth. The nature of human beings is such that they seek to know. But this desire to know does not come with a guarantee of knowing. The principle of sufficient reason, for example, only leads us to associate every event with a cause. Even if we do not know the cause of an event, this principle, combined with a speculation about a set of possible causes, temporarily calms our restless minds. It is therefore to be expected that philosophers will continue to investigate the operation of human will, knowing full well that it does not lead to the same stable and predictable pattern of knowledge afforded by the study of natural phenomena.

In an interview with Brian Magee around 1976, A. J. Ayer summed up the iconoclastic nature of logical positivism with a good laugh, declaring that nearly all of it was false. It is hard to entirely agree with this sentiment. The clarity with which logical positivism approached philosophical problems of science was a breath of fresh air that ought to be admired and preserved. But by declaring a lack of interest in the many other problems that plague mankind, they simply exposed the limitations of their logical method. Problems of human free will are more challenging than the logical analysis of experience of natural phenomena. Reflections on these problems of experience leads to noninferential insights that are broadly shared. But instead of lumping these empirical and free-will problems together, it is advantageous to clarify the way we talk about problems of the natural world and the more intricate problems of human nature. The problems of human nature will inevitably involve free will and necessitate the concept of reason in our analysis of human behavior.

We can view science and logical positivism as a special branch of philosophy that can help us to speak intelligibly about natural phenomena. There are some key words that make this discussion possible: *causation*, *laws of nature*, *logic*, *probability*, and *coherence*. We need to examine these words to come to the view that they make the use of reason unnecessary in talking about the natural world.

---

2. Russell, *History*, 835.

A. CAUSATION

Causation, or the cause-effect relation, is a central principle of change. It can more adequately explain natural phenomena in a manner that does not necessitate the use of more problematic concepts such as *reason, rationality*, and *reasonableness*. Although these rationalistic words can be used to convey the same message, the choice of causal language is more enlightening. In communication, we should aim for clarity, avoiding vague or ambiguous expressions, and embracing mechanical or physical relations that can more vividly dramatize what we intend to communicate. Let us consider the explanation of a phenomenon: when a hot block and a cold block are brought into contact, heat flows from the hot block to the cold block until both attain the same temperature. The cause of this change is that nature abhors differences in energy potential. Each block has a thermal energy potential, but the potential is higher in the hot block than in the cold block. The potential is related to the mechanical energy of the particles that make up the block. By bringing them into contact, more vigorous moving particles in the hot block collide with the slower particles at the interface with the cold block, causing them to exchange thermal energy. This collisional exchange at the interface continues until both blocks attain the same thermal potential. The absence of a thermal potential difference causes the change to stop. The goal of the change is thus attained—the equality of potential energy differences. If this account accords with the way nature operates, we can say that the explanation is causally or mechanistically sound. We could inject in our explanation the word *reason* or *rational* instead of *cause* or *causal relation*. We usually stamp such coherent explanations with phrases such as "It makes sense" or "It is logical" or "It is reasonable." The first two are more suitable.

Our basic strategy in explaining natural phenomena is to show that things have certain tendencies, capacities, abilities, powers, dispositions, or potentials to cause certain changes. We break down these pairings of tendencies of things to participate in change and reconnect them in a manner that is vivid enough to impart a sense of familiarity and ease to our listener. To attain this effective explanation, the language of causation is more helpful than vague reasonableness in discussing natural phenomena.

Although it seems intuitive that causation plays a fundamental role in the elucidation of laws of nature and in scientific explanations, it is sometimes suggested that causality is not universal. For instance, some hold that causal relations are undermined in quantum mechanics, where it is purported that determinism breaks down. Some express this reservation when they misinterpret Kant's remarkable insight into the role of causation in structuring experience of natural phenomena. Reichenbach, in criticizing the search for certainty among philosophers, asserts:

> We have seen Physics enter a stage where the Kantian frame of knowledge does break down. The axioms of Euclidean geometry, the principle of causality and substance are no longer recognized by the physicists of our day.[3]

Heisenberg, in discussing the capacity of certain atoms to undergo radioactive decay by emitting a particle, concludes that Kant's arguments for the a priori character of the principle of causality no longer applies in atomic physics.[4] But is it really the case?

This apparent restriction of causation in natural science can be neutralized by three considerations.

First, it cannot serve as a case against the idea that causation is better suited than reason or rationality in clearly discussing natural phenomena. Reason, which involves causal chains and goal or teleology, cannot afford more clarity than causation in a mechanistic presentation.

Second, the concept of causation is clearer than reason, but it is not free from vagueness. Since the time of Hume, differences can be observed in the way some scientists and philosophers use the concept of causation.

Third, quantum mechanics is still plagued by conceptual issues that can lead to absurd problematic interpretations. It is my belief that this stems from overlooking another fundamental metaphysical difference. Whereas classical physics is considered to enjoy certainty in predictions, predictions of quantum mechanics are limited by the Heisenberg uncertainty principle. According to this principle, we cannot know both the velocity and position of a quantum particle with greater precision than a certain limit. This uncertainty is wrongly elevated to the breakdown of causality.

We will return to the problem of causation shortly, but a further comment is needed in relation to the uncertainty in quantum mechanics. The equations of classical mechanics relate the metaphysical quantities of force and energy to the measurable quantities of velocity and position of Newtonian particles. Energy and force are metaphysical; their observable effects on the velocity and positions of particles allow us to initialize calculations and obtain predictions of future velocities and positions. The situation is reversed in quantum mechanics whose equations, for example in the Schrödinger presentation, describe the motion of a wave function of energy in a field. The properties of velocity and position in this framework

---

3. Reichenbach, *Rise of Scientific Philosophy*, 48.
4. Heisenberg, *Physics and Philosophy*, 64.

are derived quantities from the metaphysical quantity of energy.[5] Epistemological problems are therefore to be expected from this relation of unseen, unmeasurable energy, which is often only prescribed and measured indirectly, through mathematical relations. It is not a straightforward path to go from this difficulty to the suggestion that causality breaks down, especially if causation has a plausible alternative metaphysical theory than the presumed Humean view.

Returning to the idea that skepticism about causation in quantum mechanics arises from vagueness in our understanding of causation, it is necessary to reiterate the two main views of causation which are best considered to be complementary, albeit with the greater advantage being on the side of the metaphysical view.

Causation is the actualization of a cause-effect relation. The view arising from Hume's skepticism about causes is empirical by nature. It admits that we cannot actually see this thing called causation; we cannot grasp the necessary relation of the condition or thing called cause and the condition or thing called effect. Led by the mind's propensity to simplify observations, we fashion the constant conjunction of two events in space and time to be such that the one is a cause that precedes the other, called an effect. This purely mechanistic presentation of the matter is rather poor; it limits us from inquiring into the way things could be in nature for there to be events, change, or motion. That is where the capacity view of causation discussed in chapter 2 takes over and extends our ability to apply causal arguments to situations such as gravity, other force fields, energy fields, or fields of auxiliary variables such as those used in quantum mechanics. Causation is the actualization of the capacity or potential for change that is inherent in things. Change happens because of differences in such capacities and proceeds in such a way as to annihilate such differences. This fundamental origin of change as rooted in differences already finds its emergence in ancient Greek thought. Heisenberg recognizes this in Heraclitus's view that the fundamental principle of the variety of phenomena arises from the striving of opposite forces from which harmony emerges.[6]

The Aristotelian view that causation is rooted in the actualization of inherent potentials in things is richer than often acknowledged. Nancy Cartwright has recently challenged the apparent orthodoxy of the Humean empiricist view with her defense of capacities and how they appear in the

---

5. Heisenberg, *Physics and Philosophy*, 13–14.
6. Heisenberg, *Physics and Philosophy*, 36.

elucidation of causal laws.[7] Her view is in line with the Aristotelian idea of a capacity being involved in causation.

There is another view of reality according to which reality does not consist of concrete things; rather it consists of creative processes. This is the metaphysic defended by Whitehead, presupposing a coherence of all aspects of nature in an organic universe.[8] This makes his cosmology closer to some of the pre-Socratics. If there is any merit to such a conceptualization of the universe, one must ask how causation enters this process, and which account of causation is likely to help us gain insight into the secrets of natural phenomena. The Aristotelian capacity view of causation is better suited to deal with such complexities.

If causation is to be effectively used in explaining natural phenomena, then a composite view of causation is to be preferred. That is, each effect or phenomenon we observe should be seen as the sum effect of many weighted causal forces. These causal forces are differences of certain capacities and not necessarily distinct objects.

Most of the phenomena we are called upon to explain are effects arising from composite causes. If we assume them to be linear combinations, our judgment on the intensity of the effect must result from weighting all the causes by their contributory potential to the overall effect.

We may want to explain the acceleration of a car up a hill by simply saying that its engine is producing a forward force. If we are now faced with a steeper hill and the car seeks to accelerate from an already high speed but it fails to do so, our explanation may come up short since now, with the engine still producing a forward force whose effect can be measured, the car is not accelerating. Our effect of interest, namely the acceleration of the car up the hill, is positively influenced by the force of the engine. But it is also negatively influenced by the combination of aerodynamic drag that increases with car speed, rolling friction of the tires, and a component of the pull of gravity on the car. We can now see how the magnitudes of these four contributory forces can rearrange themselves in a way that diminishes or intensifies the observed effect—that is, acceleration.

A lot more can be said about causation and explanation of natural phenomena, but it suffices here to sum this up by noting the composite nature of causation and the complementary view of causation as being rooted in actualizable potentials. Natural science is profoundly wedded to causation in a way that makes causation a more satisfying tool for explanation than reason and its derivative terms.

---

7. Cartwright, "Précis of *Nature's Capacities*," 153–56.
8. Whitehead, *Process and Reality*, 21–22.

Laws of Nature

Laws of nature have a central place in natural science. What is their nature? Are they abstract constructs or real? Are they necessary in science? We do not intend to dwell on these issues here, but we return to our purpose—namely, to say that natural phenomena can be more precisely explained by using laws of nature in addition to causation. Nothing more is gained by invoking reason and its derived concepts.

Laws of nature and natural law are two separate concepts that cause doubts, with both suggesting a theological root. These concepts are related to causation and teleology. They also highlight our aim in this book: namely, to de-emphasize the use of reason in the imprecise discourse about the study of nature but emphasize reason in the study of human nature. In part II, where we consider how we can use our analysis of reason to improve our conduct of inferences in general, we will touch on the roles of physics, sociology, and history as sources of experience and culture. The phenomena of physics, construed as broadly encompassing the study of nature, can be understood through causal relations. In a similar manner, the phenomena of sociology and history can be understood in terms of causes. The main difference here is the nature of these causes, with the phenomena in physics arising from the sum of fewer causes with determinate weightings as compared to the phenomena of sociology and history, wherein the cumulative sum of the beliefs responsible for a single human action consists of rather complex and unstable causal contributors.

This distinction between laws of nature and natural law based on the role of causes explains why laws in natural science tend to be more stable and simpler than laws in social sciences where, in the latter case, laws of free will and rationality are involved. Liberated from free will, natural phenomena can be explained with much greater precision using laws of nature that are derived from causal patterns of experience. The subjectivity introduced by those who study such causes and arrive at the said laws can be discussed more transparently without the further complication of reason and its derived terms.

What shall we say are laws of nature? For our purpose here, we simply consider them as general statements of regularities in the causal patterns of natural phenomena, where these are obtained in well-defined conditions. This approach delimits the operative causal forces from other environmental forces and excludes, as much as possible, the intrusive participation of free will. These statements are generally such that they can be transcribed into equations. We understand equations to be identities of functions of physical properties. For instance, Newton's second law posits the equality of resultant forces acting on a system and the time-rate of change of the system's momentum. The system's momentum is further defined as the product of the system's mass and its acceleration or rate of change of velocity. If two cars of equal weight separately collide with walls of similar construction, we can explain the greater damage done to the faster one by its higher rate of velocity reduction from the higher speed to zero. We do so by invoking Newton's second law and saying that if mass and rate of change of velocity are known, we can determine the net forces on a system, these forces being abstract relations or capacities of the cars.

Laws of nature are thus closely related to causal relations of natural phenomena. They benefit from the power of numbers on which mathematical relations are built. Whereas, for instance, it is useful to say the first law of thermodynamics states that energy is neither created nor destroyed, it becomes even more powerful in scientific explanation to say that the energy of an enclosed system increases by the numerical amount of heat added and/or mechanical work done on the system. A mathematical equation can be written with terms whose contributions can be quantified numerically and then compared. It is this clarity that attracted the logical positivists to the use of science for logical analysis of experience. Laws of nature, through their relation to causal patterns, allow for the development of what Hempel calls bridge principles, by means of which these principles can be verified.[9] The concept of laws of nature expands the conceptual possibilities of describing natural phenomena with greater precision. We can thereby avoid the vagueness associated with reason and rationality. This point is worth repeating throughout this chapter.

B. LOGIC

Although logic is often confused with reason in ordinary conversation, logicians have a more precise picture of what they mean when they speak about their subject. The logical positivists who placed great emphasis on verification and logical analysis of experience seem to have willfully opted for the adjective *logical* rather than *rational* in describing the kind of philosophy they were advocating. While we may be tempted to say logical analysis and rational analysis are the same thing, we would not extend the same generosity if someone suggested that logical analysis is the same as *reasonable* analysis. An air of approximation and subjectivity surrounds the latter name. Logical analysts therefore seem to have intentionally avoided reason.

---

9. Hempel, *Philosophy of Natural Science*, 72–75.

It can be argued from the use of words such as *logos* and *logistikon* in ancient Greek that the English rendering of the word *logic* is synonymous with *reason*. This position does not stand up to scrutiny, although the interchangeable use of words to refer to reason has been noted in the first chapter. In the modern use of the word, *logic* is concerned with rules of inference in such a way that a logical exercise may be declared valid or sound. It is valid if the premises necessitate the conclusion, without considering whether the premises are true propositions or not. When the premises are indeed true propositions and necessitate the conclusion, we speak of a sound logical argument.

Another way to look at logic and how it succeeds in discourse about natural phenomena is to consider its relation to taxonomy. The premises deal with sets that are within other sets in a nested way. As extensively nested sets with other sets, it is difficult to keep track of relations using our ordinary memory. Our working memory holds content for just about ten to fifteen seconds, the average length of a sentence. We cannot therefore keep track of three or more relations that appear as relations of sets, each expressible in an average sentence with a duration of our average working memory. As a bookkeeping method, logic therefore enables us to work out complex relations and discover hidden implications. Let us look at the famous example of a syllogism:

P1: All men are mortal.

P2: Socrates is a man.

C: Therefore, Socrates is mortal.

P1 is a set of all things that share the common property of mortality—that is, men belong to the class of mortality, perhaps just as other animals; P2 indicates that from the set of properties of the thing called Socrates, the idea of being a man is one such property. C helps us to see that Socrates is a member of the set of mortality by virtue of his sharing the property of being a man. Logic therefore helps us to see the relations of subsets to sets in such a tractable manner that surpasses the mind's unaided attempt to track implied relations.

Although logic may deal with sets of mathematical, linguistic, and other objects or definitions, it can also relate contingent facts such as the connection of causes and laws of nature in ways that avoid contradiction. When sets of properties and laws of natural phenomena are well ordered, proper inference is possible in complex relations. In terms of natural phenomena, as described in causation, we often deal with composite causes that are weighted by their influences on the effect. Keeping track of these composite causes can benefit from the power of logic as a connective tool. Logic, and not reason, appears to be a more transparent and precise methodological tool to guide inferences about nature. We are therefore better placed if, for once, we follow the practice of the logical positivists to recognize the central role of logic in the discourse of natural phenomena.

C. PROBABILITY

It is unfortunately the case that our means of completely characterizing natural phenomena are limited. The logical analysis performed on such knowledge cannot lead to sound deductive systems. It is here that science embraces probability. In fact, E. T. Jaynes devotes an entire book to making the argument that probability is the logic of science.[10] But rather than interpret this probability as a means of coping with our limitations in accessing knowledge about nature, some may see probability in science as a highway to skepticism about causation and deduction. This fear is not founded in practice, given the extent to which modern science uses probability theory.

If we consider logic to be dealing with the connection of sets and their subsets is a nested manner, we can see how it becomes useful to combine logic and probability in analyzing natural phenomena. That is, logic, which deals with deduction involving certainty, can be brought together with probability, which is a quantitative treatment of degrees of certainties. Although we may be tempted to say that such a combination is best described as reasoning, we must look to the analysts of natural sciences who still consider the union of logic and probability as extended logic. In this extended fashion, one conducts a logical analysis of experience and its laws. Reason may be invoked but it only obfuscates what extended logic clarifies.

D. COHERENCE AS A TEST OF TRUTH

Coherence is to be preferred over a simple judgment of reasonableness when dealing with explanations of natural phenomena that involve concepts of methods of science, causation, laws of nature, and logic. Coherence here serves a higher purpose as a theory of truth.

The nature of truth is an ongoing debate. It is easier to understand the problem as that of the truth of a proposition. This proposition is a thought or an assertion about the way things are in the world. To enquire of the condition for truth is to ask for the criterion by which thoughts about the

---

10. Jaynes, *Probability Theory*.

world do indeed latch onto things that exist outside the mind. Some identify competing theories of truth as being correspondence, coherence, and pragmatic theories of truth.

The difficulty with the correspondence theory of truth is already highlighted by Berkeley and Kant, who point to our reliance on impressions from phenomena. There is no mechanism of experience that directly connects us with the way things actually exist in the world. Only from the perspective of a Supreme Being or from the perspective of degrees of correspondence can one hope to establish truth. But once we are talking about degrees of truth, then the coherence theory of truth becomes a more powerful theory than the impossible correspondence theory. The pragmatic theory of truth makes truth dependent on expediency. Truth depends on the pragmatic situation. This is theoretically less interesting, and the mind is less willing to stop at this. In fact, it can be said that the debate about truth is mainly between correspondence and coherence theories.[11]

According to the coherence theory of truth, a proposition is true if it coheres with another set of propositions, such that this combined set of propositions constitutes a unity. The cognition of this coherence becomes a question of aesthetics. That is, the cognition requires an ability to see a certain unity in the relation of a proposition to other propositions such that this proposition enjoys, separately or together, a greater degree of credence. We usually declare the coherence of propositions with such expressions as "It makes sense to me!" To make sense in this manner is to aesthetically strike the mind with a coherence, a purposiveness, a general suggestion that things hang together in the way they are supposed to be. If one is interested in the stability of this coherence, the set of propositions considered can be perturbed by making alterations in the arrangement. One can then observe whether a stronger or weaker sense of coherence emerges.

Through coherence of various propositions, for example, we can conclude that human activities may lead to rising sea levels in the future if these activities are not corrected. To elaborate the supporting network of propositions, we can point to increased release of carbon dioxide (CO_2) into the atmosphere since the industrial revolution. We also know that CO_2 is a greenhouse gas, whose net effect is a rise in the global temperature. With this rise in temperature, more ice can melt, and the resulting water can find its way into the seas and oceans. Low lying coastal regions are therefore in danger. We know these auxiliary propositions with greater certainty and placing the proposition of interest in this context—namely, the causal

---

11. Strawson, *Analysis and Metaphysics*, 85–86.

link between human activities and rising sea levels—we grasp that it makes sense. This is coherence at work.

The logical positivists, with their commitment to verification of propositions, did not escape the debate about the theory of truth. Neurath and Hempel came out in favor of the coherence theory of truth, against the correspondence- or foundational-theory advocate Schlick.[12] In addition to Kant's reasonable defense of the idea that we can only know phenomena of things and not things-in-themselves, the extensive use of probability in science, and the composite nature of most causes, make coherence our best judge of how close we come to truth. All knowledge of phenomena is thanks to the interaction between significations from nature and our senses. There is no practical way of establishing the correlation between our senses and the things-in-themselves, except by imagination that leads to coherence. Coherence of these significations and general laws are our best point of access to degrees of truth about nature.

We have thus looked at key concepts that can facilitate discussion about natural science without appealing to the vague concept of reason. But with the discussion about probability and coherence, we realize that our knowledge, even if conveyed with these clearer concepts, can only be in degrees of truth. To end our discussion about the clarity afforded by avoiding the vaguer concepts of reason, rationality, and reasonableness, we need to address some serious challenges to the objectivity of scientific knowledge.

E. PROBLEM OF REFERENCE AND CONCEPTUALIZATION IN SCIENCE

We are often concerned with the relation between what we think, say, or write and the way things are in the world. Kant's separation of things-in-themselves and things as they appear to us seems plausible enough that we need not defend that view here. Throughout this work, it will be presupposed and understood to be somewhat related to Plato's theory of Forms and appearances. This is the first level of our failure to get at nature itself. The second problem is using the right concepts or coming up with new concepts to describe new natural phenomena. Here we draw largely from the technique of analogies and descriptions that are used in languages. Whereas we may use the notion of an *atom* today, it differs from various stages of the development of science where this term was used. If we leave out the problems of memory for now, we must first recognize the plausible truth that we know more than we can say. Despite this handicap, human beings

12. Hempel, "Schlick and Neurath," 181–98.

still try to express themselves approximately. It is hard or very limiting to heed Wittgenstein's counsel, "Whereof one cannot speak, thereof one must be silent."[13]

The names given to natural phenomena may draw too liberally from analogies and mislead our understanding. Our explanations can then veer off from the impressions of phenomena and take us much further from things-in-themselves. In this sense, we see subjectivity introduced into the scientific enterprise by the very agent carrying out science—that is, the observer and theorizer. One may add to these limitations ethical issues that arise from a natural selfish desire to secure credit for arriving at knowledge that remains elusive. Scientists may be too impatient to get recognition for new knowledge that remains uncertain. Some scientists may introduce new concepts to capture known phenomena simply because science prices novelty much higher than bringing precision to uncertain but known facts. Any knowledge we gain about natural phenomena is filtered through a subjective apparatus where the question of goals of the scientists may come into play.

F. PLACEBO AND NOCEBO EFFECTS

From our discussion of causation, a more helpful account of causation was the idea of actualization of inherent potentials in things. This actualization often proceeds in the direction of annihilation of such differences. But with placebo and nocebo effects, we are confronted with situations where, in the absence of capacities or potentials in certain things, psychology still induces change.

A placebo is something that stands for another thing, with the latter having some causal power. Typically, this is a substance taken to represent a medication. Believing that they have taken a medication, a patient responds positively to a disease, much to a degree comparable with the improvement of another person who actually takes the medication with the required causal powers. A nocebo, on the other hand, is a substance with no causal power but given to a person with the mislabel that this is a substance with the power to cause an unpleasant feeling or illness. Based on this belief alone, the person develops the unpleasant or sick condition. We thus have causation without the causal powers we would normally have isolated in an experimental study of causes and laws of nature.

Placebos and nocebos pose a problem to our suggested scheme of sticking to causation, laws of nature, logic, and probability in describing natural phenomena. Psychology must now be drawn into the explanation of

---

13. Wittgenstein, *Tractatus Logico-Philosophicus*, 108.

placebo and nocebo effects. Desires and fears must now be drawn into the explanation of observed natural phenomena. But these operate according to the subjective will that we have sought to exclude from the discussion about natural phenomena.

Notwithstanding the elements of subjectivity introduced by scientific language and the effects of placebo and nocebo, we still recommend the use of these key concepts discussed in this chapter in discussing natural phenomena. We should recognize the fundamentally subjective nature of reason and exclude it from the discussion of science. The implications of the analysis of reason offered in chapter 2 will be discussed in relation to religion and ethics in parts III and IV. What we must recognize beforehand is that although human moral actions are decided in accordance with free will, the human body and its interaction with nature follows the causal pattern of natural phenomena. Reason, being concerned with human thoughts as they relate to actions, must consider truths about natural phenomena and possibilities that can link the circumstances of the agents to their desired goals. Part II is therefore devoted to knowledge of contingent truths and how that knowledge can improve inferences during reasoning.

PART II

IN THIS PART WE discuss how the discovered structure of reason can be used to strategically improve inference about key components. Improving how inferences are made about contingent truths can benefit from (1) developing intuitions about part-whole relations and the Principle of Sufficient Reason (PSR); (2) drawing from the scientific study of natural and human phenomena, and (3) understanding the role of memory and imagination in reasoning. These aspects are only part of the reasoning process, given that they are concerned only with proper inference about the chain of contingent facts that connect a given situation to a desired goal. The determination of the goals of a reasoning process will be addressed in parts III and IV. In part II we are thus concerned only with contingent truths that can be improved by developing one's intuitions about part-whole relations and the PSR (chapter 4); knowledge of physics, sociology, and history as representatives of knowledge of natural and human phenomena (chapter 5); and understanding the vital role of memory and imagination (chapter 6).

CHAPTER 4

Compositional and Causal Analyses Can Enhance Reasoning

WE CAN DEVELOP SKILLS in conducting inferences about contingent truths through part-whole intuitions (compositional problems) and the Principle of Sufficient Reason (causal relations).

We want to consider in this chapter how two intuitions can be used to sharpen one's reasoning skills, especially that part of reasoning that is concerned with contingent truths. These two intuitions are intuitions about part-whole relations and the PSR. The first has to do with the general feeling that any object is made of parts, and that the object itself may be part of a larger whole. This hunch is useful for relational analysis. The PSR is the disposition to believe that all events have causes.

We are starting from the idea that, in reasoning, we are concerned with connecting a given circumstance to a certain goal by means of contingent facts and compositional relations. In logical analysis, we are concerned with connecting all sorts of ideas using rules of inference, without considering the reality of the content of the participating premises. While the ideas in this chapter may relate to both reasoning and logical analysis, we must bear in mind that logic and reason are different as discussed in part I. We do not intend to go into logic here; we shall only consider issues of common interest to logic as general rules of inference, and reason as a motion of thoughts that is goal-directed, with the goal being a value judgment.

To discuss part-whole relations and the PSR, we need to be acquainted with some concepts.

A. THOUGHTS

In reasoning and logical analysis, we are concerned with elements of thoughts. If we want to be very precise with our language, we will soon run into problems. This is because anything we say makes presuppositions about many of the concepts we use, even if our intention is to investigate one of those concepts. We can take *thought* here to be sufficiently basic and not in need of further definition. In psychology, one distinguishes between folk or common psychology and scientific psychology. Folk psychology is very practical in terms of communicating our intentions as well as predicting the behavior and intentions of others. Scientific psychology goes further to study thoughts in terms of brain states. While much is learned by relating human behavior to the function of brain cells, it remains a mystery how physical sensations are transformed into ideas about those sensations. An active debate is going on in psychology, with scientific psychology questioning the truth of folk psychology. Were they to be successful, our language would have to be rewritten to properly communicate the neuroscientific processes associated with a simple wish such as "I'd like to have dinner now." Articulating this in speech would be quite a task.

We have seen in chapter 1 that one of the points of disagreements between empiricists and rationalists was the relation of ideas to the impressions received by the subject's senses. Rationalists and Kantians hold that we are endowed with certain capacities to organize impressions into ideas. In chapter 6 we will return to some of the mysteries of the mind when we talk about memory and imagination. The storage and retrieval of past thoughts during remembering or the synthesis of new thoughts during imagination affects inferences. If all our knowledge arises from experience, in the mind, then, that knowledge takes the form of thoughts. The business of philosophy is to examine the relation of these thoughts to reality.

B. PROPOSITIONS

Several ideas or units of thoughts can be assembled into a proposition. We consider a proposition to be a statement, an abstract object, with a true/false value and to which a person can relate. A person can relate to this statement by thinking, believing, saying, doubting, etc. If P is the proposition "It is raining now," then it is either true or false that it is raining. My relation to P could be that I doubt P—that is, I doubt that it is raining. My doubt, my psychological attitude to P, is called a propositional attitude toward that proposition P. Propositional attitudes take the form of *subject + verb + that*

P, with the verbs represented by such words as *think, hope, doubt, expect, desire, believe*, etc.

The contingent truths we invoke in reasoning are generally propositions and propositional attitudes. Being able to distinguish between a proposition and one's relation to that proposition can therefore be very helpful in our analysis of the truth value of the proposition. Most often, we do not have enough information to determine the truth or falsity of a given proposition. With the diversifying branches of knowledge, we increasingly rely on the testimonies of others to inform our attitudes to most propositions. For example, someone could tell us that playing classical music to dairy cattle increases their milk production capacity. Some of us may think that this is plausible, but others may doubt it, and many may take it seriously if this is reported by a scientist specializing in the science of cattle emotions. This turns out to be a true proposition but everything I know about the proposition came from testimony.

By its nature, a proposition has an author. This author either synthesizes it from direct experience of the world or acquires it from another person. If the proposition is true and relates to the physical world, it must have been acquired at one point by direct contact with the physical world using one's sense organs. If we come to know a proposition from a person, that person may be the author or may simply be transmitting it as part of a chain that started with the author. One can maintain a psychological attitude to a proposition in one's mind, such as doubt, belief, hope, etc. or also communicate that proposition. When we communicate the proposition, we may indicate our judgment about its truth value.

C. ASSERTIONS

An assertion is a speech act in which it is claimed that something is the case. That is, an assertion is an act that makes public a proposition that is believed to be the case. "It is going to rain this afternoon," someone says. If we ask the person how they know, they may say, "I heard the prediction from the weather station." This implies that they maintain a propositional attitude of belief toward the weather station and now simply transmit the weather forecast. We may also hear, "The meteorologist predicts rain this afternoon, but I don't expect that it will rain." Here, a complex assertion is made, the one being a prediction and the other being the speaker's assessment of the truth value of the first proposition. How do we deal with such a situation? It comes down to credibility with respect to weather prediction. We can conclude from the assertion that it is likely going to rain this afternoon based on the simulations of the meteorologist and discard what we take to be the gut feeling of the speaker. We may also turn out to have erred in our judgment. This example involved the future situation, with respect to which the prediction remains problematic until future verification. Other assertions involve enduring states of affairs, and present or past events. In these cases, with sufficient information, we can determine the truth value and thereby verify the asserted proposition.

There are other speech acts of interest such as questions and commands. A speech act from someone in authority, though expressed as an assertion of a proposition, may carry the intention of a command. The teacher who declares, "There shall be no class tomorrow," may be interpreted as commanding the students not to come to class the following day. Propositions, propositional attitudes, and assertions with their associated challenges, are all the subject of philosophical investigations to which the reader can refer for more insight. Although this may appear confusing, it shows the continuous attempt to render more precise our discussion about the mind and its interaction with natural phenomena. It also shows our attempt to express truth about such interactions in language. The chances of being mistaken about the truth value of a proposition can be very high, given the modes by which these propositions come from nature to the first authors, and from those authors down to us.

D. THE NATURE OF A QUESTION

If we look at the way we compare our thoughts to reality in order to ascertain the proper connection of ideas, we will be struck by this thing we call a question. What is a question? This is not an attempt at being witty by asking a question about a question. A question is a concept of central importance in philosophy. We speak of the Socratic method in education, where we imagine a teacher gently guiding a student toward the independent discovery of new information by just asking questions. By so doing the teacher promotes critical thinking, evaluating the answers obtained, and asking new questions. We are told that in such a process a student remembers what they always knew in the world of ideas but had forgotten. Or the student is led to the discovery of completely new ideas.

Just like the nature of reason, the nature of a question has attracted far less interest in philosophical analysis than the nature of a proposition, an assertion, or truth.

A proposition is distinguished from a question by emphasizing the fact that a proposition has a truth value whereas the question does not. In a proposition, we say something is this way or that way. It is then left to us to verify using an appropriate theory of truth, whether it is indeed the case. But the quality of our public and private debates can be improved by reflecting on the nature of a question.

A question is also not a command; it is not an imperative to do something, although circumstances can be designed to effect indirect communication in which a question acts as a command. For example, suppose Ali sends John to the post office to mail a package. An hour later, Ali finds John still hanging around the office with the package, and asks, "John, are you still here?" John may react by simply saying, "Sorry, I'm going right away," and he may then leave for the post office. "Are you still here?" is a question, and the answer appears as if it is a response to a command. This is actually a truncated conversation in which John answers Ali's question affirmatively, followed by another demand for an explanation from Ali, yet followed perhaps by a poor explanation, to which an apology is then attached. After this exchange, the original command is then repeated, and John obeys it. This is the hidden role of commands posing as questions and vice versa.

Even without a clear theory of what a question is, we seem to be aware that there are good questions and bad questions. We think that bad questions make it difficult to answer or do not propel a discussion forward. If the answer to a question takes the form of a proposition, written or asserted, then it has a truth value. Now, folk wisdom tells us that "a good question is half the answer or half knowledge." If folk wisdom is correct, then, while a question does not have a truth value, it has elements that contribute to the construction of a proposition that does have a truth value. With these observations in mind and with any rudimentary understanding of what a question is, we can refine our reasoning or logical analysis about a situation by asking such questions as would spur us on to more critical thinking and discovery of connections.

The usefulness of this analysis may be questioned on grounds that the concept of a question is basic enough. But if we distinguish between good and bad questions, then we should reflect on the general features of a question. This can help us to consider how, in each situation, we can improve the quality of our question to propel discussion or inquiry toward discovery.

Our first ideas about the general features of a question may come from two types of answers we may expect to a question. The answer may be a simple confirmation, Yes, or a simple refutation, no. "Is Germany in Europe?" "Yes." "Are there trees on the moon?" "No." In the first case, it seems that the question contains elements of a true proposition and in the latter case, the question has elements of a false proposition. The second type of answer is a proposition, articulated such that the questioner feels a kind of satisfaction. In this second type of question, the proposition typically includes part of the question, in order to create a logical flow in conversation. Even if that part is not explicitly stated in the answer, both the questioner and the answerer tacitly assume a restatement of part of the question for comprehension. For instance, "When did the coronavirus pandemic start in China?" "It [the coronavirus pandemic] started [in China] in December 2019." We see that both the question and the answer contain many elements in common. Questions of this second type vary a lot, with some questions being substantially longer than the answers and vice versa.

To get closer to a tentative account of what a question is, let's consider what happens at conferences or public debates. During the question-and-answer session, we may have encountered a situation where someone takes the floor to ask a question. They then plunge into an elaborate explanation of a certain matter. The moderator, desperate to get the question-and-answer session back on track, may press the speaker to conclude their extended account and actually pose a question: "Thank you for that observation, but what is your question?" A little embarrassed, the speaker may ask the panel, "What is your reaction to what I have just said?" This type of exchange is sometimes followed by laughter and a simple confirmation, "I agree," "Not quite," or an elaborate explanation.

From these few observations, what can we say a question is? A reasonable attempt would be to say that a question is an incomplete picture of the way things are in the world, seeking completion from the answerer. This means that to ask a question, one needs to know something about that which is being asked.

It might be objected that this is not a general feature of a question. A possible example would be to refer to brief questions such as "What is this?" Or a simple reaction question such as "Why?" The first objection stems from a first acknowledgment that there is something to which the questioner is pointing. Thus, they perceive a thing which is unknown to them, or which should not be at that location. The second question, "Why?" acknowledges part of the story the questioner has just been told. It could take a longer form. Suppose someone has just said, "I'm not going to watch that movie!" To which another person reacts with the question, "Why?" In the elaborate form, the question is "Why do you say that you're not going to watch that movie?"

There are questions that present a partial picture of a nonexisting world or seek confirmation of a proposition that has no truth value; these involve presuppositions that are not true. An example of this is given by Bertrand

Russell in his *On Denoting*: "The present King of France is bald."[1] Rephrased as a question we have "Is the present King of France bald?" This question is not satisfied with a yes or no confirmation of the worldview that is being interrogated. France currently has no king, and so the imagined kingdom of France with a king who is either bald or is not can only be dismissed as fictional. But were someone to write a fiction in which present-day France is a kingdom and the king in the narrative is bald, then a question about the baldness of the king strictly relating to the possible world created in the novel could be answered in the affirmative. Thus, a question that presupposes a faulty picture of the world must first be confronted based on the presupposition, rather than completion of the faulty picture of the world.

A special type of question is the rhetorical question; the author does not expect an answer from the listener. In fact, the author may follow this question with an answer as a form of emphasis. The question is used to indirectly assert something. In philosophical reflections, rhetorical questions direct one's thoughts in a certain path or they establish competing alternatives. For instance, we find this style of philosophical reflection in Augustine of Hippo's *Confessions* and Wittgenstein's *Philosophical Investigations*. Some writers use questions to grab the attention of the reader and then follow up ordinary questions with comprehensive answers or analyses. But in works such as the two mentioned, rhetorical questions play a dramatic role, propelling reflections forward and unravelling new questions and new possibilities. Sometimes the reader is left to think about these questions. As philosophical questions, some of them may not have answers but their simple asking is valuable.

From the consideration of what a question is and the rhetorical question, we therefore see that a question contains some insight on a certain matter. The question is a partial picture of a situation; the more complex the situation, the more connected the parts, and the more we need to carefully reflect before completing that partial picture then the more we credit the question as a good one. Our reasoning about a connection between a circumstance and a desired goal should not only proceed with picking and connecting causal links from our library of contingent truths; it can be enriched by questions that are either substantial or rhetorical. The substantial question launches us into further reflection on how to answer it while the rhetorical question may increase our confidence or doubt, and thus propel us toward other possibilities.

It was important for us to talk about questions for another practical reason—namely, to highlight the business of philosophy to society.

---

1. Russell, "On Denoting," 485.

Philosophy is often castigated by some scientists and many people in society who have a bias against liberal education. The charge is that philosophy never solves problems of consequence, or it never produces a useful good or service. Philosophers in turn try to defend the field by pointing to some successful people, especially in the business world, who at one point studied philosophy. This misses the point of philosophy: philosophical questions are pursued to clarify them, to show a range of possible answers, and to show why each of them maybe doubted. The process generates new questions that bring us further, toward a more complete picture of reality. Whenever we confidently state a position as being the solution to a certain philosophical problem, we are simply stating our intuitions which may differ from the intuitions of those who approach the question differently. There may be consensus on some matters but that is hardly the common situation. By clarifying what a question is, we are better equipped to defend philosophy as fulfilling a useful task in society, even if its solutions are not conclusive or its products are not tangible. Philosophical questions induce a critical look at what we know, and they propel us toward seeking a fuller understanding of nature and human nature.

Questions, assertions, and propositions involve things related by action words or verbs. These verbs, carefully analyzed, will turn out to be some type of motion: "Mary *sings* Lieder," "The children *built* a snowman," "Ahmed *checks* his email every hour," etc. These verbs all signify some specialized forms of motion. Our reasoning is concerned with thoughts as they appear in propositions, assertions, questions, and other speech acts. *Mary, Lieder, children, snowman, Ahmed, email,* and *hour* in the examples above are things. Some of these are material things and others are abstract. We briefly discussed about names in chapter 3. *Substance* is another thing with a long history of philosophical inquiry. It would be useful if we knew something about substance before we talk about how intuitions of part-whole relations and the PSR can be made more useful in our inferences.

E. THINKING ABOUT SUBSTANCE

When we speak of things or entities in general, we refer to both abstract and concrete things. A useful taxonomy of entities is offered by Hoffman and Rosenkrantz.[2] According to this scheme, an entity can be an abstract or a concrete thing. An abstract thing can be a proposition, a relation, or a property. Here, a *proposition* can be understood to include assertions, questions, and commands. Concrete things include substance, event, time,

2. Hoffman and Rosenkrantz, *Substance: Its Nature*, 48.

place, collection/set, limit, privation, and trope (instantiation of a property). An important problem is to properly differentiate substance as an entity from other entities. Substance can either be a material object or a spiritual entity. In reasoning, we invoke concrete, material objects using abstract things such as propositions, assertions, and questions, as discussed above. Knowing the nature of each of these things is important for making distinctions and connections, and avoiding incoherence. It should be of interest to us if we want to improve our reasoning about an issue to be aware of the subtleties involved. We cannot afford to blindly presuppose certain meanings and further obfuscate the issue at hand.

The classification we have offered assumes the existence of concrete particular things. This is not without contestation. How many things are there in the world? On this question, intuitions differ between monists and pluralists. Monism holds that there is only one thing, and the appearance of things we see are simply parts of the giant whole. Pluralism, on the other hand, upholds the existence of different particular things in the world. This second view is both closer to our common intuitions and useful for analysis and reasoning. We shall therefore not pursue the debate but should maintain suspense with respect to the usefulness, if not plausibility, of monism. The notion of things consisting of parts, and being themselves part of a larger whole, seems compatible, and we shall later explore how this can be used in reasoning.

Let us consider one contrast that seems important—namely, the contrast between substance and events. This is important because there is also the view that concrete things don't exist; events are more fundamental. According to this view, incessant motion is the more fundamental reality of all that we observe. As metaphysics is continuously improved by better scientific observations and discoveries, it seems that this view ought to be addressed rather than simply dismissed. Modern science views material things as consisting of atoms, and at the level of atoms at temperatures above zero degrees kelvin, constituent particles are in incessant motion, whether they are arranged as a solid, liquid, gas, or plasma. But philosophy begins from speculation and observation, and as Kant rightly maintains, for speculation to rise to knowledge, it must accord with experience.

When we perceive the physical world, we have a sense that there are concrete things—that is, substances that differ from events. The main difference between a substance and an event appears to us to be their nature over time. Substances maintain their independence over time, continuously, whereas events are marked by changes to their material, spatial, and causal relations over time. But if we follow this independence over time as the marker, what shall we say of things such as rain and fire? Are they substances or events? Rain is condensed water vapor falling from the sky in droplets under the effect of gravity. We have found it useful to name it *rain*, rather than offer a lengthy description of the things involved and their motion.

As it is clear by now, we can hardly make a statement in philosophy without presupposing something that is the subject of an ongoing metaphysical debate with various contrasting viewpoints. Hoffman and Rosenkrantz defend the view of a substance as an entity that has a single instance of its category throughout an interval of time. The question arises whether conventional physical objects that are aggregations of other simpler things can be viewed as pure substances. The tendency among some philosophers, such as Hoffman and Rosenkrantz, is to exclude artifacts from the class of substances. While this resolves difficulties in articulating how constituent parts of a physical substance relate to the whole, it creates problems in reasoning exercises. The commonsense view is that if artifacts can form a consistent arrangement that maintains itself through an interval of time, it is useful for us to consider that as an instance of a substance. While cars, planes, refrigerators, etc. may not be pure substances as in the philosophical classification, they are not events, places, or time, and therefore they can be used in analysis as substances.

With respect to the relation of a substance to its properties, two views are offered. One holds that a substance is made up of a substrate in which its properties subsist. The other view holds that a substance is just a bundle of all its properties; there is nothing beyond this collection of properties. The first view suggests then that the substrate has no properties but how exactly the properties are related to the substrate is hard to grasp. The second view presents a problem since we usually talk of the properties of something but if that something is nothing but a collection of properties, it seems that the very concept of property becomes vague or circularly defined.

It seems, however, that the bundle theory of substance, according to which a substance is just the bundle of all its properties, is more useful. It allows us to explore further relations of substances to other entities such as events, places, and time. The substrate illusion may arise when we consider an object that consists of a very large number of properties. Focusing on one of these properties in relation to the rest of the properties, we can get the impression that most of the object's properties form a substratum in which the property that is being examined inheres.

When we identify things by their properties, we usually do so in a probabilistic manner. If we are acquainted with someone who has an identical twin sibling unbeknownst to us, we are likely to mistake the twin for the person we know if we come across that twin sibling, because of the striking similarity and our ignorance about their existence. The confusion can only be overcome by acquainting ourselves with the two twins and seeking out subtle differences between them, so that it becomes easier for us to tell them apart. Apart from the use of probability in this way, we consider an organism with a missing part to still be that organism. We still consider a person who has lost a leg as an organism of the human species. We do so because we can imagine an organism being made up of parts. If all the parts of the organism are separated, that organism ceases to live, whereas loss of a single noncrucial part (such as an arm or a leg), may still lead to a sustainable life. This means that it is reasonable to view a substance as a bundle of properties that cohere to confer persistence over time.

From our discussion of substance, we find it useful to broaden the concept of substance to include artifacts and to view the bundle theory of substance as more insightful. In the theory of substance, the appeal of the substrate theory is embraced by thinking of a collection of properties acting as the substrate background from which a property of interest is considered. This approach can be viewed as a part of conceptual engineering, such as defended by David Chalmers.[3] This practical approach to dealing with thoughts arises because of the challenges we face in analysis of absolute concepts that often tend to be inconclusive. New concepts or old ones can be engineered for use in a new circumstance. Adopting this view can be helpful in dealing with complex reasoning exercises where imprecise concepts may fare worse than redefined or newly designed concepts. The downside of this approach is the potential proliferation of concepts in such a way that impedes communication or useful debate. This weakness can be alleviated by clear definition of one's engineered concepts when using them in substantial conversation.

F. DEVELOPING PART-WHOLE INTUITIONS

With the foregoing discussion, we can now turn to the question, "How can our intuitions about parts and wholes be used in reasoning about complex things?" To address this question, let us first take the concept of composition to be basic. The problem of part-whole relation is treated in metaphysics under mereology. It is concerned with the truth about parthood and the relation of parts to wholes in very simple terms. This academic approach seems too abstract for the practical purpose of making good inferences during reasoning about ordinary life. It necessarily generates many more unresolved debates such that it is hard to build consensus.

3. Chalmers, "What Is Conceptual Engineering."

An important question in metaphysics, attributed to Peter van Inwagen, concerns the conditions under which several things compose a whole made up of those things.[4] Mereological nihilists deny the existence of objects with parts. This view is sufficiently abstract to fail to convince all. Mereological universalists maintain that any material objects are parts of another material object. To mereological moderates, there are conditions under which parts fuse to form a whole that is an aggregate of those parts, and there are conditions under which they don't fuse to form a whole.

Although mereology is largely a problem in metaphysics with many competing views, its value for commonsense analysis of our thoughts lies in its connection to our natural instinct to side with the mereological moderate. We feel that things are made of parts, and we investigate what these parts are. We also guess that certain individual things we see belong to a complex whole according to a certain relational rule. We further feel that there are conditions under which certain parts never fuse to form a whole. These intuitions align with the mereological moderate.

The compositional question can be used in inferences in two ways. The first is to consider as wholes those things with which we are confronted. These things are therefore made up of other parts, which themselves could be made up of other parts. A decompositional analysis can break down an entity into its constituent parts to reveal useful relations and properties. The second is to consider the thing of interest as part of a larger whole and figure out what the larger whole is and how this part is connected to that whole.

What we are suggesting is that we should invoke our part-whole intuition whenever we encounter concrete things in our reasoning or logical analyses. We may, for example, be attracted to a close examination of a flower. We would notice that this complex whole is made of parts: a stem, sepals, petals, stamen comprising filament and anthers, and a pistil comprising a visible stigma and hidden internal parts. These are features that are accessible to our naked eyes. But if we have access to microscopes and nanoscopes, we can further probe the constituents of each of these parts, right down to molecular structures. Until recent advances in modern science and further taxonomy, philosophical analysis had mostly relied on what we can see with our unaided eyes or with telescopes. The existence of unseen things and their features were attained through metaphysical speculations about how nature must be for us to see what we see.

The analysis of the flower above may help us to make inferences about pollination and further development of fruits. But the flower itself may be

---

4. Koons and Pickavance, *Metaphysics*, 127; Van Inwagen, *Material Beings*, 21; Loux and Crisp, *Metaphysics*, 255.

part of a branch of a blossoming tree. Our attention can then turn to the branch, and then to the tree. This tree may be one of many of the same or of different types of trees on a farm. There would be certain propositions about the farm that require no explicit invocation of the nature and role of flowers. But other aspects of the farm, such as pollination, would require us to invoke the structure of the flower in order to make inferences about fruit production on the farm.

Although we have focused on concrete things, the intuition about part-whole relations can equally apply to abstract things. The main point is that thinking about things as being made of parts or belonging to a larger thing is a powerful way to improve our ability to conduct proper inferences during reasoning or logical analysis. We are only limited in such analyses by our inability to see at much smaller and much larger scales. We are also not able to decompose certain things without a proper study of their nature. The flower we just discussed requires that we possess some knowledge of plant biology. But even where knowledge of specific technical concepts is lacking, we can distinguish by experience parts that unite to make a whole or a whole that can be decomposed into parts.

Part-whole intuitions lead us to compositional relations of things. If the question is asked why a certain thing is made of certain parts, an appropriate answer will point to a natural or functional existence. It may appear that the compositional relation is causal, but this is not the case in a more general sense.

If two atoms of a hydrogen gas combine to form a molecule of hydrogen, we may explain it as an existence or causal issue. Existence-wise, two atoms combine or react to yield an aggregate which is then in the more natural state of two hydrogen atoms. Causally, we may refer to a certain potential energy difference between their isolated state and their combined state. This difference is such that greater stability is found in the reacted state at a given temperature. A lower potential energy is attained by the rearrangement that brings them into a bonded state.

The relation of various parts of the flower to form a whole is only existential. A causal account of the composition is hard to discern, although a biological teleology may be imagined. But it is safer for us to consider as a general principle that part-whole relations are concerned with preferred or more natural existences in certain compositions. During inference, we therefore identity parts which can fuse to form wholes or wholes which can decompose into parts. Whether our train of thought linking a situation with a desired goal is reasonable may come down to whether the intermediate ideas consist of properly ordered part-whole relations.

G. DEVELOPING INTUITIONS ABOUT THE PRINCIPLE OF SUFFICIENT REASON

We may follow Leibniz to recognize the principle of noncontradiction and the PSR as the workhorses for the general conduct of inferences. These inferences may feature in logical analysis or reasoning, as previously discussed. Leibniz rightly condenses the problems of inference to these basic principles. They deal with the general problems of existence and change.

The principle of noncontradiction can be used in the part-whole analysis that is largely concerned with the possible existence of wholes and parts. If parts cannot combine to make a whole, they cannot at the same time be considered to be decomposed from a composite whole. It is possible that parts which cannot combine at certain conditions to form a whole, can do so at different conditions.

But wherever motion or change is involved, we are naturally inclined to think that causal forces are involved. As Leibniz rightly noted, we don't often know the reasons behind events.[5] That is, we don't know the causes, even though we instinctively grasp the idea that these events result from causal forces.

What we are suggesting here is that if we desire to develop our reasoning skills, we need to actively develop this intuition that all events (motions or changes) have causes. Although we may not know these causes, we need to be aware of their existence and be curious about their nature.

But what is this thing called an event? Events are best understood as distinct from material objects, which we discussed before considering part-whole relations. Material objects exist; parts come together to make a whole that exists at a more self-sufficient level than the parts. But events take place, occur, happen, or come to pass. This view of events suggests the participation of material things; they undergo change in space and time or change relative to other participating things or their parts. We have also noted a school of thought that supposes events to be more natural and more fundamental than objects. Subscribers to this school would view objects as illusionary frozen snapshots of the underlying incessant motion. These snapshots are then presented to the mind for ideation or cognitive processing. But as we said before, there is merit in embracing the distinction between material objects and events. It makes inference about contingent truths easier. Even where it is manifest that we are dealing with motions, a sufficiently slow motion may be treated as a substance in contrast to a much faster motion relative to the slow motion. The choice is a pragmatic conceptualization.

---

5. Leibniz, *Monadology*, para. 32.

The PSR pulls us away from notions of chance or superstition. It is tempting to cover our ignorance of causes by embracing chance or invoking superstitions. This temptation ought to be rejected. We can interpret any suggestion of chance to mean the involvement of many hidden causes. It could also mean the operation of composite causes in a manner that we cannot evaluate and predict their net effects with a high degree of certainty. Our ability to infer relations of things will improve if causes, rather than chance, are offered as grounds for events. This has the benefit of turning our attention to speculation about those causes. It is true that our speculation about causes may be wrong in certain instances. But this is corrigible through better causal analysis, and it is to be preferred over an embrace of chance or magic as a guide to proper inference. Composite causes may add up in ways that lead to apparent randomness in effects. If we are committed to the PSR, our commitment will lead us in such circumstances of apparent chaos to suspect the operation of multiple causes.

One of the achievements of philosophy is to separate the causes of events into natural causes and causes originating in the will of sentient beings.

Although the study of causes in natural philosophy is rendered difficult by their multiplicity and complexity, once discovered, such causes are stable. The case is different for causes that arise from the thoughts of sentient beings. Here, even generalizations from behavioral studies can be subject to strong variations. It is therefore useful to identify in any given event those causes that are of a natural kind and those of a volitional kind.

If causes are grounded in capacities that inhere in things, then what we observe in events are mostly a sequence of intermediate effects. The Humean account of causation is limiting when we try to understand events mechanistically. Hume's account rests on the analysis of simple events, usually of the binary type where spatial and temporal separation of sequences are possible and where a single cause produces a single effect. If a pressurized vessel explodes, the sequence of cause and effect, as a sequence of objects, is not clear. But viewed from the perspective of differences in certain capacities of things, we can come to appreciate causation in what may otherwise appear to be self-initiated, isolated events. These are triggered by inherent capacities in things.

With a capacity-based account of causation, our ability to infer causal relations can also be improved by distinguishing between events and substances. Causal capacities are associated with a pair or group of substances. These substances undergo change that manifests itself as an event. Being able to resolve events into the participating substances can help us speculate on, or identify, the possible causal capacities.

The helpful distinction between events and substances also makes it easier to disentangle complex phenomena. For instance, when a magnet is moved into a coil of a wire, an electric current is induced in a resistor connecting the ends of the coil. The phenomenon of induced current can only be understood by appreciating the properties of the magnet, the wire, and the connecting resistor, and the idea that moving a magnet closer to the wire activates the motion of charge carriers in the wire.

It might appear as if this PSR meets an exception in events such as placebo and nocebo effects. The existing belief that makes possible these effects can be viewed as the underlying cause. That is, the mind can act on the biochemistry of the human being. In an extended fashion, ideas that form one's worldview can influence one's behavior. Even if we do not know these ideas and how they translate to action on the body, we make progress by grasping that our behavior is influenced by our beliefs and/or other external triggers. This fact poses a challenge to the distinction we made about causal laws in the study of nature and laws in the regulation of the will of sentient beings.

Here, we emphasize the service we can get from the PSR and part-whole intuitions. In the next chapter, we want to show that our library of causal relations or, in general, our library of contingent truths can be strategically increased to facilitate reasoning and logical analysis. We do this by pointing to representative fields of study that are best adapted to enhance causal thinking.

We have covered in this chapter mostly relational issues that can improve our ability to draw inferences. Taking thoughts as basic, we highlighted the role of a proposition and of an assertion. These are treated in the literature and can be further pursued. We addressed the nature of a question as a special tool that can advance our thinking about contingent truths. We viewed a question as a partial picture of the world seeking completion or a potential full picture of the world seeking confirmation or refutation. The discussion of substance led to emphasis on the need to develop intuitions about part-whole relations. These ideas address existence problems. Distinguishing events from substances, the PSR was then highlighted as a useful tool to make sense of events. The challenge that Leibniz observes remains—namely, that we are often in the dark about the causes responsible for observed events. How we can improve our inventory of causal relations to better understand events is the subject of the next chapter.

CHAPTER 5

Reason's Contingent Truths Can Come from the Knowledge of Natural, Social, and Human Sciences

NATURAL, SOCIAL, AND HUMAN sciences can furnish us with the causal relations needed in reasoning and general inferences. They can be represented here by physics, sociology, and history, respectively.

Let us recall our objective in part II. In part I, we have offered an account of reason as the motion of thoughts from a given circumstance to a desired goal, integrating a series of intermediate contingent truths. The goal that is embedded in the reasoning process is a question of value, and we shall consider this in parts III and IV. In part II, we are looking at ways to improve our inferences about the relation of contingent truths. If I give the goal of my reasoning to be saving the life of someone dying from hunger, I must discriminate among the physical objects I can give to the person and how to obtain these objects. That means I need to know which of the objects around can act as food. I further need to know whether some foods are likely to harm the person I intend to help. There are series of questions that are strictly concerned with the properties of things and the causal relations of things. There are others that are concerned with normative principles. Suppose this person is of the Muslim or Jewish faith; certain food stuffs, though they may save a starving person, would not be appreciated by a person of Muslim or Jewish faith.

There are questions concerning the means by which a stated goal can be attained, and these questions can be answered by drawing from an inventory of properties of things and the causal relations of things. Conducting inferences about contingent truths requires knowledge of the existence of things and their properties as well as causal relations among things. In the previous chapter, we separated the powerful and intuitive PSR from the question of knowing the causes of events. The lack of knowledge about causes of various phenomena should spur us toward discovery. How does one come to a knowledge of causes? How many causes are there? How does one determine effects, if one is given a set of composite causes that may act contrary to one another? How should one deal with an incomplete inventory of causes associated with a phenomenon? Or how does one deal with lack of complete understanding about the nature of a given cause?

Thinking and nonthinking things that participate in causal interactions may lead to different regular patterns. Social phenomena involve thinking things, especially human beings. Can we apply to the study of social phenomena the same approaches to causal thinking and development of laws as in natural sciences?

In the history of philosophy, rapid progress in our understanding of the natural world and human societies has come through increased specialization of philosophy. Only very general speculative answers to the questions above can come from philosophy. To obtain concrete answers about causes of events and properties of things, we need to draw from various branches of knowledge.

Natural sciences furnish us with contingent truths about natural phenomena, where the free will of participating objects does not matter. But social sciences study populations of human subjects and their interaction with the natural world. They proceed on the presupposition that although free will is involved, regular patterns can be discovered, such that predictions about the future are possible. Whereas the natural sciences seek to discover stable causal patterns that remain invariant with time, the dynamics of human societies evolve with time so that their generalizations may also be variable. The world is a laboratory where human interactions play out; major events can be observed and recorded as history. One must wonder whether causality is relevant in this historical motion of human society.

These sciences—natural sciences, social study of contemporary society, and historical account of past events—are a rich source of our knowledge of contingent truths. Building a rich library of these can improve the quality of our inferences about a set of these truths. Such improved inferences can then elevate our reasoning toward truths about nature and moral human nature. We therefore need to explore these branches, at least in outline.

A. KNOWLEDGE OF CONTINGENT TRUTHS THROUGH PHYSICS AS THE MOST FUNDAMENTAL NATURAL SCIENCE

As discussed in chapter 3, science enables us to explain natural phenomena and equips us with tools to make predictions about the future state of systems. To do this, we need to acquire knowledge of the nature of various objects, the principles of change in the form of causal relations, and mathematical methods to compute changes. The successes of science in the last couple of centuries cannot be denied; our inventory of phenomena, their causal relations, and the properties of things involved continues to grow exponentially.

Because of the vastness of the field of natural science, we cannot engage in discussing specific phenomena and causal relations here. We do need to talk about the merit of acquainting ourselves with the advances of science in a more general way. We also need to see the challenges we are likely to face. The vastness of the inventory of scientific knowledge and the growth of narrow specializations are among these challenges. For our purpose of identifying the general approach of natural science, we can view physics as the most fundamental of sciences.

It is not a controversial position that physics is the most fundamental natural science; from it, a mechanistic understanding of other natural sciences can be derived. That is, chemistry, biology, geology, and astronomy all involve the motions and transformation of aggregates of elementary particles. The properties and mechanics of these particles are studied in physics. It is also in physics that the most extensive use of mathematics can be found. The other sciences then use results and methods of physics in addressing problems specific to their domains. For instance, chemistry studies the composition of substances and the changes that these substances undergo. These are rooted in the physics of subatomic particles.

But what is physics? Physicists concern themselves with the study of material objects; they seek to understand their structure in terms of constituent parts, the changes that these objects undergo in space and time, and the capacities (e.g., forces, energy, and fields) that are responsible for such changes. To develop predictive knowledge from these studies, we need controlled experiments, measurements, and generalizations.

Since when did mankind start studying physics? We must appreciate that mankind has been studying physics from very ancient times. This view is based on a consideration of the type of problems that physics is interested in, not just a limited focus on the modernized methods of the subject. The discovery of fire is said to be at least a million years old. Early humans were able to cognize a phenomenon initiated by bringing together objects under certain conditions. They saw the warmth produced by this phenomenon. They saw that it could chase away predators. They equally realized that this phenomenon could be used to make better tools and to cook food, thereby making food more tasteful and easily digestible. These human beings grasped the repeatability of the phenomena and thus could anticipate effects in future. Repeatable phenomena thrust the mind into the direction of science. A causal account and a predictive scheme are attempted. It is therefore justified to see the discovery and use of fire as part of physics and that it occurred in the distant past.

From such early times as the discovery of fire to the start of philosophical inquiry in ancient Greece, the store of human knowledge of phenomena continued to grow. Cultivators developed knowledge of the conditions that improve crop yield. They anticipated the seasons based on signs in earlier seasons. Thales, and the Greeks who followed him, thus introduced innovations in an existing field of commonsense physics. Based on such accumulated knowledge, the Egyptians built pyramids and other innovations. Seafarers built their boats based on the knowledge of buoyancy.

Less frequent phenomena, especially those that occur on a very large scale, usually raised the possibility of divine causes among the ancients. People are less likely to seek supranatural explanations for common diseases in each culture for which cures, such as medicinal plants, have been developed. But infrequent phenomena often elicited supranatural explanations. The gods, alone or in partnership with a Supreme God, could decide to act directly on the world. This approach to interpretation of natural phenomena does not immediately mark the ancients as antiphysics.

In very general terms, it can be argued that all events in the world are traceable to the actions of a will on material objects. A car driving down the street can be explained naturalistically but a human will is still involved. Even if this vehicle is a self-driving car, it does not take away the feeling that there is the will of a sentient being behind the motion. This view might be countered with such examples as accidents. Suppose something accidentally falls on a computer keyboard, activating the code for a self-driving car; it may be argued that the motion is a series of causes that do not originate in a will. The fact that a potential cause can be dormant for a long time before activation does not negate a causal link between the subsequent event and the cause of the suspended action. The programmer of the self-driving car is part of the causal chain of the ensuing motion.

The idea that all changes can be regressed to a cause originating in the will of a sentient being can explain why the ancients tried to account for events in terms of divine causation. Theirs was a crude but not totally unreasonable physics, given that we are often unaware of the nature of causes responsible for the events we see, but we do speculate on these.

The revolution ushered in by Greek philosophy was to separate naturally caused events from those that are supranatural. This separation was initially not a clean one. Thus, Aristotle attributes to Thales the view that substances cause change because they have a soul. This intuition persists into the modern era of philosophy with Spinoza holding the view that God and nature are one. According to him, individual things are just modes by which God's attributes are expressed in a necessitarian manner. The soul of things is the origin of the will that causes perceived changes in the world. The definitive separation of natural causes from supranatural causes takes the clearest form in the British empiricism of Locke, Berkeley, and Hume. From then on, scientific epistemology examines how we gain knowledge of natural phenomena. The methods and results of science have produced a large body of contingent truths about the natural world. Although the methods of science are debated, and some results are best presented as tentative conclusions, natural science can be said to be closer to its mission of establishing knowledge about natural phenomena than other fields of inquiry.

While natural phenomena can now be accounted for, purely on the basis of invariant causal patterns in material objects, the actions of human beings, however, resist a naturalistic account. Human free will can be influenced by ideas. Anthony Flew makes this point more lucid by distinguishing between movings and motion, where the former involves choices by a will.[1] This makes impossible the doctrine of universal physical necessitating determinism, says Flew. If this is true, then ideas of, or ideas originating from, a supranatural being can influence human behavior as they act on things in the world and set them in physical necessitarian motion. The source of this tension between physical necessitarian and willful choice-like causation can then be seen in the general attempt to infer causes from effects. Suppose we observe an apple falling from a tree. Without looking up, we may think that the apple fell naturally, the retaining force of the apple on the branch being less than the gravitational pull. It may also be that a squirrel on the tree caused the apple to fall. Or there may be a human being on the tree harvesting apples. In ancient times, the idea that gods have pushed the apple did not therefore seem too far-fetched given the possibility of willfully as well as physically determined causation. Without additional evidence, we can only infer probabilistically, but not determine with certainty, what caused

---

1. Flew and Varghese, *There Is a God*, 63.

the apple to fall if we only analyze the observed falling at a later stage of the motion.

The success of modern science has increased our confidence in invariant natural forces as the drivers of natural phenomena. Even if a person kicks a ball or the ball is pushed by a falling object, we do not implicate the human will beyond the generation of the force that initially acts on the ball. After such an action, or moving as Flew would call it, the motion can then be described naturalistically, without reference to the psychology of the person who kicked the ball.

You may wonder what all this discussion has to do with our attempt to improve our skills in making good inferences. We want to emphasize the fact that natural science is necessarily the study of phenomena that are caused by natural forces and whose effects can be experienced. We leave out the operation of the will and treat the interaction of any will with a physical object as a boundary condition. Natural science then proceeds to generalize causal relations, as Karl Popper rightly suggests,[2] by conjecture and refutation. According to the falsifiability criterion of science, if a hypothesis is scientific, a test can be conceived such that the hypothesis is either confirmed or refuted. That human factors can affect results of natural phenomena is not to be denied. The phenomena themselves are understood to be caused by forces in a manner that is repeatable, provided the boundary conditions between a will and physical interaction can be maintained.

Separating natural from supranatural causes in physics is the main, but not the only, achievement of modern natural sciences. Advanced mathematical tools and controlled experiments have equally propelled the natural sciences such as physics. These controlled experiments and mathematical devices help to detect new phenomena, isolate various causes, and identify various properties of things while also supporting the development of quantified relations among properties. With these developments and progress, more clarifying concepts have been developed with the aid of metaphysical thinking about the generalities. For example, mathematics and clean room experiments can now be combined with a nomenclature of subatomic particles and their energy levels to investigate particle mechanics at the nanoscale, a scale that is not visible to the naked eye. The mind and fine mechanics can access the secrets of nature at such scales.

These advances in mathematical devices and measurements at fine scales explain the very general nature of insights about phenomena offered by ancient or commonsense physics concerning their causes and their properties. The advances also help us to refine the collection of commonsense

---

2. Popper, *Logic of Scientific Discovery*, 17–18.

ideas about nature, since some of these ideas are only inferences from our experience, rather than observed experiences themselves. For instance, while common sense suggested that heat is a substance that flows from one body to the other, a mechanical foundation of thermodynamics has now disproved that view, pointing to the motion of billions of invisible constituent particles in a body.

To enlarge our library of contingent truths about naturally caused phenomena, we can therefore draw from both commonsense physics and modern physics. Where can we find these contingent truths of physics that can help us in connecting various phenomena when we conduct inferences? This is a tough question because increased specialization in the natural sciences makes it difficult even for professional scientists to keep track of the avalanche of new results of science. The situation must be more hopeless for the nonscientist who needs to incorporate contingent truths in their reasoning process.

The difficulty in keeping track of the expanding sea of scientific knowledge can be overcome by effective use of questions. In chapter 4, we discussed the nature of a question. The first path to enlarging one's library of contingent truths is by developing a curious mindset and learning how to ask a good question about natural phenomena. Taking advantage of science books, the internet, and special programs on TV and radio stations, one can seek answers to questions of interest. In pursuing this process, one's library of contingent truths about natural phenomena and one's ability to generalize without losing accuracy can grow. Conflicting views about a scientific truth are best resolved by experts from that branch of science. This should determine how we increase certainty about questionable scientific facts. This breadth of knowledge from an enlarged inventory of contingent truths then comes alive in a reasoning process where inferences and discrimination among competing truths must be made. But as we can see from the vast sea of information, our inferences would still be fallible. It is left for us to do our best, be humble and honest about our limitations, and avoid self-deception through prior commitment to political positions that may resists the force of careful inferences.

While physics gives us a good view of the mechanism of change, the other subjects—chemistry, biology, astronomy, and geology—offer us more parsimonious ways of discovering phenomena at larger scales and larger populations of things without delving into the motion of much smaller particles. From these different branches of derived sciences or applied physics, units of material objects with varying sizes can be obtained for analysis. These are also linked by causal relations, but they have emergent properties that are not immediately obvious from the mechanics of particles. These objects, their properties, and their causal relations are a tremendous help to us in inferences that involve contingent truths of practical import.

Our modest goal to enlarge our library of contingent truths about the natural world differs from the focus of philosophers of science and some science popularizers. Philosophers of science are concerned with the methods and foundations of science. While particular contingent truths of science may be discussed, it is not the objective of the philosophy of science to duplicate scientific knowledge. Also, some popularizers of science focus on the latest results of science, especially those that are more likely to be sensational. But if our goal is to improve our ability to make inferences by drawing from a large library of contingent truths about natural phenomena, we must take a broader approach as recommended above. The mundane things that confront us in daily life are not as sensational as the material that interests the science popularizer; they also require a greater degree of confidence than is to be admitted by the philosopher of science for whom skepticism is a powerful investigative tool.

Some branches of physics are more accessible to the nonspecialist than others. Mechanics, for example, is more intuitive. It is concerned with the equilibrium or motion of bodies under the action of forces. These bodies can be solids, liquids, gases, or plasmas. Although the mathematics of complex motion may be too involved for the nonspecialist, the resulting motion—equilibrium or lack thereof—can be grasped easily. It is because of this intuitiveness that mechanistic explanations of scientific phenomena are easily grasped.

The intuitive nature of mechanics also accounts for the fact that other branches of physics generally invoke mechanical language in their fundamental theories. Electrodynamics is thus concerned with the motion of electric currents as they interact with magnetic fields and other material motions. The modern theory of quantum mechanics invokes the mechanics of subatomic particles subject to quantization of energy storage and exchange. Statistical mechanics eschews the study of individual particles and studies the behavior of large populations in mechanical terms. The dominant role of mechanics in physics and our ability to relate to the motion or equilibrium of material objects justify the role of physics as a fundamental natural science.

If we are to benefit fully from the power of physics in other natural sciences, we must appreciate emergence. Emergence is the process by which the properties of a macroscopic system arise from the aggregation of smaller units or microscopic particles. These properties differ to some extent from the simple sum of properties of the constituent particles. Whereas we may know all the atoms of which a butterfly is made, the characteristics of the butterfly are not reducible to the properties of those atoms. It is the manner in which they are arranged that gives rise to new properties. In addition to our intuition about the existence of part-whole relations, we add this emergence of new properties from the fusion of parts into complex wholes—molecules, organisms, or astronomical objects.

This discussion complements what was said in chapters 3 and 4. But most importantly, it underscores the importance of knowledge about the natural world in our reasoning processes. We have defended the view that reason has to do with circumstances and goals, with the two being connected by an integrated chain of contingent truths. When we act in accordance with a will, whether good or bad, we operate on physical things. Their response to our interaction is determined by scientific principles. To predict their response, especially when this involves the connection of different physical things, we must possess knowledge of their contingent behavior under different constraints. While we may question whether science can tell us what a good or bad will is, it is a futile exercise to attack the system of scientific knowledge from without, as some religious folks may attempt to do. Because of its foundations and methods, scientific knowledge is best scrutinized from within science. But thanks to the mechanistic intuitions with which we are endowed, we are able to understand and use many of the contingent truths established by the ongoing scientific process.

As successful as the natural sciences are in providing us with knowledge of contingent facts, their limits must be clearly discerned. There is the mistaken view of scientism: it takes a hyperbolic approach to what natural science can tell us. It is asserted, without convincing evidence, that natural science can lay down foundations for human behavior, for the operation of human free will. It peddles the false hope of naturalistic ethics. Contingent truths about the behavior of human beings and their societies come from the social sciences, and the study of human beings in society shows the limit of necessitarian thinking when it comes to human beings and sentient things.

B. KNOWLEDGE OF CONTINGENT TRUTHS THROUGH SOCIOLOGY—THE STUDY OF HUMAN BEINGS IN SOCIETY

If our reasoning from a given circumstance to a desired goal involves interactions with human beings, then we need to know something about human nature and be able to predict human behavior. It is indeed the case that in addition to contingent truths about the natural world, the means that leads us from our given circumstance to a desired goal can involve interactions with other human beings. This involvement can be direct and active, or it may simply be the society observing our actions and judging the external actions against the structure of our reasoning. But if human behavior is influenced by free will, then can we really talk of the predictability of human behavior? Social sciences boldly answer this question affirmatively. They are encouraged by an innate human tendency to infer regularity from repeated experiences, and a tendency to use that regularity to anticipate future behavior. This disposition appears to be a very vital skill that promotes self-preservation and intelligibility of the chaotic world of human affairs.

Among the social sciences that have as their subject matter the societies of human beings are sociology, psychology, anthropology, economics, political science, and geography. It can be argued that many of these specialized sciences intersect with sociology, making it a reasonable representative of the social sciences. The term *sociology* is attributed to Auguste Comte (1798–1857 CE). Comte offered a hierarchy of the sciences, going from mathematics to sociology in the following order: mathematics, astronomy, physics, chemistry, biology, and sociology.[3] The first four, as he argues, can be studied as discrete independent systems. These systems are less complex than those involved in biology and sociology, where the systems studied are necessarily interrelated.

The success of scientific predictions depends heavily on the invariance of the principles of change within the time frame of the prediction. What methods and what foundations can guarantee the emergence of law-like generalizations from sociology? How stable can these generalizations be? Can we discern directional progress in sociology such as in the case of the natural sciences? These are questions that challenge sociologists and determine the degree of confidence that society can accord to their results.

In terms of the methodology of sociology, we find positivism and interpretivism or methodological individualism. Positivism follows the methods of the natural sciences closely, albeit operating on more complex human social systems. They observe and measure social phenomena from which theories are then developed. Just as in the natural sciences, where hypothesis-driven observations and measurements are more likely to lead to more credible theories, sociology also uses theories to guide its inquiries. Comparative analyses of societies or several phenomena can lead to generalizations.

The interrelated nature of systems in sociology would seem to suggest the futility of studying individual human beings. But interpretivism

---

3. Comte, *Positive Philosophy*, 48–55.

proceeds from the observation that human actions, though greatly influenced by one's social location, are also preceded by personal beliefs. Understanding these beliefs as driving forces is missed in positivism, where only black box analyses of inputs and outputs are pursued to established generalizations about the society. It can be said that positivism is concerned with how society works from the study of society as coarse systems, whereas interpretivism pierces into the nature of the human agents in society. This contrast can be seen in the positivism of the early sociologists such as Emile Durkheim versus the interpretivism in Max Weber's theorizing on the Protestant work ethic, or W. E. B. DuBois's work on the social conditions of African Americans. It is fair to say that interpretivism also uses data on social phenomena as confirmatory checks on the interpretive results.

Social sciences, by their devotion to the study of human behavior, face a peculiar task. Sociologists point out that theories produced by their science tend to modify the behavior of people in society once they come to understand these theories. We can see how this is the case. Since sociology generalizes the current behavior of people within the society, it is admitted that our society as it is falls short of a certain vision of a perfect society. There is no doubt about this conviction since the idea of fighting for change, whatever that means, generally attracts admiration and approval. Simply articulating the present situation in a clear theory of behavior is enough to induce dissatisfaction in the listener. If a wider section of the population is brought into that state of regret about the present situation, a perceptible change in social behavior is possible.

But the change in behavior within a society, induced by a certain social theory, also falsifies the theory that initially induced that change. For instance, in nineteenth-century America, slaves were treated as if they were not fully human and women were denied the right to vote as if they were not responsible co-citizens. If one considers the activists of those times as representatives of the sociological approach, they revealed to the political system a prevailing truth that fell short of the ideal of a society in which all human beings are created equal and endowed by their Creator with certain inseparable rights. This tension, between an empirically driven generalization of social behavior and an idealistic view shared by the people of that society, is the driving force for the instability that we observe in sociological theories.

This instability of social theories invites criticism from philosophers who examine the social sciences with the same rigor accorded to the methods and results of natural sciences. If sociologists present their positivist program to be as naturalistic as the natural sciences, then the uncertainty associated with the complex field of sociology is a stumbling block. Alasdair

MacIntyre attacks the weak predictability and lack of stable law-like generalizations in social sciences by blaming them on the conception of explanation and prediction.[4] He questions the positivist view that to explain a social phenomenon is to retrospectively invoke law-generalizations, whereas to predict is to invoke a similar law-like generalization in future terms. He then offers an interpretive view of the social sciences, with Machiavelli's political science as an example. This interpretive view is closer to Weber's methodological individualism, but Weber is not as pessimistic as MacIntyre about the prospect of a science of society.

By attacking the positivist program, MacIntyre sides with Karl Popper, whose demarcation criterion would seem to exclude sociology from the sciences. The reason for this is the lack of clear conjectures and hypotheses that are unambiguously falsifiable. The interpretive approach advocated by MacIntyre can be viewed as causal explanations that can benefit from a better understanding of human nature. Even this approach cannot fare much better, if the complexity of the social location of people within a given society is considered. A human being is defined by many characteristics: religious belief, gender, age, race, sexuality, education, geographical location, etc. With this complexity, we may wonder how groups of people may be considered to share a causal feature that explains social phenomena of interest. The collection of their defining features will lead to many permutations that are unlikely to perfectly overlap.

What the social locations of people in a system tell us is that our notion of individual freedom may hide many influences that bear on our behavior in profound ways. For example, in chapter 1 it was suggested that the Pietist Lutheran faith of Kant and Kierkegaard had a strong bearing on the way they incorporated religion into their philosophical theorizing. In like manner, Hegel's Lutheran understanding of Christ's presence at Holy Communion profoundly influenced his absolute idealism.

Despite these profound influences on our behavior, society still changes, and we have the feeling that we do make choices that run against certain standard norms. Criticism of the predictive power of social scientific theories does not negate the profound insights that sociology has produced. The instability of the models is understandable, given that there is feedback between the researchers and the people being studied. The people being studied are capable of being influenced by ideas of perfectibility or freedom. But the general possibility of sociology as a science of complex social systems rests on the nature of free will and the range of possibilities to choose from.

---

4. MacIntyre, *After Virtue*, 88–108.

If the will of individuals is free, and the possibilities to choose from are limited, then, as can be expected in the study of large populations of a few types of things, a statistical distribution emerges. If this distribution attains a certain regularity, something can be said about the average behavior of the society. The point here is that those who present sociology as a science like the natural sciences are disproved by the instability of their theories. But the weak predictability of social theories does not detract from the fact that many social phenomena can be explained and anticipated in qualitative terms. The theory of probability comes into play when we have statistical distributions of limited possibilities.

The foregoing discussion has many implications for the use of contingent facts about human behavior in the reasoning process. Three of them can be mentioned. First, the instability of social theories injects a degree of uncertainty in our reasoning, if they are used in connecting various contingent facts. Second, just the awareness about the subject matter and methods of sociology empowers us to seek sociological explanations from our observations of society. Some who embrace the interpretive method of social research immediately see that we can include among early sociologists such ancient philosophers as Plato and Aristotle. Third, knowing some of the causes of the failure of sociological models, such as people changing their behavior upon acquaintance with theories, we can develop intuitions about the dynamics of a society undergoing change and cautiously go beyond the given theories and circumstances to anticipate the future. That is, we can estimate the degree of uncertainty associated with a sociological fact.

If we are to be interpretive sociologists for the purpose of our reasoning exercise, paying attention to the social location of the people involved in our analysis can help. People's religious beliefs, race, education, gender, etc. will inform their behavior. While a broad understanding of the relation of some of these characteristics to behavior may attain a predictive status, we should still guard against stereotypes. It seems that the problem turns on whether or not the behavior we ascribe to people of a certain social location is positive or negative. If it is positive and we turn out to be wrong, the problem is limited to us and our attempt to predict. In that case, the consequences are not as serious as when we assume negative behavior based on our interpretation of people of a certain social location in society. Herein lies the serious problem in our society. Discrimination based on race, gender, sexuality, height, geographical background, etc. is and should be against the law. But this very fact conflicts with the innate human disposition to interpretively impose order on social phenomena, seeking correlations between certain behavioral acts and social locations. The result of this tension is uncertainty in any reasoning that involves human behavior, especially in a sociologically heterogeneous society. The uncertainty can, however, be reduced through further interactions which allow us to experience life from a sympathetic position of others in society. In a nutshell, reasoning in a heterogeneous society is fallible, where we understand by *heterogeneity* any difference in social locations, such as men and women, different religious denominations, etc.

When we embark on more social interaction, we are methodologically improving our amateur sociological research skills. Travel, conversation, and social events are valuable sources of contingent truths about human behavior. With the internet today, it is possible to experience virtual travel and to participate in the social lives of others without physically travelling. By engaging in these perspective-broadening activities, we partly follow Pythagoras's analogy of people at Greek festivals. That is, we participate in life while also gaining wisdom through careful observations of other lives.

When our worldview is limited, and when we shun reflection on our observations of society, we fail to see the overarching commonality in the cultures of the world. We may judge a particular action of a certain human being without understanding the goal of the action. But if goals are grasped, it can be understood that the same goal is attained by different means in different cultures. For example, whereas in some African communities it is disrespectful to look at your elder when they are talking to you, in some European cultures it is disrespectful to look away when anyone, let alone your elder, is talking to you. But the two contrasting behavioral recommendations both aim at the moral recommendation to listen to your elder respectfully.

Our discussion of sociology as an example of social sciences has shown that social sciences, carried out by specialists or reflective ordinary people, are a source of contingent truths about human behavior. If we are to properly connect given circumstances to certain desired goals such that the train of thought rises to reason, we need to arm ourselves with knowledge of human society. We also need to grudgingly admit the fallibility of such knowledge of contingent social truths.

C. KNOWLEDGE OF CONTINGENT TRUTHS THROUGH HISTORY

A third source of contingent truths that we can use in conducting inferences is history. It differs from physics and sociology. Physics is concerned with the motion and equilibrium of material objects according to unchanging, law-like generalizations. Our knowledge of these generalizations grows with time, but the natural order, the causal disposition of things, we take to be invariant. It is this idea that Plato seeks to convey in his separation of unchanging knowledge of the Forms of reality from the unstable opinions of change or experience. Sociology studies the contemporary society. While interpretive sociology may rely on historical data, positivist sociology attempts to devise hypotheses and test these through designed experiments. But the subject matter of history is the past.

Human beings are endowed with the ability to preserve accounts of past events. This preservation as history can take the form of personal memory, oral history, or written accounts of the past. Our knowledge of the natural world is incomplete and our behavior within society is not yet in accordance with the vision of the good, the just, the beautiful, and the true. This means that along the way, we create models of our partial understanding and leave behind traces of our actions. In this, Kant sees the greatest advantage of cumulative knowledge. While the life of one investigator of the world may be limited, the transmission of acquired knowledge to younger generations can result in a general cumulative growth of mankind's knowledge of world—past and present. History is therefore of profound significance for our project of understanding ourselves and the natural world.

Regarding the methods of history, it is debated whether history is a science or an art. Because the subject matter of history is evidence of past events, if evidence is elevated as the hallmark of science, then, it is argued, history should be a science. But it does not devise hypotheses and set up experiments to obtain the crucial validating evidence. Rather, it waits for human actions and time to create the material for historical investigation. But history is often presented as a narrative account of past events. Is this narrative account of history, then, closer to the arts? Here again, the creative imagination that is characteristic of the arts cannot be entertained as belonging to history. Memory, and not imagination, should produce historical narratives.

Supporters of the view that history is akin to the sciences go beyond evidence and emphasize the possibility of generalization. Hempel, for example, discusses law-like generalizations, or what he calls universal hypotheses, in history, showing how they are like the laws in the natural sciences.[5] Opposing this view of history are the historicists, who argue for historical explanations that do not aim at general laws.[6] This view is closer to interpretivism in sociology.

---

5. Hempel, "Function of General Laws."
6. Nielsen, "Historicism."

To understand what is at stake, one needs to look at the methods of history. According to Hegel, we should recognize three different ways of studying history: original, reflective, and philosophical.[7] Original history is the raw collection of data about events as they occur. Accounts of war in Greek states by the early historians are given as an example. The second way is reflective: it embeds accounts of particular events in a broader context, attends to some pragmatic present need for that history, and critically engages with the material in terms of its accuracy. Hegel's interest is in the third, philosophical history, where reason is used to analyze historical events. While Hegel's definition of reason is vague, a central element in his view is the directedness of history toward a goal, a higher moral and epistemological state than in the past.

By positing the motion of history toward a goal as a principle of history, and offering an interpretive account of world history, Hegel can fit into one of the two contrasting camps. The problem lies in the understanding of law-like generalizations and the failure to realize that laws arise from causation. Historicists who resist general laws do invoke causal relations in explaining history. Generalized, these amount to laws, albeit unstable laws, that are perhaps more unstable than the laws of sociology.

That the laws or generalizations of history may be more unstable than those of sociology is seen in the bias of historical data toward the lives of great people. The lives of ordinary people play a role in social dynamics but have not been properly documented in history. Sociology, on the other hand, studies the common people far more often than the great people who eventually enter the more visible sections of history. In history, some sections of society, such as women, slaves, conquered nations, etc. have not been sufficiently or unbiasedly recorded to reconstruct the psychology that caused those events of the past. Nationalism and other biases are also known to influence historical narratives. It is only through more historical research and freedom of the press that historical bias can be reduced in the generation of material for the history of the future.

But even with all the limitations of history in the current state, human society and human knowledge are impossible without drawing from historical accounts. If we are concerned with connecting a certain circumstance to a desired goal through contingent means, we will need knowledge of the natural world and knowledge of human behavior in present and past societies. We cannot do so without history. We must therefore endeavor

---

7. Hegel, *Philosophy of History*, 1–10.

to stock up our library of contingent truths with historical facts, remaining conscious of the possibility of biases and the possible instability of its generalizations.

Where can we find historical knowledge? Books and credible internet sources for historical information are an obvious source. Documentaries and movies are also alternatives. In historical movies, it is more likely to find embellishments of the original historical accounts for dramatic effect. Unfortunately, audiovisual presentation of history has a very strong appeal without forewarning about possible embellishments or bias. If getting at contingent truths about the past is our goal, we must seek to minimize the uncertainty that is necessarily inherent in historical knowledge.

Thus, we have discussed physics, sociology, and history as key sources of valuable contingent truths that can benefit reasoning exercises. But we have also been introduced to sources of errors and our limitations in this area. We can only do our best and exhibit both humility and honesty in the way we use these probable contingent truths to make inferences associated with reasoning.

Since we will not always have immediate access to the natural, social, and historical sciences during a reasoning process, we must recognize our inescapable dependence on our ability to retrieve from our memory knowledge that we once had in the past. In making inferences, we may need to connect different ideas that have never been connected before. This calls for use of our imagination. As we wind up our discussion about how we can improve our skills in conducting reasoning exercises, we will consider the role of memory and imagination in the next chapter.

CHAPTER 6

Memory and Imagination, Though Fallible, Are Necessary for Reasoning

MEMORY AND IMAGINATION ARE necessary for our acquisition of knowledge. They are also necessary for knowledge of the past and for comparative analyses during reasoning. But by their very nature, memory and imagination are fallible. Consider this statement:

> There is no logical impossibility in the hypothesis that the world sprang into being five minutes ago, exactly as it then was, with a population that "remembered" a wholly unreal past.[1]

This provocative hypothesis about a five-minutes-old world by Bertrand Russell demonstrates the challenging nature of memory. Our working memory is said to be about ten to fifteen seconds, corresponding to the time taken to make an average sentence of twenty to thirty words. We may define the instant we call "the present" as the working memory duration of ten to fifteen seconds. Anything outside this time window is either the past or the future, the knowledge of which is not immediately available to our minds.

But if we are to reason from a circumstance to a desired goal by connecting a string of our stored contingent truths, we must bring those things we knew in the past to our working memory. We must also create different patterns of reasoning, briefly keep them aside, then compare with other patterns, and then make a judgment about the most reasonable network of ideas. But how is it possible to know ideas we once knew in the past? What is this thing called memory?

We generally do not get bogged down with questions such as the nature and possibility of memory. We seem to have a general idea of what memory

---

1. Russell, *Analysis of Mind*, 116.

is and can invoke knowledge of the past in our discussions of the present or our planning for the future. People can testify in court about events that occurred in the past. On the strength of those testimonies, accused persons can be exonerated or condemned. But in the context of improving our ability to carry out reasoning exercises, we must examine all those things that may make us go astray. Our goal is to connect given circumstances with their desired goals using the most feasible and dependable strings of contingent truths about the natural world and about human nature.

Skepticism can either be a crippling attitude or a methodical tool for improved understanding. With respect to the relation of our knowledge to time, we can identify three types of doubts in philosophy. Knowledge of the present can be challenged by such a skeptical thought experiment such as the brain in a vat. According to this thought experiment, our consciousness may be the result of a disembodied simulation of a brain. This challenges us to examine the causal connections of our thoughts about the present to the external conditions that are supposed to be causing those thoughts. The second doubt is about the future. Knowledge of the future is successfully challenged by the skepticism about induction as highlighted by David Hume. Our plans about tomorrow involve contingent truths based on generalization of regular patterns we have observed in the past. By what principle do we extend these generalizations to the future? We bet on a certain changelessness in the operation of the laws of nature and patterns of human behavior. This faith in changeless preservation of certain regularities is innate or it arose in our cultures from a theological view about a Supreme Being who assures the changelessness of certain truths. In engaging with doubts about induction, we may identify certain generalizations that do not strongly suggest changelessness. We may weaken our expectation of regularity in the future. The third doubt concerns knowledge of the past, where we rely on memory.

Regarding the past, memory skepticism challenges us to consider how we can bring back to life those thoughts that arose from direct experience of the external world. If we are concerned with how memory can help us in reasoning, we must avoid the crippling effect of skepticism because reasoning as a prelude to action cannot afford such luxury as suspending judgment. But we need to embrace the enabling aspect of skepticism—namely, its ability to spur us toward greater clarity, even if we do not completely resolve all our doubts about an issue. This calls us to consider the nature and mechanism of memory in order to guide our reasoning with the help of knowledge of, and from, the past.

Apart from memory, imagination also appears in our reasoning. We do not only remember and connect past pieces of knowledge; we need imagination in order to connect separate ideas and form a logical structure that links a given circumstance to a desired goal. Imagination is the means by which alternative trains of thoughts are synthesized, juxtaposed, and judged for their potential rational character.

The empiricist account of knowledge acquisition, either in the Humean or Kantian fashion, suggests that memory and imagination are not only important in the analysis of knowledge of the past and analysis of possibilities. Memory and imagination are also involved in sense experience of the world insofar as concepts acquired in the past are needed to make sense of the impressions from without and transform them into ideas.

Although memory and imagination are challenging as separate concepts, their joint consideration can lead to mutual enlightenment, with one shedding light on the other.

A. MEMORY: BETWEEN DOUBT AND CERTAINTY ABOUT REMEMBERED FACTS

Some people speak of the faculty of memory. The complexity of the human mind sometimes leads theorists to imagine the existence of specific faculties for each complex cognitive process. This approach does not clarify the situation. One can therefore sympathize with the position of Gilbert Ryle who argues against the notion of a faculty of memory, like his refutation of the existence of faculties of imagination and reason.[2] The value of this simplification is that one can focus on memory as a process or an event that involves other objects and processes of the cognitive system.

In talking about memory and other mental activities, some may adopt dramatic or pictorial language aimed at introducing intuitive mechanistic features. In his *Confessions*, Augustine speaks of palaces of memory into which he enters when he wants to remember something.[3] The things being remembered then spring forth in a certain order, with certain things inquiring whether they are the things being recalled, others making way for images from the back to come to the front while awaiting their turn as the next in the chain of things remembered. This vivid stream of images is not the real picture of remembering; it only helps to communicate a certain subjective feeling of remembering. It also suggests the complexity that arises when we reflect on how we remember.

Dealing with the complexity of the mind is approached through conceptual engineering. That is, we must break down this complex cognitive

2. Ryle, *Concept of Mind*, 249–54.
3. Augustine, *Confessions* 10.8.

system using concepts. By *concepts* here we mean abstract ideas that are used to describe substances, events, and relations that may be real or imaginary. These concepts are embedded in a network of other concepts and expressed in language. This sort of modeling is aimed at simplifying a complex system by isolating those things that matter in describing the main functions of the system. The resulting simplicity is an advantage, but two disadvantages can be mentioned. The first disadvantage of unbridled conceptual engineering is the proliferation of concepts with different meanings. The second disadvantage is that we are still left with unresolved debates on whether the substances, events, or the relations captured by the concepts do really exist, and if not, then, how do they relate to reality?

In memory research, one distinguishes three types of memory based on how their process of remembering works: procedural memory, declarative episodic memory, and declarative semantic memory.

Procedural memory deals with the memory of how to do something. For instance, if we have learned how to ride a bike, when we get on a bike, that skill is recalled without consciously thinking about what we need to do. Another example could be an opera singer who instantly recalls the techniques of breathing, vocal-cord opening, and mouth placements that are needed to produce a high-quality sound. Here, remembering appears as a tacit or subconscious process; one does not think much about it. Procedural memory can be doubted by suggesting that one performs an action for the very first time through imagination and trial and error; any feeling of having performed the act before may be said to be illusory. But compared to other memory doubts, this doubt is not very common or, when it occurs, it is easily dispelled.

Declarative episodic memory refers to the capacity to store and recall past personal experiences. It is declarative or explicit in that the process of remembering is intentional, explicable, and distinct from the process of procedural remembering by doing. For example, Andrew recalls having lunch with his friend yesterday at a certain Starbucks coffee shop. Episodic memory can be doubted by suggesting that such an experience never occurred in the past or it occurred in a totally or slightly different way. Perhaps Andrew had lunch the day before with his brother, not his friend, and at a Burger King restaurant, not a Starbucks coffee shop.

The third type of memory, declarative semantic memory, is concerned with the storage and remembering of knowledge about the world. It is concerned with impersonal, general facts about the world. For example, Anna remembers that France is in Europe. Hasan remembers that the sun is stationary, but the earth revolves around the sun. The content of semantic memory may be a necessary or contingent fact.

The definition of memory as procedural, episodic, and semantic allows us to appreciate the possibility of memory contents moving from one type of memory to the other. For example, Anna may just have learned from Wang this morning that France is in Europe. With repeated usage of this knowledge and the passage of time, and perhaps a personal visit to France, she may come to completely forget how she first learned that fact but will still remember the impersonal fact that France is in Europe. In a similar manner, the engineer and the mathematician may go about solving an algebraic problem without giving much thought to the identities invoked in their simplifications. The recalled identities are elements of declarative semantic memory, but they are tacitly invoked in solving a given problem procedurally.

The content remembered is related to knowledge from the past. The conceptualization of memory categories allows us to imagine how information is encoded during the learning process, later consolidated in a network of previously acquired ideas, and retrieved at later time in the same or modified form. The retrieval may result from an external prompt, an intentional desire to recall that content, or a spontaneous suggestion of that material to the mind. If we are prompted by an external question or circumstance, we remember. But whether we assert exactly what we remember is a different question. For instance, prompted by the question whether Juan has seen José, Juan may choose to say yes or no, even if the prompt brings to mind the instance where he chatted with José in the recent past.

But how are memory beliefs related to the events remembered? Here, at least in philosophy, two main positions are in tension: the direct realist theory of memory and the representational theory of memory. The direct theory asserts that, in memory, we remember the actual events that we experienced at an earlier time. On the other hand, the representational theory of memory, such as held by Hume, asserts that, in memory, we recollect ideas that are linked to the experiences we had in the past.

If these two positions exist, it means that there are reasons for each view that are not fully defeated by the competitor: both advance arguments for their position. But nonetheless, it seems that the direct realist theory of memory is misled by the facility and speed with which remembering is done. The fact that the natural capacities of human beings are relied upon in philosophical theorizing does not mean that the nature of what is being theorized cannot be better understood using other tools beside human natural capacities. For instance, an eyeblink lasts about one third of a second. This is rather short, almost instantaneous, we may say. But with a high-speed camera and other equipment, we can break down this fast process into a series of processes where we can observe the complex mechanism of an eyeblink. We can play back the recorded process in slow motion and appreciate the complexity of the otherwise simple act. In observing processes of philosophical interest, modern philosophy must welcome the aid of tools that help us make sense of the phenomena being studied.

The directness in the direct realist's theory appears to be not so direct. Since we experience many events in the past, remembering one of them would at least require a mechanism to match our trigger to the desired event. If the events reside in a memory palace as Augustine says, we must follow his recalling process to see that it involves sorting through the pile of past events.

According to the representational theory of memory, when we remember, we bring to life in our minds those ideas that are connected to past experiences. The question arises: how do we know that the images or the ideas recalled are not just the products of our imagination? Supporters of the representational theory address this challenge by asserting a certain familiarity or pastness that is stamped on those images that are indeed reflections of the past. But if our best adjudicator between memory and imagination is a feeling of pastness, we must admit the possibility of being fallible. Uncertainty is therefore intimately bound to what we remember. If the remembered facts are constituents of our reasoning, we must entertain the possibility that our reasoning may be fallible in ways that are linked to memory and cannot be eliminated without invoking memory in a circular manner.

Some memory theories attempt to secure memory beliefs from doubts about what is remembered. The epistemic theory of memory asserts that to remember a proposition is to believe that proposition at the time of remembering and at an earlier time of acquisition. This view introduces another difficulty. It is said that when a lie is repeated many times, the fallible human mind is likely to elevate it to a truth. This popular view has some truth in it, given the way media and marketing experts tap into it. It is therefore possible that a proposition acquired at a certain time may transform its truth value between the acquisition and a later remembering of it. For example, suppose someone asserts that Mr. Barack Obama was born in Kenya and Peter entertains this proposition with some doubt. The proposition is false, but through contact with a conspiracy source, Peter may come to hold the view that Mr. Barack Obama was indeed born in Kenya. These challenges can be retraced in episodic memory where we can retrace initial and intervening experiences of the fact being remembered. They become more difficult to disentangle in the case of declarative semantic memory where we remember things while forgetting where and when we first came to believe those things.

The idea of a feeling of familiarity as a distinguisher of memory from imagination deals only with the judgment of the image presented to the mind. The question of how that image is synthesized from past experience calls for a mechanism of its representation or direct realization. The direct theory has limited avenues for exploring the mechanism of our natural capacity to remember. But simply admitting the simple idea of representation in the representational theory opens up opportunities for further exploration of how remembering is realized.

Since representation occurs in direct experience, memory, and imagination, a principle is needed to determine whether a representation under consideration qualifies as memory. In the direct theory of memory, we are dealing with a retention theory. This suggests that the memory content is present in the mind, waiting for a prompt to recall. Some remembering processes take time, while others follow almost instantaneously the prompt to recall, yet other remembering processes do not succeed to reestablish the past content.

A causal theory of memory considers a recall to be connected to a past representation through a causal process. Sven Bernecker defends this theory using the approach of argument to the best explanation.[4] Alternatives such as the retention theory discussed above are found to be more problematic in connecting memory to the past experience. The nature of this causal process can, however, be debated. The concept of memory traces is advanced to illuminate the causal process. These traces are supposed to propagate information and bring about the recall of that information at a later time.

Although the idea of memory traces appears to be the best explanation for the causal connection between remembered material and past experience of that material, it faces some challenges from recent scholarship on the neurobiology of memory. Given the complexity of memory, and the idea that the philosophical investigation of memory is mostly conceptual at the moment, any new insights need to be brought to bear on tentative accounts.

Based on studies of the part of the brain associated with remembering, the hippocampus, Katherine Akers and coauthors have suggested that the brain appears to be wired to forget.[5] Neurons are generated as the learned information is encoded but the neurons generated at a later time appear to clear away the previous memory neurons, preparing for a new learning process. This puts into question the idea of memory traces as entities that persist and propagate information from a past to a recalled state.

---

4. Bernecker, *Metaphysics of Memory*, 9–10.
5. Akers et al., "Hippocampal Neurogenesis."

The support for memory traces as key in the causal theory of memory seems to be influenced by how causation is understood by the proponents of traces. If a Humean account of causation is embraced, then the need for contiguity between the cause and the effect necessitates an entity such as the memory trace. But we have previously argued in favor of the capacity account of causation as more metaphysically satisfying. If we agree that a recalled state must be causally connected with the past experience that is being recalled, we can look for that causal mechanism in the activation of certain potentials or capacities of the cognitive system.

It seems that the capacity or potential account of causation recommends itself quite well when we consider the different memory types: nondeclarative procedural, declarative episodic, and declarative semantic memory. Let us consider the case of a classical guitar player and their teacher. The teacher possesses both procedural and semantic memory of guitar playing. But that teacher may teach the student without holding a guitar! This is possible through instructions to the student. The student, on the other hand, acquires procedural memory from trying out the instructions from the teacher. The student also remembers episodically the previous lesson in which the teacher explained other playing techniques. As the years go by, the student will also become a guitar teacher, capable of instructing other students on playing the same guitar pieces they learned from their teacher.

The guitar learning process is only one example. A similar situation occurs with the professional training of singers. It can occur that a soprano acquires singing skills through the instructions of a baritone singer. She learns by aligning her actions with propositional instructions from the teacher who can't sing the same high notes as the soprano. This soprano may in future train a tenor singer by also using propositions while the tenor conditions his body to produce the right sound. Thus, we see the interplay of semantic, episodic, and procedural memory. What kind of memory mechanism is at play in this dynamic migration of memory from one type to the other?

It seems that during the learning process, memory is encoded as a training process. The body is trained in such a way that it acquires new capacities. The impressions on the senses excite and communicate certain vibrational patterns. It is through the reactivation of this pattern, as a kind of drama, that past experiences are recalled. That is, when we experience something, that experience amounts to an algorithm that teaches our body to mimic some motion from which certain ideas or thoughts are deduced by the mind. An appropriate recall triggers this reconfiguration of the cognitive system to produce a similar image. Hume considers the remembered ideas not to be as vivid as the initial impressions. This is possible if the remembered ideas are indeed a reconstructed motion based on previously acquired capacities to move in a certain way, with respect to neighboring cognitive cells.

In terms of improving the retention of past experiences, certain actions and attitudes seem to favor recollection. Research shows that if the learning process is active and focused, and the learner gets good sleep, the new material is well encoded and consolidated in a network that interlaces with past knowledge. It is indeed true that we do not only recall the exact material encoded in a specific past experience, we often recall integrated memory material. This integration seems to be better explained by the view of impressions as triggering the senses to learn and incorporate new skills or capacities. The connective motion of thoughts that recreate the motion must be complex, but it is best understood by abandoning the idea of memory as being preserved in entities rather than capacities of existing or generated entities. Neurons may contain instructions from a given learning process, but after passing that information on to other memory system components, they can degenerate. The neuroscientists may well be right to interpret new neural generations as depleting previous neurons. These previous neurons have fulfilled their task of training the cognitive system to acquire the capacities to reenact the original impressions.

If this account of memory causation is true, then one can view the process of forgetting as failed consolidation of the encoded material in an existing network, or neurons degenerating without transmitting their acquired capacities to more permanent parts of the memory systems. This account is indeed plausible, if we consider that the human body makes new cells and kills off old ones. It is held that the human body can completely replace its cells within a couple of years. Irrespective of whether one is committed to the dualistic, or the reductive materialistic, or nonreductive materialistic view of mind, brain cells do participate in memory creation and recall. It seems that if we are to remember anything from our childhood after the complete replacement of our body cells, then the only way to transmit experience from old cells to new cells would have to be a form of teaching these new cells or transmitting certain capacities to them. These learned skills or capacities then participate in latter recollection processes.

Given that our goal here is not a reasoned account of memory, we should consider our goal of knowing in general terms how memory works to be partially attained. We have shown that memory is complex; concepts are needed to break it down to a level that we can clarify what we mean when we say we remember something.

Let us return to the question of how we distinguish between a mental representation that is memory and one that is the product of imagination. Other analysts advance the idea of a feeling of familiarity or pastness that is supposed to accompany a mental representation that is memory while this familiarity is absent from that which is imagination. This is the best we can hope for, it seems—that is, a certain intuition that this image is memory, but that the other image is imagination. At once, this is disappointing, but it also illuminates the phenomenon of misremembering or forgetting the past.

It is often hypothesized that while certain things may be easily forgotten, more dramatic events are not forgotten that easily. This does not seem to be generally true. Ten years after the September 11, 2001, terrorist attack in New York, psychologists found that most people could not accurately remember their personal experiences on that day.[6] This was a dramatic event of common focus, and a few weeks later memories were clear about the event. What was remembered with greater accuracy about the event were general facts that one can read in a newspaper or glean from a movie such as Michael Moore's *Fahrenheit 9/11*. This case reinforces the fact that the feeling of familiarity of the image presented to the mind for memory judgment is fallible with respect to recovering events experienced in the past.

We could imagine that among those interviewed about their personal experiences on September 11, 2001, if some people had kept a diary of the events of that day, they would consult their diary and give a more accurate account. This would still be true even if they had never consulted the diary between writing their experience and a decade or more later. Ideas arising from our subjective experience of the world can thus be stored more faithfully in external objects: books, inscriptions in statues, vinyl records from the early twentieth century, laptop computers, mobile phones, etc. This possibility has therefore attracted the attention of the philosophers of cognition to suggest the idea of extended cognition. If a causal connection to the past is the criterion for memory, we must embrace the opportunity presented by external memory storage while also acknowledging the possibility of manipulation of such externally stored material between storage and retrieval. That is, we are still left with fallible methods of recollecting past knowledge.

We are indeed faced with skepticism about memory that cannot be resolved without resorting to memory in a circular manner. Even if we store our experiences in external devices, we need to remember this fact. We also need to acknowledge that the stored information can be manipulated; a diary can be forged, information stored on a computer can be changed, a video of an event can have its content modified. Once an event is separated

---

6. Hirst et al., "Ten-Year Follow-Up."

by time, an account of that event based on internal or external memory remains fallible. But this does not mean that we are not prudent enough to reduce the odds of our being mistaken. In fact, our use of memory is often accompanied by knowledge of the fallibility and strategies to minimize the chances of being mistaken. We are required to be humble and honest about our use of memory.

Research on memory is progressing at the psychological and neurobiological level. As new insights are gained, the complex nature of memory will continue to astonish us and cause us to be less confident in our memory judgment. But such research will also show practical ways to improve our memory. Based on the findings of memory research, we are told that frequent use of memory elements and good sleep are helpful in recalling past events or past knowledge. In an age where less sleep is praised, it cannot be emphasized enough how vital sleep is for the consolidation of memory elements, improved deep learning, and easy recollection of past events. Also, alcohol is found to render memory less effective. As one ages, memory becomes less effective than in youthful years but with exercise, the reduction can be controlled. It is noted how easy it is to recall the words of familiar songs. In addition to other pattern effects in songs and poems, the fact that we repeat these very often inscribes an easily retrievable pattern in our minds. If we play a music record long enough, we tend to anticipate the order of the songs being played. We can thus tap into the results of memory research and make small cumulative improvements in our use of memory.

To sum up our excursion into memory, we have learned that memory plays a vital role in our reasoning. While this memory is fallible, it is also improvable in terms of accuracy and speed of recollection of knowledge of the past. Through the exercise of our memory, we can also build larger units of memory and relations of ideas that become useful when we recall contingent truths or connect them during a reasoning exercise.

B. IMAGINATION: NEW THINGS FROM CONNECTION OF UNITS OF THE FAMILIAR

In reasoning, we are not simply perceiving or recollecting past experiences. We are synthesizing, comparing, and making judgments about a series of contingent truths with respect to how they connect a given circumstance to a desired goal, an end, an aim, or a desired telos. Imagination is therefore central to this complex process of thought called reasoning.

Although imagination and memory are different concepts, we said earlier that their joint consideration can enlighten us more than an isolated analysis of each of them. But as we have seen in our observations about memory, there is a sense that memory is realized by synthesizing ideas that are supposed to be caused by past experiences. But the synthesis introduces the potential of omitting or introducing new information into the remembered past experience. Bernecker, in his *Metaphysics of Memory*, relates the study of memory among people of a Canadian Indian tribe.[7] A complex folktale is narrated and memory of the tale is tested at later times. As time passes, more difficult, unfamiliar elements of the tale are omitted, and, to make it a more relatable tale to people of this tribe, new elements are introduced. In general, it seems that, propelled by the need to make sense, we tend to straighten out difficulties or oddities during recollection of the past by incorporating new ideas.

In what way is imagination like memory? How do they differ? Hume's account of perception is rich, in the sense that it implicates many elements of the cognitive system, including imagination. We have impressions from which ideas are formed. Imagination is also active as a versatile connector of ideas, and memory presents to us at later times the ideas formed from earlier impressions. Hume distinguishes between memory and imagination based on the forcefulness and distinctness of memory as compared to the languidness of imagination. He says:

> When we remember any past event, the idea of it flows in upon the mind in a forceful manner; whereas in imagination the perception is faint and languid, and cannot without difficulty be preserved by the mind steady and uniform for any considerable time.[8]

Rather than a clear criterion for distinguishing memory from imagination, we need to see Hume's observations as suggesting that imagination and memory can enter the mind with interchangeable qualities that make their distinction difficult. This suggests the aphorism that a lie repeated many times becomes the truth. If there is some truth in this, it points to the possibility of transforming an imagination to a memory. A lie is an imagination without a basis in nature or in past experience. But by repetition, it can attain the forcefulness that Hume sees as characteristic of memory.

Imagine a spy trained to assume a different identity. At the beginning, the imaginary biography of the spy is told with difficulty and with great attention to avoid being discovered. But as time goes by, the spy may come to a situation where the details of the imaginary past are recalled with the same

---

7. Bernecker, *Metaphysics of Memory*, 149–51.
8. Hume, *Treatise of Human Nature*, 12–13.

vivacity that Hume attributes to memory. We may say that it is still imagination since the narrator is aware that they are lying. It is possible, according to the aphorism, that a time can be reached where the spy indeed views the imagined biography as theirs or at least they begin to struggle to distinguish their true biography from the imagined one.

To Hume, it is the forcefulness and distinct nature of the representation that makes it memory as opposed to imagination, while to Russell it is a feeling of familiarity or pastness that sets memory apart from imagination. In Russell's case, we see that the proposed familiarity can also accompany a repeatedly remembered imagination. That is, an imagination remembered can feel like a past experience remembered. That is, the markers suggested by Hume and Russell do not seem to be robustly discriminatory.

There is another problem with the distinction between memory and imagination illustrated by the nature of a dream. If Hume considers imagination to be marked by weakness and lack of distinctness, we can see how contrasting imagination with a dream may elevate imagination to a memory. In the mental state of a dream, our thoughts are less constrained, and their motion is altogether involuntary. In the Rapid Eye Movement (REM) stage of sleep, dreams are more intense, and the mental activities increasingly resemble conscious thought. It is held that if we are awakened amid such a REM dream, we can retain a significant amount of the dream content. By contrast, imagination commands a greater control of thoughts than in dreams and people in the creative arts can willfully create a representation from basic elements of the art form. Memory content that has not been remembered for a long time may be weak upon renewed remembering. This weakness may be like that of an imagined assembly of thoughts. Thus, we see that in dreams, ideas can be even more intense than remembered or imagined ideas and if we awakened in the REM stage, we may remember the content of our thoughts distinctly. But memory content can be recollected with greater weakness than the ideas of a REM dream. Here again, the marker for imagination as weakness can fail us, even in discerning what ideas are memory, imagination in a conscious state, or a clear and distinct dream. Recent psychological research is beginning to tackle this similarity between memory and imagination.[9] The subject is expected to continue to attract more attention in psychology.

How does imagination come to share such similarity with memory that the two cannot be distinguished with certainty? This is a difficult puzzle, but some clarifying observations may come from two different perspectives

---

9. Schacter and Addis, "Memory and Imagination."

of imagination—namely, the role of imagination in sense experience and imagination as synthesis of novel information.

Imagination is central to the acquisition of knowledge through experience. Kant's distinction between the phenomenal world of experience and the inaccessible noumenal world is praiseworthy and reasonable. We come to have an idea about things which are far from us and much larger than our sense organs through an indirect process. It is the imagination that conjures up a relation between the sense data we receive from our senses and the external cause of these data. When we talk of imagination, we think of a synthesis that is not the object of our present or past experience. As Bishop Berkeley rightly points out, our immediate contact in experience is the significations of external things as they strike our senses and generate ideas.[10] Imagination, in the context of direct experience, is the capacity of the mind to conjure up the missing link between phenomena as perceived by the senses and the inaccessible things-in-themselves that cause these phenomena.

In the case of imagination mediating experience of phenomena, we can think of this motion of thought as consisting of an innate disposition to seek coherence, causality, and purposiveness in things. It can also incorporate, to some extent, elements of past experience. Imagination furnishes the judgment that correlates perceived phenomena with the cause of those phenomena. No other standard is convincing as a source of judgment, apart from this feeling of coherence, causality, and purposiveness that accompanies the imagined correlation, and induces a state of ease in the mind as it contemplates the relation of experience to reality.

When imagination occurs separate from direct experience, it is a synthesis of elements of experience, but it is done in such a way that the synthesized whole is novel. This novel whole is not the product of past experience such as in the case of memory with its constituent elements. Some professions thrive on imagination. Among these imagination professionals are novelists, movie producers, actors, singers, composers, and engineers. They depend on proposing to us a possible world that has not been realized before, but that is convincing enough as an actualizable possibility. We praise these imagination professionals if the imagined world they present to us is very convincing. We ask whether their imagined world has the air of something that could have existed or that currently exists. But we sometimes also judge the imagination produced by these experts as not convincing. We do so by pointing out certain features which strike us as impossible, incoherent, or lacking in purposiveness. We also become disappointed when a movie that

---

10. Berkeley, "Principles of Human Knowledge," 163.

is supposedly based on a true story is later found to have contained too many embellishments that mislead us to label imagination as dramatized memory or dramatized history. These embellishments, though convincing at the time we first watched the movie, become distasteful imaginations of the movie producers because of the distortion brought to the reality being dramatized.

After this survey into imagination, we must ask ourselves how these observations help us in reasoning exercises. It seems that imagination has two roles in reasoning: determination of the desired goal and search of an optimal path from a given circumstance to the desired goal. First, it is involved in setting the desired goal of our reasoning process. This goal has the character of a value judgment and if the will is needed to determine it, we have competing options from which to choose. We are dealing with a moral question which is regulated by choice from competing options. Second, imagination is crucial in the search for the optimal combination of contingent truths connecting the given circumstance to the desired goal.

Regarding the use of imagination to set the goal of reasoning, we shall see later that this comes down to intuiting the goal or making a comparative judgment involving two or more plausible goals. Ethical, legal, and other social principles or considerations come to bear on the operation of the imagination in fulfilling this duty.

In the case of using imagination to infer the most reasonable chain of contingent truths connecting a given circumstance and a desired goal, we must consider how imagination combines with the central concepts discussed here in part II—that is, the role of part-whole relations, PSR, and the various disciplines responsible for the study of causes and characteristics of natural, social, and historical phenomena. Also, the more we exercise our imagination, the easier it becomes for us to employ it in reasoning. With practice, it becomes easier to discern between two arrangements of contingent truths that both appear plausible, though one may better align with the desired goal.

C. EMBRACING UNCERTAINTY IN REASONING

One of the consequences of the theory of reason proposed in this work is that we must become comfortable with the limits of reason. The untenable view of reason as entirely objective only hides too badly its potential to generate falsehoods and unethical consequences. When the noninferential kernel of a reasoning process is hidden, anything can be rationalized away. Suppose two noninferential kernels of reason are used by two conflicting sides, the outcome of such supposed rational discourse is cynicism among those who already have a low regard for philosophy.

There are many contingent truths and concepts that are needed for reasoning. We cannot cover them all without digressing from our current goal of analyzing reason, looking at the constituent elements, and investigating the implication of religion and ethics in reasoning.

Any substantial statement we make in philosophy is the result of commitments to some unsettled philosophical debates related to the issue. We rely on the sympathy of our audience regarding our choices, or, at least, we ask for the benefit of doubt. The concepts considered in part II could not be debated at length with extensive arguments and counter arguments. The positions we have taken in order to advance the discussion are reasonable, while not dismissing the challenges surrounding the concepts considered.

The account of reason in part I and the issues discussed in part II also furnish us with tools for metaphysical research. Metaphysics as a speculative search for truth can benefit from the moderated view of reason as being fundamentally subjective. It can also benefit from a careful engagement with theories of the concepts in part II. Possible world and counterfactual analyses are among problems that can be helped by this fresh view of reason. Combined with memory, imagination, and the coherence theory of truth, plausible speculative theories can be arrived at.

Having looked at the theory of reason and contingent truths, we must consider the desired goal toward which reasoning is propelled. Religion is relevant in the discussion of this value judgment. If we can see that religion is not only relevant but indispensable to reason, then the debate between reason and faith is an ill-posed problem. We can all agree that ethics is involved in setting the desired goal. But ethics itself is a field of active debate about methods and principles. There is a possibility that religion, much better than any other noninferential fact, is the proper basis of ethics. These issues then, need more attention and to them we shall now turn in parts III and IV. It is useful to first discuss religion so that any implication of religion in the foundations of ethics may then be easily discerned.

PART III

RELIGION IS EVERYWHERE: FROM a universal minimum religion to systematic religion with doctrines of salvation (soteriology). Atheism is impossible; even religious pluralism is not a successful argument against theism. The power of religion's soteriology must be appraised, and its differences properly understood.

We have now arrived at a point where we consider the relation of reason to faith and the foundational role of religion to ethical theory.

In the debate between reason and faith, faith is a concept from religion. Here, we may tentatively follow William James to construe religion broadly as the experiences of individuals insofar as they see themselves to be related to whatever they regard as divine. We will revisit the idea of religion later. But to talk about the relation of reason to faith, then, is to discuss the relation between reason and religion.

Although there are competing principles of ethics today, most of these principles share the common point of not taking religion seriously as a source of noninferential ethical principles. Joseph Butler's sermons are an exception to this dismissive attitude toward religion as a basis for ethical theory. We should go against this dismissive current. Let us just start by intuitively supposing that there is a link between ethics and religion.

We may therefore consider parts III and IV of this work to be addressing important religious and ethical questions that concern all humans and are expressed by Socrates and Kant:

Q1: How should one live?

> The answer is that one should live by following, and further developing, the religion with which everyone is naturally endowed. That is, we proceed from the thesis that everyone has a religion, which we can call the universal minimum religion. True atheism is not possible. This minimum religion can be, and is often, further developed. We can then consider two important questions posed by Kant to be arising from within the religion that already binds all:

Q2: What ought I to do?

Q3: What may I hope?

These three questions are intuitive enough to warrant our attention. The answer to Q2 is the imperative: love! And the answer to Q3 is the promise: eternal life or life after death. You may be asking, "Love what?" Or, "What life after death?" Even more problematic to you may appear to be the answer to Q1, which recommends the practice of religion as a way of life. Let us develop these answers in parts III and IV, then consider whether they strike us as a plausible complement to the new theory of reason and its related ethical theory.

In part III, we are concerned with religion. We shall argue that all human beings have, and do practice, some form of religion. This basic form we shall call the universal minimum religion. Human beings respond differently to the innate impulse to further develop this religion toward a systematic religion that has a more explicit ethical foundation and a vision of personal salvation or soteriology. Chapter 7 will defend this idea of a universal minimum religion. We are led to recognize that true atheism is impossible.

Chapter 8 will discuss the further development of this universal minimum religion toward a systematic religion as a way of life. One possible further development of the universal minimum religion exclusively uses philosophy and the arts, in contrast to the others that rely on divine revelations. This critical philosophical religion expresses itself as atheism or agnosticism but does not defeat the thesis that true atheism is impossible. These minimum and systematic religious stages can provide the basis for an ethical theory. As diverse as the realizations of the systematic religious impulse are, it can be shown that there is consensus on the seed of extended religion that can ground ethical theorizing.

Chapter 9 will focus on religious rituals and the different soteriological outlooks that result from various systematic religions. More differences emerge here among the religious systems. The teleological nature of ethics means that some of the differences in soteriological perspective can feed back into the system of ethics. A clear analysis of the dynamics of this relation can help to moderate the consequences of differences in the further development of the universal minimum religion toward different visions of human salvation.

CHAPTER 7

On the Universal Minimum Religion of Conscience as the Source of Reason's Goals or the Impossibility of True Atheism

ALL HUMAN BEINGS PRACTICE a minimum religion that consists in a sense of the divine and a meaning to life; true atheism is impossible. Properly considered, the minimum religion enjoys a consensus; observed religious differences in the world are a manifestation of innate human desires to further develop this minimum religion through speculation and revelation.

The sociology of knowledge examines relations between knowledge and the social context within which that knowledge arises. If such analyses are applied to parts III and IV, a Protestant influence will be discernible in the author's thought.

But the discussion in this chapter is not conducted from the position of Protestant theology; the author has no formal theological training. The main ideas cannot be offered as original, even if the classification of religion is novel and affords greater clarity. The attempt to show that reason is faith plus something additional to faith, is entirely Protestant. But this way of approaching the faith and reason debate is an attempt to refashion fideism as the seed of reason, so that it neutralizes that old view of reason to which fideism supposedly stands in strong opposition.

Natural theology, especially the branch concerned with proof of the existence of God, is not part of the discussion we want to pursue here. Our starting point is an awareness of a relation between a human being and a Supreme Being, an awareness that this relation conduces to our benefit and to the glory of the Supreme Being. This awareness, we must maintain, is a universal experience at least once in the life of a human being. We should follow John Calvin here to refer to it as a sense of the divine (*sensus divinitatis*).

It should not be confused with the knowledge of God as asserted in various proofs of the existence of God. These proofs purporting to show in deductive terms that God exists have been reasonably challenged by Kant and other thinkers, mostly of the Protestant tradition. Their usefulness in intellectual discourse about religion is not to be denied but in the matter at hand they do not add further light. The sense of the divine is noninferential, it is an axiom, a universal intuition. But it can serve as the departure point for further inferences about the duties of a human being in relation to other human beings and to God.

While reason remained vague and appeared as opposed to faith, fideism reigned as a supreme protector of faith against the incoherence and sophistry of reason. In the history of philosophy, one finds this skeptical attitude not only deep seated in devout Protestant thinkers such as Bayle, Schleiermacher, Kierkegaard, Kant, and many others, but the skepticism about reason extends to Protestant thinkers who distance themselves from the Protestant faith, such as Hume and John Rawls. For Rawls, his fideism was the last Christian conviction with which he parted, and he did so purely on moral grounds. Of this, Rawls writes in "On My Religion":

> My difficulties were always moral ones, since my fideism remained firm against all worries about the existence of God. The so-called proofs of God's existence in St. Thomas Aquinas and others proved nothing of religious significance in any case. That seemed clear. Yet the ideas of right and justice expressed in Christian doctrines are a different matter.[1]

We shall first discuss this phenomenon of the sense of the divine and how it is sometimes expressed more broadly and rather vaguely as conscience. This is the seed of faith. We shall then consider and refute the possibility of true atheism, explaining its perceived manifestation in society as a form of critical minimum religion, animated by the corruption and pretensions they observe in some systematic religions. It is useful to consider the problem of divine hiddenness that is thought to undermine any noninferential basis for religious faith. The argument to unbelief from divine hiddenness fails to refute theism. We end this chapter by observing the yearning for more than the universal minimum religion. This yearning can either take a critical philosophical attitude and culminate in what is termed atheism or agnosticism or it can embrace divine revelation and further systematization of divine revelation to more developed forms of religion.

---

1. Rawls, "On My Religion," 263.

A. SENSE OF THE DIVINE (*SENSUS DIVINITATIS*) AND CONSCIENCE AS SEED OF FAITH

When we consider Aristotle's observation that all human beings by nature desire to know, we are moved to agree with him. The object of human knowledge is not only knowledge of the external world but also knowledge of the self. Know Thyself was one of the maxims inscribed at the Temple of Apollo in Delphi. This is indeed an imperative that one gives to oneself to make the self a proper object of inquiry. Human beings pursue this maxim and are consequently made aware of many intuitions. This knowledge springs forth just by considering the situation of the self.

It is a strange situation that philosophers, especially of the analytic tradition, have long grasped the central role of intuitions in our knowledge system while the public is lulled by scientism into a dogmatic belief that all knowledge is built on evidence and inferences based on that evidence. These intuitions—that is, noninferential truths—come to us with such a force that we cannot but embrace them. The general public that is not aware of this central role of intuitions in our knowledge edifice would be alarmed if one openly admitted that a certain fundamental belief in our knowledge system is an intuition. In the context of religion and ethics, we must overcome this adverse reaction and elevate intuitions to the axiomatic role that they play in practical life. No ethical theory can succeed without admitting of an intuition as a fundamental axiom.

The content of the universal minimum religion is therefore a set of intuitions. In practice, we do not only have a single intuition. It is also not a worthwhile task to attempt to demonstrate the deduction of one intuition from another, if these intuitions are properly basic, noninferential beliefs. We may therefore consider the universal minimum religion to consist of the following intuitions:

UMR1: existence of a religious seed. I stand in relation with a transcendent force.

UMR2: aim of the relation. This relation is to my benefit and to the glory of the transcendent force.

UMR3: meaning of life. I feel that my life has a meaning or purpose.

UMR4: gratitude as the proper response to the gift of life. I feel a sense of gratitude directed toward this force. This feeling of gratitude imposes a sense of duty on me.

UMR5: the force of moral law. I feel that not all actions are permissible and that this is a universal feeling also approved or acknowledged by the transcendent force.

UMR6: the social instinct. I feel that I share some affinity with other human beings whom I suspect to also stand in relation with the transcendent force.

UMR7: guilt and regret. I sometimes feel guilt and I regret those actions of mine that I judged to be contrary to the moral law.

By no means is this set of intuitions exhaustive, but those outlined above constitute what we may call the universal minimum religion. From it can spring, not only a foundation for ethics, but also a meaning for personal life. Taken together, these intuitions also lead to the ritual of worship of the transcendent force as an act of gratitude.

Since these constitutive elements of the minimum religion are intuitions, they cannot be defended in the same way as inferential assertions. They are the result of inner experience that, we can all agree, rises to the level of universality. The method of cases can be used to refute them, but this method cannot succeed against the minimum religion. The intuitions are based on universal religious feelings.

It may be argued that while these intuitions make sense, the notion of religion is forcefully injected into the discourse. We have referred to the relation as one between a human being and a transcendent force. The transcendent force refers to a Supreme Being, the divine. This universal minimum religion is theistic. In a developed version, we can have monotheistic, polytheistic, and pantheistic feelings. The view that some human beings are not theistic at all can be refuted by showing at least the presence of some theistic assumptions in their felt or expressed worldview.

The suggestion that we all have a universal minimum religion may strike some people as false. The idea that the transcendent force is a Supreme Being, a personal God, would leave even more people disagreeing with the intuitions of the minimum religion. The problem lies in the concept of God.

Can we know God absolutely? The answer is negative but not for the same reason held by those who have problems with intuition UMR1. If God is other than the human mind, and if Kant's epistemology points in the right direction, then we can never come to a full knowledge of God as a thing-in-itself. Some may pretend to do so on the basis of reason but as we argue in this work, reason is nothing but contingent truths arranged to cohere with intuitions of permissible or desirable goals. This view of knowledge of the true nature of the external world is a Kantian injunction against any pretention to the absolute knowledge of God through experience.

If experience cannot fully grasp the nature of God, then reason falls even far shorter. The first intuition of the minimum religion is not primarily about the existence of God; it is the existence of a religion—that is, the existence of a relation between a human self and a Supreme Being. The self is only vaguely aware of this relation and the presence of the other, the presence of the Supreme Being. It is for this reason that we consider this feeling to be the manifestation of a minimum religion. This is the mustard seed of faith from which a blossoming and fruitful tree of reason can be grown.

Human understanding of the nature of God can range from the certain but vague feelings of the minimum religious person to the deep awareness of God experienced by prophets, mystics, and the deeply religious. But even in this deep awareness, we cannot pretend to have gained absolute knowledge of God. What we know of God is what he reveals and his goal for us is primarily moral knowledge, not knowledge of all truths about the natural world which we are encouraged by our very human nature to pursue. For this knowledge of God, the seed of faith is far more powerful than a learned defense of all sorts of proofs of the existence of God. It is also accessible to all—the learned and the not-so-learned human beings.

One can bemoan the impossibility of knowing God fully or one can express profound gratitude for the little that has come down to us through historical revelation. The latter is the more profitable path that already expresses itself in the intuitions of the minimum religion. A profound sense of gratitude for life is the first approach to dealing with the mysteries of the divine nature. It is mostly pride and excessive confidence in human capabilities that move people in two wrong directions. First, it is a misplaced priority to set as the object of the philosophy of religion a quest for proofs of the existence of God. And second, it is a wrong turn to mischaracterize the realization that the mission of proof of God's existence is doomed. We cannot take the shortcomings as a demonstration of the inexistence of God or as proof of the absence of love and goodness on the part of God.

We will consider the objection to theistic religion from the perspective of divine hiddenness. As long as our minimum religion is concerned with the existence of a relation with the divine, and the minimum religion is viewed as the seed of ethics, the argument of divine hiddenness cannot prosper. The existence of an original moral predisposition in the minimum religion points directly to the existence of another self in the religious relation—that is, the existence of God.

If we took a survey of people on the question of religion and spirituality, we would find interesting opinions. These opinions do not necessarily capture the feelings or the doubts faced by people when they attempt to put into words their most basic minimum religious sentiments.

The Pew Research Center found in 2017 that, for the USA, 48 percent of those surveyed identify as religious and spiritual, 27 percent are spiritual but not religious, 18 percent are neither religious nor spiritual, and 6 percent are religious but not spiritual.[2] It is true that the USA is more religious than most Western countries. From this research we see that about 81 percent of the population is religious and/or spiritual. This is a common pattern to be found around the world with some people declaring a spiritual outlook but no religious convictions. What they refer to as *religion*, or what is negated by the atheist, is mostly systematic, organized religion that is a further step above the universal minimum religion. Those who therefore say that they are spiritual but not religious can be said to be expressing the religiosity of the universal minimum religion. That the self-declared atheists may hold these intuitions too may be seen in their approval of the arts as essential in life. The membership in the minimum religion cannot be judged by the assertions of people; it is a religion of feelings and moral intuitions. Its precepts are not always expressed in words, but they are discernible from actions.

It may be said that the sentimentality of being spiritual is not something shared by most Western Europeans, who proudly declare themselves to be atheists. Sweden is often presented as an example of an atheistic society. In 2009, Peter Steinfels of the New York Times reported on a series of interviews that Phil Zuckerman conducted in Sweden and Denmark. The benign indifference to religion that he encountered is contrasted with the moral foundation of the two societies. He finds an explanation in the words of a 68-year-old interviewee:

> We are Lutherans in our souls—I'm an atheist, but still have the Lutheran perceptions of many: to help your neighbor. Yeah. It's an old, good, moral thought.[3]

This sums up the worldview of most of Protestant northern Europe. If we were to take the northern Europeans at their word, then we would have to admit that the minimum religion is not universal. The judgment of the existence of minimum religion in a person must be considered carefully. When that minimum religion has been raised to a systematic religion, and then to a culture, the tendency is to forget the foundation of that resultant normativity. This acculturation through a systematic religion is consistent

2. Lipka and Gecewicz, "More Americans."
3. Steinfels, "Scandinavian Nonbelievers."

with the existence of the minimum religious spirit in that society. The minimum religion leads to a foundation for ethics and meaning in personal life. A set of contingent facts may be raised to quasi-intuitions by a culture. In the case of northern Europe, their religious dispositions must be judged based on what we may call synthetic intuitions. In this case, we would be concerned with the systematic religion of the Lutherans and the revelations of the Swedish mystic Swedenborg. These have led to the unexpressed religiosity of most Scandinavian Lutherans.

B. PROTESTANT THEOLOGY AND ETHICS

The set of intuitions presented above as the universal minimum religion can be viewed as a restatement of the idea of a universal innate sense of the divine. Others call this conscience. From this seed sprang the free speculation of Protestant thinkers on matters of ethics and religious toleration during the Enlightenment.

The role of Christian humanism in the Protestant Reformation has been widely acknowledged. The first essential feature of this movement was a positive appraisal of the work of classical authors who were not necessarily Christians. In essence, the humanism of the fifteenth and sixteenth centuries can be construed as a recognition of moral value in the classical works of pagans, mostly Greek and Roman. The second essential element is a diagnosis and condemnation of the moral corruption in the Roman Catholic Church. To positively appraise pagan authors, one had to believe that they were capable of moral cognition and instruction. Here we see mutual influence. First, the observed moral discourses in pagan literature informed the hermeneutics of segments of Christian Scriptures. Second, further reading and interpretation of the Scriptures, especially Paul's Epistles, yielded further positive appreciation of moral themes in classical pagan works without compromising the distinctiveness of Christianity.

Christianity, especially Paul's theology, has been charged with Hellenization of an otherwise Hebrew religion. What is wrong with such mutual influence? Plato's literary theory emphasizes the necessity of moral value in all art. Thus, every classical work of art whose author subscribes to Plato's view is a treatise of moral philosophy. Further, if one recognizes the influence of Egyptian thought on classical Greece, and the influence of Egyptian, Cushite, and Ethiopian culture on early Judaism by way of Israel's sojourn in Egypt, one can see how these gentile systems could have reinforced the universality of a basic religious instinct ingrained in human nature.

A survey of some Reformation authors can easily confirm the illuminating power of pagan moral philosophy and the fresh hermeneutics of Christian Scripture that recognizes the religious seed in all human beings.

Heinrich Bullinger, the Swiss Reformer, addresses the laws of nature and men in "The First Sermon" of "The Second Decade" of his *Decades*. By the *law of nature*, he is referring to the law of human nature. He opines that we recognize the moral law of human nature, not because humans have a special disposition of or by themselves to do right,

> but it is because God has imprinted or engraved in our minds some knowledge, and certain general principles of religion, justice, and goodness, which—because they are grafted in us and born together with us—seem therefore to be naturally in us.[4]

In his *Institutes*, John Calvin states the basic idea behind the sense of the divine as consciousness of a relation to the divine, a consciousness that rises to a religion:

> By the knowledge of God, I intend not merely a notion that there is such a Being, but also an acquaintance with whatever we ought to know concerning Him, conducing to his glory and our benefit. For we cannot with propriety say, there is any knowledge of God where there is no religion or piety.[5]

A page later, Calvin indicates that this sense of the divine is capable of teaching us piety that further produces religion, or we should say it produces more religion in addition to the basic sense of the divine:

> For this sense of the divine perfections is calculated to teach us piety, which produces religion.

The sense of the divine also leads us to the knowledge of God's judgment and consciousness of our imperfection, from whose guilt and despair only divine grace can free us. We shall consider these issues in the further development of religion and soteriology. But this is the seed of ethics and theology of Reformed Protestantism as well as Lutheranism.

This universal sense of the divine can be viewed as a restatement of Paul's Letter to the Romans (Rom 2:14–15):

> For when Gentiles, who do not have the law, by nature do the things in the law, these, although not having the law, are a law to themselves, who show the work of the law written in their

---

4. Bullinger, "Laws of Nature and Men," ii.194.
5. Calvin, *Institutes*, 49.

hearts, their conscience also bearing witness, and between themselves their thoughts accusing or else excusing them.

By their very nature, all human beings therefore stand in a religious relation with the divine, constituting the universal minimum religion that partly manifests itself as conscience.

The ideas expressed in Rom 2:14–15 can be said to be grasped by Lutherans and all other Christians as well. For instance, Philip Melanchthon, the foremost Lutheran systematic theologian of the Reformation, in the section "On Law" in his *Loci Communes*, comments:

> Paul moreover, in Rom. 2:15, teaches by a marvelously elegant and clear argument, that within us there is a natural law. He says that the Gentiles have conscience defending or accusing a thing done; and it is therefore a law unto them. For what is conscience but the judgment of our action which is demanded by some law or common formula?[6]

But by strengthening the doctrine of conscience in Rom 2:15 with the idea of the sense of the divine, Calvin influenced many later Protestant thinkers. This influence shows forth in two ways. First, it leads to the recognition of the futility of dwelling on the proof of God's existence. Second, it leads to the emphasis on the freedom of conscience, hence, many Protestant scholars and political activists fought for religious toleration.

Similar support for the sense of the divine intimated in Rom 2:14–15 can be found in Prov 20:27:

> The spirit of a man is the lamp of the Lord,
> Searching all the inner depth of his heart.

The spirit of human beings here can be interpreted as conscience. This conscience is the light of God, and it searches and illumines the inner life of human beings even before they have a revealed religious system to further instruct them.

The sense of the divine confers an unmistakable dimension of theistic religion to the intuition of the morality that is inherent in human beings. At first glance, the concept of conscience is rather neutral, nontheistic. Thus, conscience can be used by theistic and nontheistic speakers to refer to the universal condition of the awareness, albeit imprecise, of a sense of morality. It is left to the defenders of the universal minimum religion to point out that the concept of conscience implies theistic religion. This they must do, even

---

6. Melanchthon, "On Law," 111.

if theistically minded users of the word *conscience* are unduly charged with atheism.

To shy away from using the sense of the divine in preference of conscience is considered suspect in pious Protestant circles. In the seventeenth and eighteenth centuries, Pierre Bayle, a French Calvinist, and Francis Hutcheson, a Scottish Calvinist, elevated and defended conscience in matters of politics and religion. The relation of conscience to the knowledge of God is presupposed by both. Bayle is concerned about religious toleration in a pluralistic society and within a religious group that may be intolerant of diverse interpretations of doctrines. Human conscience should be inviolable; it should only be subject to the judgment of God.

For Hutcheson, conscience is the basis of morality. As the father of the Scottish Enlightenment, Hutcheson's use of conscience in moral theorizing set the path for Scottish ethics as would later be seen in Adam Smith's and David Hume's moral theories. Conscience, as used by Hutcheson in his moral philosophy, presupposes the knowledge of God. This basic conscience is also capable of being trained toward a more virtuous nature. We find the same theme pervading the sermons and moral reasoning of Bishop Joseph Butler.

The sense of the divine is more explanatory than conscience with respect to the source of the moral predisposition being expressed. The sense of the divine is the core of the minimum religion, with two main ideas. It consists, first, in standing in relation with a transcendent force, and second, in having a practical orientation toward morality. The human being in that relation is free, and with this autonomy comes the possibility of also being controlled by an evil principle that wrestles against the predisposition to morality. Here then is a contrast between the sense of the divine and conscience; conscience appears to be too optimistic. For this reason, Bayle and Hutcheson faced accusations of atheism in their day. By accentuating conscience, it appears that, through education, moral perfection and self-reliant justification before the Supreme Being are possible. This makes conscience smell like Pelagianism, the theological doctrine that denies hereditary sin and asserts the possibility of moral perfection without divine grace. Normally, the ordinary human being knows the force with which the evil principle in them thwarts their moral predispositions.

For the universal minimum religion to succeed as a religion, it must not only dwell on the intuition of morality in the minimum religionist, it must also take seriously the propensity to evil. In this sense, Kant is closer to Calvin's and Paul's view of the sense of the divine.

"That the world lies in baseness is a lament as ancient as history." This is how Kant opens the section "First Piece" of his major work *Religion*

Within the Bounds of Bare Reason.[7] One must not only explain the origin of morality in human beings but one must also come to terms with the evil in human desires and actions. One must then proceed to show how good, with divine help, can overcome this tendency to do evil.

We can say that Kant is demonstrably committed to the universal minimum religion and understands it through his Protestant outlook. In the preface to the second edition of the *Critique of Pure Reason*, he declared that he had to limit knowledge in order to make room for faith.[8] But it is not in that first critique that he delivers on the role of faith in his moral philosophy; it is much later in *Religion Within the Bounds of Bare Reason*. What he calls bare reason is indeed the universal minimum religion, the foundation of reason. This is evident when he says:

> But there is one thing in our soul which, if we duly fix our eyes upon it, we cannot cease regarding with the highest amazement and where the admiration is legitimate and simultaneously also elevates the soul: and this is the original moral disposition within us, as such.[9]

After doing justice to human nature by addressing the disposition to good and what he calls a propensity to evil, Kant establishes a conflict that needs to be resolved. He holds that the good principle can overcome the evil principle in us. But for good to win this battle over evil, a liberator is needed. Further, Jesus Christ is presented as the personified good principle, the ideal moral perfection to whom we should elevate ourselves.[10] This thinking is already deep into extended, systematic religion, beyond the mere recognition of minimum religion.

When we consider the influence of the idea of the sense of the divine on Kant, we can see how the moral argument, to him, is the most powerful argument for the existence of God. In the preface to the first edition of *Religion Within the Bounds of Bare Reason*, he writes:

> Morality, therefore, leads inescapably to religion, through which it expands to the idea of a powerful legislator, outside the human being.[11]

The presence of God is felt within an innate religious relation. It is strengthened by embracing morality in general and considering God as

---

7. Kant, *Religion*, 17.
8. Kant, *Critique of Pure Reason*, xxxiv.
9. Kant, *Religion*, 56.
10. Kant, *Religion*, 66–87.
11. Kant, *Religion*, 4.

a powerful legislator. Only universal intuitions can arrive at this religious sense.

The sense of the divine, as presented by Calvin, is founded on Christian Scriptures. But the Scriptures themselves lay out, as in Rom 2:14–15, the core of the universal minimum religion. This universalization of the minimum religion must be taken seriously before the diversity of systematic religious practice is used as evidence against the implausibility of religious knowledge.

What Calvin and Kant also make us realize is that the universal minimum religion cannot be completely optimistic if it seeks to capture the reality of the human condition. But to understand and overcome the presence of the evil propensity, as Kant calls it, this universal minimum religion must be further developed. And by what means can it be developed? Through revealed religion, accompanied by a critical attitude, perhaps?

When human beings respond to the need for further development of this universal minimum religion, different religious systems emerge. Some partisans go the extra mile to deny the existence of a common foundation of their edifices; they disown the universal minimum religion. Because of Rom 2:14–15, Christians cannot do so without contradicting their Scriptures. Some critical minimum religions take upon themselves the name of atheism as a philosophy, often expressed with a militant attitude comparable to that of other fundamentalists of systematic religions. Other critical minimum religions argue from divine hiddenness to a despondency in their state of minimum religion, assuming agnostic or benign atheistic postures. What these critical voices target in their criticism is the systematic religion, without the distinction between minimum and systematic religion that we have adopted here. These critical voices must be considered and shown that their criticism is unfounded.

C. IMPOSSIBILITY OF TRUE ATHEISM FROM A MORAL PERSPECTIVE

We have suggested that there is a universal minimum religion. True atheism is therefore impossible. And that is a good thing. The position that is referred to as atheism benefits from the union of two forces: (1) those who call themselves atheists, and (2) those of partisan systematic religion whose primary interest is conversion of others to their specific systematic religion. People who call themselves atheists are manifesting a reactionary attitude to systematic religion, not a denial of the universal minimum religion. While they do not explicitly profess the universal minimum religion, they live according to its precepts. Some systematic religions may pay lip service to the universal minimum religion but do not rise to defend it in their apologetic debates with self-declared atheists.

What can we say about those who declare themselves to be atheists? Well, we must first recognize that we experience and feel much more than we can express in words; we sometimes say that which we neither experience nor feel. This is the position of those who call themselves atheists. We cannot rely completely on what a human being says to believe what they feel. This is not always a suspicion that they are deceiving us; it is an acknowledgment that certain deep truths are only felt but remain inexpressible or are deformed in attempted expression. Art may sometimes go further than simple language, but it is manifest that the self is a lodge of mysteries that sometimes remain inexpressible.

Atheism, as professed by those who believe to be characterized by it, is a negative project. It negates theism—namely, the view that there is a Supreme Being, a moral legislator who stands in relation to human beings. To buttress the case for atheism, one must first understand that which is being negated in terms of their attributes. One must then stand from outside the universe and scan it simultaneously to establish the absence of that entity. This is impossible. If we have a full description of God, it would still be impossible for the atheist to demonstrably establish that the entity referred to as God does not exist.

To advance atheism as a viable worldview, then, one must look to the theist's account of God and how they come to believe in God's reality. Having established the basis of the theist's faith, the atheist must then try to undermine it.

We have approached our idea of a universal minimum religion from a Protestant tradition. That tradition de-emphasizes the proof of God's existence through rational arguments, an intellectual activity necessarily dependent on the dubious and vague concept of reason. As discussed, the Protestant view emphasizes the existence of a religious relation with God as properly basic. The self-declared atheist, whom the traditional Protestant cannot consistently acknowledge, therefore approaches the debate on Roman Catholic terms. The presumed atheist claims to be able to establish, using reason, that God does not exist; the Protestant may as well react to their use of reason with the colorful language of Martin Luther that reason is the devil's whore.[12] On that basis of demonizing any supposedly nontheistic reason, the presumed atheist cannot even begin the debate they long for, because it is in the company of theists that the presumed atheist springs to life.

---

12. Blanshard, *Reason and Belief*, 130.

In this work, we have purified reason beyond the objectionable view of it professed by Luther. We have done so by rightfully snatching it away from the hands of the presumed atheist. This is right because reason is fundamentally subjective and teleological. Knowing this, we pay attention to its subjective operation and that limits the abuse of trust through the wrong view that there is such a thing as objective reason outside a community of common values and contingent truths. In the objective presentation of reason, it can only be a vehicle that is used to channel the prejudices of the speaker. The use of reason in this way therefore has the power to deceive us, and even deceive the speaker without their knowing it. We uphold that the teleology in a reasoning process is furnished by faith, either directly or indirectly, through a chain of inferences that ultimately rest on matters of faith. Where does that leave us? It leaves us in the moral territory, at the very foundation of morality, where there can be no reason without a kernel that consists of faith. That is our main argument.

So, the universal minimum religion is intricately bound up with our original moral predisposition as Kant says, or with a moral sense according to Francis Hutcheson. We are aware of this moral predisposition and, associated with it, a sense of the divine. But along with this moral predisposition, we are also aware of the depravity of human nature—that is, the human soul is a battlefield, where the good predisposition wrestles against an evil propensity. The presumed atheist is acutely aware of the universal moral predisposition. They may acknowledge the attendant presence of the evil propensity but quickly dismiss it or attribute it to the fault of the society (almost always blaming religion for this). In the rest of parts III and IV, we will interchangeably use *presumed atheists* with *atheists*. Our position is that the sense of the divine is universal; it may lessen in intensity, but the minimum always remains in the form of a moral sense, even if we go against this sense under the influence of the evil principle or critical philosophy. There are no true atheists.

That morality is important for human flourishing is not disputed by presumed atheists. If we accept that reason is subjective, that there is a universal minimum religion, and that our moral predisposition is bound up with that universal religious experience, then the presumed atheist must attempt to do two things to justify their pretension. First, they must refute the fact that morality is bound up with minimum religion, and second, they must offer an account of how they come to their innate sense of morality outside the framework of the minimum religion.

The first task is accomplished indirectly: they deny the existence of God. To defend this view, they first ask the theist to defend theism, followed by their refutation of such a defense. Even if we suppose that all the reasons for God's existence advanced by a theist are wrong, we can see that their wrongness does not logically exclude the possibility of God's existence. Seeing the power of this argument, the presumed atheist then argues from the hiddenness of God to his nonexistence. That weakened argument is not without its own challenges. It proceeds by ascribing attributes to God and then demonstrating that God does not live up to those attributes. We shall consider this point again later. But we must now acknowledge that the atheist's reliance on the theist to establish God's nonexistence fails in the first task.

What is the source of the atheist's morality? Open to the atheist as a source of morality, we have the concepts of reason, conscience, and naturalism. Reason, we have argued, is fundamentally subjective. We pointed out in chapter 1 that if all human subjects are connected to God, such as through a universal minimum religion, and if they are endowed with the same cognitive capacities, then their subjective judgments can, but not always, rise to objective judgments. Compared to scientific epistemology, this is synonymous to having a material standard by which thermometers are calibrated. These calibrated thermometers can then be said to be measuring with the same accuracy without further demonstration. But the atheist cannot accept this theistic path to the theoretical possibility of objectivity in reason. An atheist cannot argue to morality using reason, without acknowledging the universal minimum religion.

As for *conscience*, we have argued that it is another name for the *sense of the divine*; it is conducive to an original moral sense. Extended or systematic religionists can admit that further development of minimum religion can elevate conscience to a more discriminatory moral tool. At this elevated level, it may seem that conscience is not universal because of observable gradients in its exercise among human beings, with and without further moral inculcation. For instance, a Christian who comes to the consciousness that war is evil and must be avoided, and another minimum religionist who espouses a just war theory, or even advocates war as an evolutionary tool that aids the survival of the fittest, may appear to have different consciences.

This further development of the conscience associated with the minimum religion is akin to Rousseau's blaming of human moral corruption on civilization. Systematic religion develops within a society and, unless care is taken, new principles of the systematic religion may conflict with the original undeveloped conscience in which is lodged a sense of the divine. It is this purer undeveloped conscience that Rousseau praises. If the atheist takes refuge in conscience as the source of morality, they still have a hard time showing that such conscience is not derived from, or bound up with, the intuitions that constitute the universal minimum religion.

The third refuge for the presumed atheist is to deny the existence of religion, and with it, the existence of God, by pointing to naturalistic ethics as the basis of our moral predisposition. Proponents of rational nontheistic ethics may go as far as saying that there are no moral facts; our moral maxims are convenient societal constructs that we arrive at using our reason. But moral naturalists see the problematic nature of such a view. To these moral naturalists, there are objective moral facts that exist independent of the human mind. Further, they hold that these facts are natural objects, and that their essence can be grasped in the same way we come to know scientific facts. But is there any truth to naturalistic ethics?

The most challenging objection to naturalistic ethics remains the question whether we can obtain value judgments from the description of natural phenomena. In terms of ethics, we need to come to terms with what a natural moral phenomenon is. Defining such would require us to draw from a capacity of judgment that is not dependent on experience for its determination. Some would point to reason, but reason depends on ethics and thus brings us full circle to the original difficulty about judgment. But if we leave these aside, we must still push back against objective facts obtained through experience. Kantian epistemology strikes us as largely correct or closer to the truth. In this case, even if there were natural moral phenomena from which we can glean moral truths using the senses, our imagination and cognitive system would have to assist in correlating the natural moral phenomena with the natural moral objects-in-themselves. An innate capacity to organize and establish moral facts from moral phenomena would still be needed in naturalistic ethics.

If the atheist cannot successfully defend the nontheistic origin of the human moral predisposition, they must at least entertain as plausible the existence of universal minimum religion from which springs innate morality. It is hard for us to see how they can succeed, based on our consideration of reason, conscience, and naturalistic ethics above.

If religion first appears to us as an entirely private matter, morality cannot be. If morality is grounded in a universal minimum religion, then that minimum religion is not entirely private; it rises to the level of a community. Legislation and politics, insofar as they are concerned with the welfare of the citizens of a community, must draw from a moral source, and implicitly from a shared religion. This fact has been recognized in the history of political and legal theorizing.

By asserting existence of a universal minimum religion that can serve as the foundation for law and politics, we eliminate the danger of persecution on the charge of atheism. Where such intentions or laws exist to punish atheism based on assertion of some citizens as being adherents of that view, our refutation of true atheism must liberate and protect such citizens. Their speech is incoherent and at variance with their obvious practice of the minimum religion, by virtue of their demonstrating innate moral predisposition in their interactions with society. They are bound by innate theism.

Atheism, if it were possible, would indeed be incompatible with a properly grounded legal and political system. Strong atheistic views of morality or advocacy for morality without principles, especially theistic principles, can only dissipate when the proponents of such views are confronted with the task of legislating a political system. This is because the challenge posed by atheism is severe, given that nontheistic foundations of morality cannot prosper sustainably. A negative project such as embraced by atheism must give way to the demand for a positive one, but this is hard to fulfil without resorting to ethical principles rooted in a sense of the divine or tyranny.

Law and politics that eschew morality or advocate for morality without rules cannot be sustainable. This fact has been recognized by many political theorists. For instance, it is this insight that moves Plato to censor atheism in his *Laws*. The same insight moves Rousseau to propose the concept of a civil religion for all citizens of a state. Furthermore, we find in John Locke's *Letter Concerning Toleration* the unmistakable injunction against tolerating atheists.[13] However, the apparent harsh treatment they all prescribe for atheists need not be feared because of the view we advance here: there is a universal minimum religion shared by all, and further developed by others.

In Plato's *Laws*, a theory of punishment is offered for those we would qualify as atheists.[14] Plato considers the source of unlawful acts and speech in a society to arise from those who hold that: (1) the gods do not exist, (2) gods exist but do not care about the affairs of human beings, or (3) gods exist, care about the affairs of men, but are corruptible with gifts from unjust human beings, thereby making injustice part of the nature of the gods. What should the law do with such people? Should they be punished? How severe should their punishment be?

According to Plato, those who profess atheism are not well in their soul. They ought to be redeemed from that position through intellectual discourse on the view that there are gods, they care about us, and that justice is in their nature; they are incorruptible. Plato offers an extended discussion of how supposed atheists should be tried and punished. They ought to be aided to freely come to the acknowledgment of the incoherence of their views. Failure to repent of atheistic inclinations deserves punishment that ranges from life imprisonment to death after preliminary imprisonment in

---

13. Locke, *Letter*, 93.
14. Plato, *Laws* 10.

a house of reformation as a last attempt to cure them of atheistic illness. The tenor of Plato, through the voice of the Athenian in this dialogue, is not that of a zealous punisher; it is that of a reformer who is deeply convinced that atheism is a mortal crime in a city. It is also the voice of a legislator who lays more weight on moral education than on punishment and is convinced that supposed atheistic confessions are incoherent utterances.

We can see that our view of the universal minimum religion makes these extreme punishments unnecessary. The situation with the atheist can be likened to that of someone who appears before the court to plead guilty for the murder of someone who is alive and well. While the supposed murderer pleads guilty, we see the supposed deceased appear in court to say they are alive and well. If our self-declared guilty person continues to plead guilty for premeditated murder, shall we condemn that person according to the code for murderers? Obviously not. We must refuse to believe the assertions of the self-declared murderer. This is the situation with the supposed atheist; the elaborate method of demonstration of their error is intended by Plato as a warning for those who are overzealous about punishing nonbelief. Nonbelief is won over by pointing out its lack of any defensible theoretical foundation, since we are by nature bound to the minimum religion through an original moral sense that is of a theistic nature.

Plato is not the only thinker concerned about atheism. Rousseau proposes the idea of a civil religion to protect the state from the corrupting danger of atheism, and to protect the religious doctrines of citizens from the corrupting influence of the state. Insofar as the doctrines of a religion include the minimum requirements of civil religion, the practitioners of that religion should not be disturbed by the state. This creates room for many different systematic religions as long as they are tolerant of one another and conform to the requirements of the civil religion.

Contrary to the misuse of the idea of civil religion in today's literature, the minimal doctrines of Rousseau's civil religion can be said to be a rephrasing of the Calvinist sense of the divine, also variously referred to as conscience or moral sense. Toward the end of his *Social Contract*, Rousseau writes:

> The dogmas of the civil religion ought to be simple, few in number, precisely worded, without explanations or commentaries. The existence of a powerful, intelligent, beneficent divinity that foresees and provides; the life to come; the happiness of the just; the punishment of the wicked; the sanctity of the social contract and of its laws.[15]

---

15. Rousseau, *Social Contract* 4.3.

In modern usage of Rousseau's idea of civil religion, it is common to restrict it to the last dogma in the form of respect for national symbols, the constitution, and the laws. But if we consider the context in which Rousseau is moved to propose this idea, we must come to see that the state and its citizens are protected against the threat of atheism by adopting this civil religion. Rousseau is hard on those who, after pledging to uphold the dogmas of this civil religion, adopt a behavior that proves contrary to the dogmas. Against such, he recommends punishment by death, just like Plato's last resort.

Although we may discern a similarity between Rousseau's civil religion and the universal minimum religion, there is a major difference. Our view is that atheism is impossible; a minimum religion exists in all and predisposes all to a moral sense. That people are inclined to act in evil ways is not negated by the presence of the minimum religion. In the case of Rousseau, the dogmas of civil religion ought to be set up by the state and citizens are required to come to a profession of these dogmas. It is coincidental that the content of his civil religion aligns with the main ideas of our proposed minimum religion. If the content of Rousseau's civil religion is innate, then the need for a state to set up the religion and punish contrary behavior seems unnecessary. It would be more logical to assert minimum religion as a universal religion against which the state can do nothing. What the state may legislate is incorrect speech about universal religion, not the absence of its essence in an individual.

Atheism, though a real threat to society, is not to be feared because it does not actualize in men and women. By nature, they are members of a universal minimum religion because of their original predisposition to morality, notwithstanding the ongoing battle with the attendant natural propensity to evil.

D. THE UNIVERSAL MINIMUM RELIGION CANNOT BE SUCCESSFULLY CHALLENGED BY THE ARGUMENT FROM DIVINE HIDDENNESS

We have just said that true atheism is impossible based on moral arguments. We should at least consider another argument for atheism, or benign atheism. We can call this benign because it has the tone of one in a state of nonbelief but with such a longing to believe that is only frustrated by the hiddenness of God. This frustration makes nonbelief appear reasonable.

Universal minimum religion asserts that human beings stand in a relation with a Supreme Being who grounds their moral sense. In the language of existence, God exists, all human beings are aware of him, and this is made manifest in their universal moral predisposition. A minimum belief about the existence of God therefore exists as part of an innate religion.

On the contrary, the argument from divine hiddenness to nonbelief is that there is nonbelief in the world, and this is incompatible with the existence of a God who would normally make himself known to those in a state of nonbelief.

Schellenberg is one of those who argue for the reasonableness of nonbelief from the hiddenness of God. His main argument can be characterized as follows:

1. If there is a God, he is perfectly loving.
2. If a perfectly loving God exists, reasonable nonbelief does not occur.
3. Reasonable nonbelief occurs.
4. No perfectly loving God exists (from 2 and 3).
5. Hence, there is no God (from 1 and 4).[16]

The second premise is further explained to mean that a perfectly loving God would be open to a relationship with the loved. This love would dispel nonbelief, but Schellenberg asserts that we have evidence that nonbelief occurs. This argument fails because of points 2 and 3. We should also note that we are looking at this argument from the perspective of the universal minimum religion.

The second premise turns on two things. The first is the meaning of reasonable nonbelief and the second is the relation between a loving God and reasonable nonbelief.

Reasonableness is a matter of degree and, given that reason itself is entirely subjective, we need to come to an agreement on the threshold for something to count as reasonable. It is possible to see how it may strike us as reasonable that we do not agree with the standard of reasonableness set by supposed atheists. But before one can debate on the threshold required for reasonableness, we need to see that for something to be reasonable, it must exist.

It would clarify things further if we knew the time frame within which nonbelief can be said to exist. Let's suppose that it exists. If someone has believed all their life until the last hour, and now they say they are in a state of nonbelief, does that qualify as the nonbelief referred to in 2 and 3? This question is important because doubt and faith are compatible in the lives of some theists—for example, Christians. We meet this in the lives of the

16. Schellenberg, *Divine Hiddenness*, 83.

apostles of Jesus Christ, such as Thomas and Peter. If we construe nonbelief broadly to be the state of mind that a person has from birth to death, then according to the universal minimum religion, this is impossible. Nonbelief does not exist in that sense and so we cannot qualify its putative existence as reasonable. That which does not exist cannot be in a state of reasonable existence. What is being pursued in the argument is doubt, not nonbelief as an enduring state.

But if it may be granted that nonbelief can be a fluctuation between belief and doubt, then our analysis is focused on the state of nonbelief. Since doubt and faith in God are compatible in the lives of some believers, it cannot be concluded that a state of doubt, or occasional nonbelief that was preceded by a state of belief or that is soon to be succeeded by belief, is evidence for the lack of God's existence. The Christian religion is full of accounts of faithful people who go through a state of doubt only to emerge invigorated after yearning for God's return. In the story of the cross, when Jesus cries out to God, his Father, asking why God has forsaken him, this is an entirely different question than asking why God has stopped existing or why God has never existed. The absence of a sense of God's presence in the vicinity of a person at a particular time cannot surely be taken to be a proof for the nonexistence of God.

Regarding the relation between a perfectly loving God and the absence of reasonable nonbelief, Schellenberg's commitment to epistemic rather than metaphysical issues is evident. Even though he clarifies that relation to be of a loving God being open to a relationship such that it dispels nonbelief, he unreasonably holds that the relationship can only be actualized by evidence of the sort required by empiricists. What sort of evidence of God's presence counts as dispelling the hiddenness of God? If we admit that God and the human being are of different natures and spatiotemporal dimensions, then the manner in which the one appears to the other is not predetermined. Were God to appear as a sublime object, then we'd be overwhelmed by his presence, as an analysis of perception of the sublime would suggest.

God does appear to all human beings. He does so in the sense in which a relation between him and the human is cognized as universally conducive to the presence of an original moral predisposition. God appears in a feeling, one that is strong enough to determine the will or to make the conscience cognize the rightness and wrongness of an action.

What Schellenberg is getting at is not the proof of God's existence as cognized in the universal minimum religion. Rather, he is examining a yearning for more of God—that is, a yearning for more revelation and more knowledge of God than the experience of the universal minimum religion. That feeling or awareness is weak, but strong enough to endow us with and sustain an original moral predisposition as being grounded in God. We yearn for more of God, but we approach this in different ways. It is this that can lead to doubts. These doubts notwithstanding, the situation does not amount to proof of the reasonableness of nonbelief and absence of a loving God.

E. THE YEARNING FOR SOMETHING MORE THAN UNIVERSAL MINIMUM RELIGION

We may say that three impulses lead to human yearning for something more than the universal minimum religion. The one is an innate metaphysical urge, the other is a sense of guilt about our moral shortcomings, and the third is a human disposition to ritualistic life and belief in afterlife.

Regarding the first impulse for more religion, we grasp that human beings by nature desire to know and the world of phenomena does not satisfy that urge. If our innate thirst for metaphysics was properly recognized, the attacks on those in search of metaphysical grounds for experience would not be as sustained as they are. Deep down in us human beings, we are convinced that reality is not the simple vision presented to us in observed phenomena. With respect to our self-knowledge, we seek to know, but whatever we know we suspect that there is more to it that we do not yet know. This "more to know" is partly empirical but also partly metaphysical. God is a proper object of the quest for knowledge, but this quest can proceed on the solid basis of the universal minimum religion.

Like Augustine of Hippo stating that our hearts are restless until they rest in God,[17] Calvin writes in the *Institutes*:

> For though our mind cannot conceive of God, without ascribing some worship to him, it will not be sufficient merely to apprehend that he is the only proper object of universal worship and adoration, unless we are also persuaded that he is the fountain of all good, and seek for none but in him.[18]

The second impulse to go beyond universal minimum religion recognizes our guilt and helplessness in the internal court of morality before which we appear very often. We feel a sense of guilt that is not overcome by a simple commitment to do better. No, in fact, we realize that no matter how resolved and how hard we try, we still seem to be caught in the situation of imperfect knowledge and imperfect desires that ultimately lead to more

---

17. Augustine, *Confessions*, 1.1.1.
18. Calvin, *Institutes*, 51–52.

regretful outcomes. It is surprising that many supposed atheists become very passionate in condemning any systematic religion that dwells on sins and possible eternal punishment.

Atheists criticize the good God who punishes sins, the religious bodies that commit sins (or what society generally views as wrongdoing), and the religious bodies that recommend corrective or punitive actions against its members. Their criticism is presented from the point of caring humanists, who present themselves as kinder than God and religious organizations. In this behavior, there is a manifestation of the universal minimum religion.

There is an indication that those who have a more optimistic view of human nature are generally misled by the universal minimum religion to assert that the original human predisposition to morality should, and does, translate to a coherent moral lifestyle that is free from vice. Where evidence speaks against such optimism, the society is blamed for the moral failings of the individual. But surely, those social forces emerge from the forces of individual wills. Bertrand Russell condemns the moral lesson of Augustine's story of stealing pears for no practical reason.[19] Augustine sees the motivation that led him to steal pears as child as a manifestation of hereditary sin. He did so not to eat the pears, but for the simple pleasure of stealing and frustrating the owner. Russell calls this story morbid, quite characteristic of his vehement rejection of what he views as a Christian obsession with sins.

But even if the story is morbid, is morbid-minded religion bad? William James, in his *Varieties of Religious Experience*, contrasts between healthy-minded and morbid-minded religion. The healthy-minded religion is the morally optimistic one. James rightly considers the healthy-minded optimistic religion to be inadequate:

> There is no doubt that healthy-mindedness is inadequate as a philosophical doctrine; because the evil facts which it refuses positively to account for are a genuine portion of reality.[20]

According to William James, morbid-minded religion such as Calvinism is more in tune with the reality of human life. Evil is here and some or most of it is caused by other human beings. But the human being wants to know how to deal with this problem. More systematic religion is needed to discover doctrines of grace and salvation.

The third impulse to go beyond minimum religion speaks to our nature as ritualistic, artistic beings who also feel that there is an afterlife. Art speaks to us in ways that words alone cannot. Through the arts, we can

---

19. Russell, *History*, 345.
20. James, *Varieties of Religious Experience*, 148.

transcend cultural barriers to live out our universal minimum religion. But to reach that level of religious feeling through the arts, more religion is needed. We need religious symbols and propositions that further deepen the moral sense with which we are endowed. We seek burial rituals that hint at what we can hope for in a possible afterlife. But what precisely is the form of this systematic religion? We want to know.

The yearning for more religion moves us to seek to expand the horizon of the universal minimum religion on which we securely stand. But we are full of passion for more. Perhaps we may say that feeling—that is, a sense of a religious connection—far exceeds propositional knowledge, as William James observes in his *Varieties*.[21] We must now turn to explore the various ways in which this universal minimum religion can be further developed into systematic religions or critical but dissatisfied religion that adopts the name of atheism or agnosticism.

---

21. James, *Varieties of Religious Experience*, 372.

CHAPTER 8

The Universal Minimum Religion Develops Toward a Systematic Revealed or More Critical Minimum Religion

UNSATISFIED WITH THE UNIVERSAL minimum religion, human beings often further develop it toward a more systematic religion. The approach is either based on divine revelation or critical (philosophical) speculation. The critical or philosophical speculation assumes the form of so-called atheism and agnosticism, but it cannot satisfy the initial desires that propelled it toward a more systematic religion. The adherent of the new critical religion is, however, still anchored in the universal minimum religion.

In the preceding chapter, we said that although we all practice a universal minimum religion, we are not satisfied. We desire more. We identified three motives that propel us toward an extended or more systematic religion. These forces are an innate desire for metaphysical knowledge, our sense of guilt and helplessness because of inescapable evil inclinations in our will, and our need for rituals and a doctrine of salvation. Systematic religion therefore builds on the universal minimum religion and attempts to satisfy these three desires.

We arrived at the idea of a universal minimum religion through intuitions of a moral nature. But what methods can human beings use to pursue their deeply felt desire to deepen and systematize this minimum religion? This is not an easy question. We may say that anything goes; but the vindication of any method adopted should lie in the resulting systematic religion. This may not seem like a satisfactory answer. Before any methods can be suggested, it is useful to divide extended religions into purely philosophical religions versus revealed religions.

Philosophical religion is not possible without an element of revelation in the form of a myth or an inspirational historical figure. The teachings of most inspirational figures are considered to be revelations insofar as the person does not explicitly engage in philosophical theorizing. Although the criterion for what counts as philosophical theorizing may still be debatable, at least we have a sense of how revelation may enter into a philosophical religion. Another name that is more descriptive of this philosophical religion could be *critical religion*. This is religion that reflects on, and corrects, its contents, based on a criterion of coherence imposed by philosophy's quest for generality and timelessness.

Even philosophers who adopt a skeptical attitude toward religion and theology concede that philosophy is closely related to religion or theology. For instance, in the introduction to *The History of Western Philosophy*, Bertrand Russell, a critic of systematic religion, asserts: "Philosophy, as I shall understand the word, is something intermediate between theology and science."[1] He claims that philosophy occupies the no-man's-land that lies between theology and science. He holds that philosophy shares with theology the method of speculation about nonempirical matters, and with science, philosophy shares the method of appealing to reason rather than to authority or revelation. Our analysis of reason has brought reason closer to religion. Russell's view, therefore, lends support to the view that philosophy and religion are closely related by speculation and a critical attitude about the same big questions, for which empiricism has no obvious or definite answers.

As for revealed religion, it cannot be completely void of philosophy. If we follow Pythagoras and consider philosophy as the love of wisdom, then it broadens what can be called philosophy. The general realm of wisdom is broader than what today is considered academic philosophy. Religion and culture are also sources of the kind of wisdom meant by Pythagoras. Revealed religion can sometimes come to a prophet or seer because of an intentional search for wisdom about the big questions with which philosophy is concerned. From the perspective of Socrates, philosophy is more about realizing that you don't know and asking the right questions, with the practical goal of advancing the well-being of individuals and society. Today's academic view of philosophy is obviously more critical and canonical, demanding acquaintance with prior scholarship on the subject. But in the broad sense of Pythagoras and Socrates, revealed religion involves some philosophy and philosophy involves religion.

---

1. Russell, *History*, xiii.

Despite this lack of clear-cut boundaries between philosophical and revealed religion, it would be useful to consider as philosophical that religion in which the initial seed of revelation is far removed and no longer emphasized. Such a philosophical religion is built on conceptual and critical analyses of the minimum revelation, supplemented by speculations. We view revealed religion as one in which philosophy plays a secondary role to a body of religious teachings, passed down from a person who presents themselves as divinely inspired and a nonphilosopher.

Without the analysis offered in chapters 1 and 2, it would be customary to say that philosophical religion is established through the extension of the universal minimum religion using reason. Revealed religion would be said to be religion that is based on faith in prophetic teachings. This can no longer work since, because of our analysis of reason, we now hold that reason is fundamentally dependent on faith. While this kernel of faith may not be invoked in every reasoning process, the premises of that reasoning process must be seen as if they are held together in a nested manner, all the way down to noninferential intuitions that are of a religious nature.

From the distinction between philosophical and revealed religion, with the qualifications considered, the methods for extending the universal minimum religion therefore include adopting a revelation, a historical teacher, metaphysical speculation, and natural philosophy, among others.

The ideas of a universal minimum religion that serve as starting points for the development of a systematic critical religion include: the original predisposition to morality; awareness of evil in the world and in our nature; awareness of the battle that sometimes occurs between the moral disposition and the inclination to evil; and our relation to the divine and the rest of humanity, where a sense of duty is felt as an expression of gratitude to God. Since the method of arriving at an extended religion involves metaphysical speculations and coherence, these starting intuitions are necessary to constrain the speculative mind from wandering too far afield.

The three driving forces that propel us toward systematic religion may be emphasized differently in the elaboration of a given systematic religion. One group of religions may emerge where the metaphysical urge leads to abstract, knowledge-based religion, where distinctions rely heavily on conceptual debates and emphasis on evidence. Some approaches may de-emphasize rituals and end up with very limited rituals whereas others may place a lot of weight on rituals and lead to a religion that is heavily based on tradition and rituals but poor in propositional creeds. In such a tradition-based religion, knowing the right rituals and manner of behavior may outweigh the significance of religious knowledge and personal-religious experience. Regarding our sense of guilt and helplessness, some developments may boldly assert the optimistic view of human nature and ignore or minimize the problems arising from evil inclinations, while other extreme approaches may tend toward a very morbid-minded religious system (to use William James's distinction of religions).

We shall first consider philosophical religion and its impacts on modernity. We will then consider revealed religion and the systems of systematic religions that are based on historical revelations. The Christian religion should be of interest to us as a systematic religion that seems to me to best address the yearning that propels people beyond minimum religion. The idea of further developing a universal minimum religion in response to the human quest for more systematic religion is not entirely correct when it comes to revealed religion. Revelation is viewed as a gift from the Supreme Being; if human beings play a role in the extension, it can only be their display of total dependence on an external source of knowledge in that attempt to move beyond the vague but inescapable universal minimum religion.

A. PHILOSOPHICAL RELIGION

Philosophy is not complete without ethics. But ethics cannot find a stable foundation that is not of a religious nature. And a realistic religion is not possible without theism.

As time goes by, many religions, especially those of the Eastern world, appear to distance themselves from theism. Some even try to characterize such religions as purely ethical systems that are void of religion and neutral to theism or atheistic. But these religions cannot stop their adherents from expressing their innate theistic predispositions in religious rituals. The truth remains that ethics is impossible without religion, and that all religions, insofar as they offer a principle of morality and a doctrine of human salvation, are theistic.

Unlike the universal minimum religion that is rooted in the nature of the individual, the development of the systematic religion cannot be the work of a single individual; a community is involved. Even if one is philosophically inspired to start a systematic religion with doctrines all worked out, one must still proselytize and form a community of fellow believers. Such is the case with Pythagoras, Epicurus, and, in the nineteenth century, such attempts as the founding of the Religion of Humanity by Auguste Comte. In the case of a revealed religion, the prophet is a messenger of the Supreme Being to the people; here, proselytizing takes on an even greater role to form a community.

This social dimension therefore makes the evolution from minimum to systematic religion a social phenomenon that can be studied historically or sociologically. But the historical approach cannot just amount to amassment of facts; the causal relations of the historical events must be sought in the beliefs of those involved. Even a sociological study of religion cannot only rely on the measurement of events as if the society is a black box. An interpretive scheme—that is, methodological individualism—must be used to understand the ideas that animate the social phenomena of the religion. As varied as these interpretive approaches may turn out to be, it is useful to recognize the universality of the minimum religion, and to grasp the forces that propel people or societies beyond that minimum religion. It is a search for meaning, salvation, and rituals.

Philosophical religion is a critical religion; within the context of an evolving religious system, it must have as its starting point some religious content that is further developed. We could follow the broad division of religions into Eastern and Western religions to understand how the minimum religion is systematized into doctrines and rituals that differ. This is outside the scope of this work. It would suffice for us to consider the evolution of religion in Greece for two reasons. First, as part of the West, the role of gods and doctrines of salvation are more clearly stated than in the variety of Eastern religions. Second, religion in Greece demonstrates a dynamic evolution from revelation and myths toward philosophy, with key theistic elements maintained. This is not the case in Chinese religions, for example.

The emergence of philosophy in Greece is clearly preceded by various religious practices where speculation plays an important role. Unless one is limited to philosophy from the modern era, it is impossible to miss the theistic themes in Greek philosophy. As discussed in chapter 1, the distance between philosophy and religion seems to arise from the emergence of Christianity as a religious system that asserts itself as *the* religion. This sets Christianity apart from pagan religion with the result that philosophy or reason now becomes synonymous with the doctrines of Greek pagan or folk religion. This is unfortunate because it renders opaque the practice of philosophy as a historical struggle of humankind to further develop innate minimum religion into a richer, systematic religion.

The philosophical religion of Greece starts with theogonies and evolves to cults such as Orphism. From Orphism emerge philosophers such as Pythagoras and Plato. The later schools of Stoicism and Epicureanism can be viewed as equally arising from this religious stream. This philosophical religion finds its way into modern life through Abrahamism, secular spirituality, and self-professed atheism. This outline of religious change is also one of the many possible paths taken by a universal minimum religion as it grows into a richer religious worldview.

Hesiod's *Theogony* and the Gods of the Greeks

Hesiod's *Theogony* demonstrates the fertility of the speculative mind of the Greeks. There are many Eastern and Western theogonies, but in the Greek *Theogony* a dramatic and highly imaginative landscape is displayed. This is unlikely to be the product of a simple revelation or dream; it is the free flow of the imagination. This free speculation percolates and modifies itself among the people, with the result that when accounts of it are written at later times, variation in the narrative is more common than unity.

Hesiod, of whom little is known, declares that his song is a divine revelation from the Muses at Olympus, intended to tell the story of the immortal gods of the Greek pantheon.[2] It is possible that the *Theogony* is a written account of one version of many oral accounts of the origin of the Greek gods. This *Theogony* is placed around the eighth or seventh century BCE. Hesiod's account is both about the origin of the gods and the origin of the universe, even if the latter takes backstage to the drama of the gods. This origin of the universe is different and less moral in tone than Plato's *Timaeus*, whose content is supposed to have come to the Greeks from Egypt through Solon. Egyptian cosmogonies and theogonies would thus appear simpler but not as simple as the Gen 1–11 account of the Abrahamists (Jews, Christians, and Muslims). The Abrahamic cosmogony can be considered to be simpler and more stable on account of the number of personalities involved and the absence of competing cosmogonies among the Israelites and other Abrahamists.

We may rightfully ask, How is Hesiod's *Theogony* an extension of the universal minimum religion? We find this answer in the role of good and evil in the four gods and descendants of Gaia and Ouranos. The Greek mind first seeks to establish the place of Zeus as the king of all gods, in charge of law and order, among others. The battle between good and evil that is well known to human beings is conjectured to have been the origin of the gods as well. The gods mimic the lives of mere mortals through their greed, intrigues, and injustice. It is not the idea of a Supreme Being who is morally perfect that drives the Greek narrative, but the central idea of strife between good and evil forces and how this strife engenders vengeance. The Greeks who speculatively arrive at the pantheon of gods with Zeus as the king of the gods therefore anthropomorphically attribute evil dispositions to the lower

2. Hesiod, *Theogony* 20–34.

gods and goddesses while allowing for the emergence of a clearer vision of a Supreme Being, Zeus.

But why is the starting point in Greece one of polytheism, rather than a Supreme Being as we have been discussing in chapter 7? In the seven intuitions presented as the core of the minimum religion (pp. 117–18), we spoke more generally of a transcendent force. We morally sense the existence of a relation between us and that force. We also see phenomena in nature and among human beings that may seem to stand in relation to a force different from the one we sense morally. It is therefore conceivable to think of reality as consisting in many deities with similar conflicting predispositions to good and evil as human beings. For there to be ultimate justice and benevolence, the possibility of a Supreme Deity presents itself. From this possibility, we therefore have the idea of gods but also of a king above the gods—be it Zeus among the Greeks, Osiris or Amun-Ra among the Egyptians and Cushites, Marduk among the Babylonians, or Yahweh/Elohim among the Abrahamists.

Hesiod's *Theogony* thus tries to give an account of the dozen Greek gods on Mount Olympus who play a central role in what we may call the state religion. These gods show benevolence toward mortals but are also capable of punishing them. Their humanlike behavior seems to suggest that they are corruptible, such that they can dispense a blessing where a punishment is due. But do these Olympian gods fully satisfy the spiritual yearnings that would propel a person with minimum religion to search for a more systematic religion? It appears not, because we encounter the Orphic cult in the sixth century as a new development.

Orphism, Personal Religion, and Orphic Philosophers

The sixth and fifth centuries BCE constitute an interesting period in Eastern and Western religious history. In Chinese religious history we have Confucius (551–479 BCE) developing his ethical system. Gautama Buddha (some sources say he lived from 563 to 483 BCE) also develops a new religion, breaking away from Hinduism, thus making Buddhism a sort of reformed Hinduism. This period also corresponds to the writing of the accounts of the Old Testament of the Abrahamists during the exile in Babylon. Karl Jasper categorizes the period from 800 BCE to 200 BCE as the axial period and remarks on its transformative nature in world religions. He writes:

> In this age were born the fundamental categories within which we still think today, and the beginnings of the world religions,

by which human beings still live, were created. The step into universality was taken in every sense.³

Since the state religion of the Greeks could not quench the religious thirst of all its citizens, we therefore witness the rise of cults such as Orphism. This cult leads us away from the focus on the drama of the gods to the human being. What is the origin of this good and evil in us? Which of the gods can save us? How can we attain salvation? If we answer these questions systematically, especially in such a manner that the minimum religion is not undermined, then we are dealing with a form of systematic religion anchored in the universal minimum religion.

The poet Orpheus and the god Dionysus are central figures in the Orphic religion. Dionysus is also known by other names, including Bacchus and Zagreus. Orphism, or the cult of Bacchus, is said to have Egyptian origins and its importation to Greece through the Thracians was enthusiastically welcomed by some.

Orpheus is said to have encountered the mysteries of Dionysus through a revelation from Apollo, who chose Orpheus because of his musical abilities. Orpheus, of whom it is not quite clear whether he actually lived, is said to have gone to the underworld and returned thanks to his musical genius that could even charm the underworld. That makes him a hero almost of the demigod status.

The mysteries of the Orphic religion have their origin in legends about Dionysus. Born of Zeus and Persephone, Dionysus was said to have been torn to pieces by the creatures called Titans, who then ate his body parts, except the heart. Furious about this, Zeus struck the Titans with a thunderbolt, transforming them to ashes. As Bertrand Russell relates in his *History of Western Philosophy*, conflicting accounts either hold that Zeus ate the heart or that it was given to Semele, with the final result that Dionysus was born anew.⁴ Human beings, according to Orphism, arise from the ashes of the Titans—their bodies are derived from Titanic material. But their souls are closely related to the god Dionysus, or Bacchus, whose body parts the Titans devoured. To attain salvation, human beings must purify themselves to get rid of the material part which is of Titanic origin and thus evil. This Dionysus became the god of wine, theater, insanity, and religious ecstasy, among others.

The Orphic cult admitted members by initiation and kept many of their doctrines secret. Music and ecstatic dancing were central to the practice of the religion. Men and women could become part of it. As part of their

3. Jasper, *Origin and Goal of History*, 2.
4. Russell, *History*, 17.

rituals, animals were killed and eaten raw, a practice perhaps reminiscent of the Titans tearing apart and eating Dionysus. We see that this religious community has a clear founding figure in the charismatic and musical Orpheus.

As an Orphic and a seeker of wisdom, Pythagoras unites mathematics and music. Having discovered harmonic relations in musical notes and ratios among numbers, the view emerges that reality is numbers. We see the incidental mutual relation between logic and religious experience. This is in the pre-Socratic period. After Socrates, we encounter Plato as an important Orphic philosopher who demonstrates how a moral commitment can fructify philosophical theorizing about human nature and humans' place in nature.

We can view the following as the main teachings of Orphism:

Orphism 1: Human beings are, by nature, partly body and partly soul. The body is made of earth and related to the wicked Titans, while the soul is related to Dionysus, or Bacchus, who is divine.

Orphism 2: Human life on earth should aim at purifying the self, to have less of the body and ever more of the soul, until one is purely soul.

Orphism 3: Certain rituals can help in this purification process and should be observed. These rituals are only revealed to the initiated.

Orphism 4: When one dies, the soul transmigrates—that is, it can pass from one body to another body, which could be human or beast. The aim of the soul after death should be eternal bliss in which the soul becomes one with Bacchus. Failing this aim, one faces permanent or temporary suffering.

Orphism 5: It is advantageous to live in a community of like-minded Orphics. Membership is through initiation and all are welcome, men and women.

Here we find an extended religion in which personal faith plays a key role, unlike the state religion. One is free to choose to become a member or not. We also see a speculative account of the origin of good and evil, and we have a sense of what we should hope for after we have done our duty of purification. This purification is more about sacrifices and rituals than about moral reformation. It is possible that among the dietary restrictions there are ethical precepts that build on the moral intuition of minimum religion. But superstition plays a central role, albeit not without theoretical explanations of how this relates to salvation.

In Orphism we also see the role of passion in religious worship. The intoxication identified with Orphism turns out mostly to be one where feeling is higher than reflective thought. We could say that there are some similarities with charismatic Christian or Sufi Muslim practices in this picture. Mystical ecstasy is claimed to give access to divine knowledge in a more direct way.

Pythagoreanism and Orphism are considered to share the same common elements. The Pythagoreans only appear to have been a more tight-knit cult. Although it is difficult to point to the developed moral doctrines of the Orphics or the Pythagoreans, Plato's moral philosophy and its theistic tone seem to signal the general character of their ethics. Clark and Smith suggest that there is a marked difference between an earlier Plato who viewed pleasure as the goal of life, and the Plato after he returned from Italy, where he is supposed to have met and interacted with Pythagoreans.[5] Dialogues such as the *Republic*, *Timaeus*, and *Philebus* are said to have been written after the Pythagorean encounter. Since this is plausible, we can view the ethics of Plato, with his commitment to theism, as further expression of the systematic religion of the Orphics.

In Orphism and its Pythagorean versions, we find a systematic religion with emphasis on personal faith but shrouded in secrecy. More is being uncovered through studies of fragments of their mysteries and commentaries on their practices. An example is the Derveni Papyrus of Macedonian origin, a commentary on an Orphic poem, discovered in 1962.

In Plato, we find a philosophy that is religious and engages in challenging debates, but does not often state in very clear terms the views of the philosopher. In some works it is obvious what the message is, but in others it is not straightforward or conclusive. This personal faith of the Orphic, Pythagorean, or Platonic type is not presented in a form that is easily accessible to all. But with respect to the key teachings of Orphism above, they are similar, except that the role of rituals in purification of the self is replaced by critical reasoning. Plato's tripartite theory of the soul brings out the role of reason in regulating the behavior of a person. In Platonism, the Academy plays the role of an institution of learning; it is not a place of worship and social interaction as the Orphic gatherings were. We thus find a deficiency in the communal practice of religion. This is understandable because Plato's aim is not to replace the state religion but rather to reform it through moral education and the attitude of people toward religion.

---

5. Clark and Smith, *Readings in Ethics*, 21–22.

Stoicism and Epicureanism: Summit of Religion or Dead End?

It is unlikely that a philosophical religion converges to a stable systematic religion. This is to be expected, especially if the initial revelation that kick-starts it is only one of many variants of stories that emphasize complex mythical beings, beside a Supreme Being, whose very idea constrains speculative thought. We find in Aristotle already a situation that is closer to deism. But in quite different ways, the Greco-Roman revealed religion, fused with critical and speculative thought, further develops toward personal ethical systems in Stoicism and Epicureanism. Both turn their focus to the present life and a certain materialism. For the Stoics, the materialism is deterministic and divine, and for the Epicureans, the materialism is atheistic and admits of chance events.

Although Stoicism and Epicureanism share certain features, especially with respect to the view of an afterlife, they have key differences. In the present life, Stoicism proposes a religious way of life that aims at virtue while also advancing philosophy through logic and a monistic physics. The inner life receives the greatest attention. We can take control of our thoughts and emotions and identify those things that are under our control and those that are not. We can use our reason, aligned with our will, to address those things that are under our control. Virtue, and not external things, constitute happiness. We must seek to avoid vice. But the distinction between vice and virtue is black and white; there is no intermediate. This is the Stoic worldview.

The Epicureans acknowledge the existence of gods but exclude them from the current life. Leading a tranquil life of pleasure and nurturing friendship are to be pursued. Neither determinism nor total chance should dominate our view of the future; the future is neither wholly ours nor wholly not ours. We study nature mostly in order to allay those fears that disturb our tranquility. As a coherent system that also responds to the desire for a passionate religious life, Epicureanism looks rather austere and uncertain; the possibility of vice lurks at every turn.

But the Stoic and the Epicurean are skeptical about life after death. Epicurus speaks of death in his *Letter to Menoeceus*: "When we are, death is not come, and, when death is come, we are not."[6] As for the Stoics, some admit of the soul existing after death until the next conflagration, after which the universe starts all over. Some deny the possibility of an afterlife; we become matter which is of a divine nature and determined by destiny to take its place in the universe.

---

6. Epicurus, *Letter to Menoeceus*, 88.

The doctrine of the afterlife is a major human concern as it relates to Kant's question "What may I hope?" While Epicurean doctrines easily attract criticism for their quasi-atheistic outlook, the Stoic's position on the afterlife receives greater criticism after consideration. For instance, Augustine, in his *City of God*, exclaims about the absurdity of the Stoic's position: "O happy life, which seeks the aid of death to end it?"[7]

Compared to Eastern religions that focus on ethics and less on gods, Stoicism and Epicureanism as the advanced stage of Western philosophical religion differ radically on the issues of the afterlife and ritualistic worship. Buddhism and Confucianism, for example, articulate a vision of the end goal of life that transcends the current life and motivates the ethics of the present. Though it may be said that religious worship among the Stoics and Epicureans largely follows state religion, the system promotes community life but the yearning for ritual that may motivate the search for religion does not seem to be fulfilled.

Here we have briefly considered the Greek religion developing from the universal minimum religion through the anthropomorphic gods to philosophical religious worldviews. It is hard to see how those who set out to enrich the minimum religion can find satisfaction in such philosophical religions. It is indeed true, that these contain many truths that have found their way into Abrahamism, but as a system capable of durably satisfying the thirst for systematic religion and providing a stable foundation for ethics, philosophical religions leave many human desires unfulfilled.

Nietzsche is one of the thinkers who flee from Christianity to pure philosophical religion. Though his closeness to Epicurus is noted, his opinions on the Greek religious philosophers vacillated during his lifetime.[8] The existential quest that sets Nietzsche in motion may be found in his prayer of 1864. The last verse of this prayer says:

> I want to know you, Unknown One,
> Who reaches deep into my soul,
> Who roams through my life like a storm—
> You Unfathomable One, akin to me!
> I want to know you, even serve you.[9]

It seems that philosophical religion, although it may produce truths that help us on the journey of life, fails to completely quench the thirst for more religion or give us the impulse to lead a passionate life. The role

---

7. Augustine, *City of God* 19.4.
8. Knight, "Nietzsche and Epicurean Philosophy."
9. Nietzsche, *To the Unknown God*. For the German, see "Dem unbekannten Gott."

of passion in extended religious practice must be recognized; it does not necessarily mean an opposition to the development of a more intellectual worldview. Of the Greeks, Bertrand Russell says, after discussing Orphism in his *History*:

> It was the combination of passion and intellect that made them [the Greeks] great, while they were great.[10]

If we take today's humanist movement to be the logical development of Epicureanism, we can discern from their manifestos a dismissive attitude toward the existential questions that motivate people to look beyond the universal minimum religion. The apparent systematic and self-contained nature of their principles succeed by embracing vagueness about reason, rationality, and the origin of ethical feelings. Having first presented their worldview as a humanist religion, the most recent manifesto steers clear of religious language and embraces vague pronouncements on difficult questions. The first three of the six beliefs expressed in the 2003 third manifesto, "Humanism and Its Aspirations," are:

1. Knowledge of the world is derived by observation, experimentation, and rational analysis.
2. Humans are an integral part of nature, the result of unguided evolutionary change.
3. Ethical values are derived from human need and interest as tested by experience.[11]

In the context of this work, we believe to have cast enough doubt on the meaning of reason or rationality. Whereas we can agree that observation and experimentation play a significant role in our knowledge of the world, when we invoke rational analysis we tacitly enter the world of metaphysics and, specifically, the world of religion. Such things as cannot be observed or derived from other facts feature in our analysis. Human nature belongs to the world and knowledge of the world is not complete without a knowledge of human nature. Social sciences and humanities point to challenges that cannot be resolved soon. It is easier to see that religious faith is important in understanding human nature.

That the second humanist belief is not true can best be seen in the later views of Anthony Flew, a signatory to that manifesto and the previous version. One year after the publication of the third manifesto, Flew changed his

---

10. Russell, *History*, 21.
11. American Humanist Association, "Humanism," paras. 4–6.

atheistic position to belief in a divine being, a superior mind who is at the origin of the natural order. Although we embraced here the moral argument leading to God, Flew proceeds along natural theology to deny the possibility of life originating from unguided evolutionary change. In line with Plato's advice to follow the argument where it leads, Flew writes:

> I now believe that the universe was brought into existence by an infinite Intelligence. I believe that this universe's intricate laws manifest what scientists call the Mind of God. I believe that life and reproduction originate in a divine Source.[12]

We thus see that, purely on epistemological grounds, not considering revelation or the moral argument toward God and religion, an active cosigner of the manifesto comes to the view that behind the order we see there must be an intelligence. The one who approaches the need-to-know God from the moral perspective is already aware of the role of God, not only in the natural world, but also in the moral predisposition of the human soul and the feeling of a relation to the transcendent being. The second belief is thus only a humanist wish, contrary to the evidence that Flew sees.

The third belief of the humanists asserts naturalistic ethics. We have already said that it is impossible to lay the foundation for ethics based only on a descriptive account of human behavior. Collected data do not rise to a principle without a reflective judgment on the motivation and goal of human actions.

If we only consider Stoicism, Epicureanism, and the three humanist manifestos as products of the philosophical extension of minimum religion, we arrive at a position that is not rich enough to satisfy our desire for a more systematic religion. In the case of the humanists, we also arrive at a point of intolerance since the demise of organized religion appears to be part of their aspiration, judging from the earlier manifestos. But tolerance and multiplicity are to be expected, just based on possibilities and the fact that God lays more weight on developing the moral person and not purely epistemologists.

If one is lucky to start off with a revelation that is closer to reality, one can more successfully develop one's minimum religion toward a richer systematic religion. For such revelation, the Supreme Being must reach out to us; we cannot grasp that divine light from the position of human speculation or from a mythology that is laden with the unethical impulses of our human nature. That is, we must not start from a theogony such as Hesiod's, with gods that fail to meet the morality that cries out from our very human

---

12. Flew and Varghese, *There Is a God*, 88.

nature. The Supreme Being or gods must be better and must know better. For this reason, Plato is willing to censor those poets who imagine gods with all sorts of vices and evil dispositions. Critical reflection on such a moral scene involving corruptible gods can lead to cynicism about the Supreme Being.

B. SYSTEMATIC REVEALED RELIGION

In revealed religion, the key ideas are of a supranatural origin. We have the sense of the divine, but our knowledge of the nature of the divine and human destiny cannot be intuited in the same way that we come to grasp the deep-seated moral law within us. The exact manner of revelation can vary from visions to dreams and inspirations that are distinguishable from ordinary experience. If the empirically minded skeptic takes issue with the language of revelation, Newbigin points out that to say "God spoke to Moses" is like stating in the language of experience that "Moses had a religious experience."[13] In this religious experience, God reveals himself. While one may be inclined to object to this, we are at least as puzzled by the origin of the ideas of the divine in the inspired person as we can be in the origination of a scientific theory by conjecture.

The question we may ask is whether it is possible to judge from outside the system of a systematic revealed religion the plausibility of that religious system.

To answer this question, we must say something about what it means for it to be systematic and revealed; we must also show that it accords with the universal minimum religion; and we must show that it meets, or at least advances, the three existential drives that propel people beyond the comfort zone of the universal minimum religion. To fully investigate this question would carry us far afield. It may serve us better to highlight some of these elements in a historically revealed religion. As we said before, the development toward a systematic religion occurs within a community. Also, it is thankfully not the case that everyone is required to work out their own systematic religion, starting from the universal minimum religion. In practice, very few people find themselves in a pure universal minimum religion on account of being born into a community with a culture that openly or tacitly includes a systematic religious worldview. For instance, we mentioned before that Lutheranism undergirds the supposed atheism of the Scandinavian countries.

Abrahamism, especially its Christian version, can serve as a framework for discussing the reasonableness of systematic revealed religion. By

---

13. Newbigin, *Gospel in a Pluralistic Society*, 62.

reasonableness we only understand the extension of the universal minimum religion in a way that meets the propelling existential needs for more religion. There are three reasons that support our choice of Abrahamism. First, Abrahamism currently represents a major sector of revealed religions with over 55 percent of the world population. Second, the revelation on which the systematic religion is based has the character of a universal history with a religious interpretation. This subject is dealt with in an excellent manner in chapters 5–9 of Newbigin's work *The Gospel in a Pluralistic Society*. In a broader context, Herman Bavinck develops the idea that philosophy is, as a matter of fact, a revelation, and that systematic revelation rises to a philosophy.[14] This point was implied when we discussed Pythagoreanism and Orphism and their relation to the philosophical spirit of Greece. Principles asserted by revealed religions, such as Abrahamism, are often more extensive and coherent statements than some examples of fragmentary metaphysics, such as ancient Greek thought that is unquestionably admitted into philosophy. The third reason for the choice of Abrahamism is its historical use of philosophy for systematization and adjudication of competing interpretations.

Western religions can generally be considered as various forms of Abrahamism. God calls Abram the Sumerian (later Abraham) and sets him and his descendants apart for his self-revelation. The ultimate goal is to reach and bless the whole world through that process of revelation (Gen 12:3). Jesus and Mohammed are the progeny of Abraham; both become the founders of universalized theistic religions that are scripturally connected to ancient Judaism. In Christianity, these revelations include a redemptive plan that culminates in the ultimate revelation of God through the person of Jesus Christ. The revealed message transforms a given generation, and, through prophecies, prepares the people for the next revelation. A sense of moral and metaphysical development can be discerned in the Abrahamic narratives. Because of the historical nature of the revelation, one is not only concerned with the message but also with the human source by which God reaches the people. The message is more important but through the commitment to knowledge and the desire to avoid false revelation, Abrahamic scholarship also critically comments on the sources of the sacred revelation.

The primeval history of Genesis, chapters 1–11, includes the creation account, and this primeval history differs from the rest of Abrahamic revelations where the receiver of the revelation is known. Revelation from Gen 12 onward deals with the present and future state of affairs. Revelation of the past as in primeval history is of a different nature and this fact is recognized

---

14. Bavinck, *Philosophy of Revelation*, chap. 1–2.

by many theologians of Abrahamic religions. This distinguishing fact is missed by critics of Abrahamism and those fundamentalist believers who try to build an epistemological castle out of the primeval history beyond the establishment of God as the author of the universe.

But what value is there in the primeval history of Abrahamists? What credibility? These questions can only be dealt with in a just manner by comparing the cosmogony of the Abrahamic primeval history with other accounts of the creation of the world and theogonies. Compared to Hesiod's seventh-century account of the creation of the Greek gods, the primeval history of Gen 1–11 is a refreshing account in terms of coherence, morality, and plausibility. Plato's *Timaeus*, considered to be a myth brought from Egypt by Solon, demonstrates a cleaner and more moral account of the beginnings of things than Hesiod's *Theogony*. But the *Timaeus* is still far from the simplicity and beauty of the Abrahamist primeval history, especially regarding the nature of human beings and animals. Apart from the primeval history, then, the vast system of revelations in Abrahamic religions are largely religious experiences of historical figures concerning their present and future situations in relation to God.

Curiously, some supposed atheists are moved to doubt the historicity of Abrahamic Scriptures while acknowledging the authorship of Plato, pre-Socratics, and Eastern scholars such as Confucius. Detailed historical accounts can be offered for the authorship of the different elements of Abrahamist Scriptures. These extend from oral accounts and isolated written documents to the canon of the Old Testament during Jewish captivity in Babylon, to the first-century writing of the books of the New Testament, and to the writing of the Koran after the death of Mohammed.

The spiritual nature of the Scriptures means that there is more substance beyond the written words; they believe that God and divine meaning come alive as one interacts with and contemplates the text. This is the view defended by Augustine and writers such as Kierkegaard. Hermeneutics—that is, the science of textual interpretation—must therefore play a central role in the religious life of the Abrahamist. But precisely because of this dynamic encounter with the divine through interaction with the revealed word, divisions are bound to arise. These divisions in themselves are not to be viewed as invalidations of the revelation; the question is whether they lead to a systematic religion that meets the existential needs of the seeker and accords with the core principles of the universal minimum religion.

Some may bemoan the fact that Jesus and Mohammed did not write down their teachings in unambiguous terms. Others take issue with any differences in the Gospel accounts of Jesus. But we see a similar thing in the philosophical religion if we consider the life of Socrates and how this is later related by Plato and Xenophon. What Plato and Xenophon narrate about Socrates shows the different lenses through which they looked at Socrates. If we have good reason to believe that Kant's epistemology is true, then we must see divine revelation to also be confronted with making the divine message cognizable to people living within a certain culture. Thus, when Isaiah prophesizes about the coming of the Messiah, he gets a general idea, and sometimes the ideas may be close together in narration but separated by centuries in fulfillment.

But the fact that revelations in the Abrahamic religion are cumulative points to the operation of a philosophical spirit in bringing them together. They also speak of true and false prophets, with the mark of true prophets being coherence in their message with what was said by other prophets and the nature of God. The relatedness and coherence in Abrahamist Scriptures make them a subject of serious philosophical consideration.

Abrahamic Commandments as Extension of Minimum Religion

We cannot go into the details of each of the Abrahamic religions, but we should observe that from these revelations we obtain the Ten Commandments in Exod 20:1–17 and their further simplification to the two great commandments (Lev 19:18 and Deut 6:4–7). We also receive extended teachings on how to live and act toward one another, directions on worship rituals, and afterlife doctrines. We shall consider rituals and the afterlife in the next chapter.

From the perspective of Christians, Jesus is the ultimate revelation who simplifies the law. The law moves away from codified principles whose primary guiding role can overly restrict the operation of the religious conscience. For, if a conduct is not explicitly written in the law, even if one's conscience prompts one to avoid it, one may falsely feel liberated by the law if one transgresses the dictate of conscience. We can agree that systematic religion fails in its mission if it contradicts the universal minimum religion as manifested by conscience. The revolution of Jesus is to shift emphasis from the Ten Commandments to the two great commandments. Although these two laws are found in the Old Testament, and therefore bind Jews and Muslims, they take a more systematic and firmer presentation in New Testament Christianity. In Deut 6:5, the version that binds all Abrahamists is:

> You shall love the Lord your God with all your heart, with all your soul, and with all your strength.

In the New Testament, in addition to heart, soul, and strength, Jesus exhorts his followers to also love the Lord with all their mind. Mark expresses this new commandment as:

> And you shall love the Lord your God with all your heart, with all your soul, with all your mind, and with all your strength. (12:30)

Matthew's version leaves out *strength* (22:37), but Luke has the same four capacities as Mark's version (10:27).

What does it mean to love with all your mind? Here, we have an interesting situation where love—that is, related to a special feeling, a passion—is brought into contact with the mind, an intellectual capacity. In this we find the seed of an ethical system as the union of sentiments as well as reflected thoughts that are derived from sentiments and experience. The idea of the intellect and feeling coming together is already hinted at in the imperative to love. We are asked to express a feeling toward God. This feeling arises from our memory of being under a commanded duty to love.

The second commandment is given in Lev 19:18 as part of a longer command:

> You shall not take vengeance, nor bear any grudge against the children of your people, but you shall love your neighbor as yourself: I am the Lord.

The first part forbids vengeance or bearing a grudge against someone within one's community; then comes the command to love your neighbor as yourself. It is possible to misinterpret this commandment as limited to one's community. This therefore engendered the question "Who is my neighbor?" in reaction to Jesus's declaration of this as the second greatest commandment (Luke 10:26–29).

The extension of the meaning of one's neighbor is a significant change introduced by Jesus. This extension universalizes the commandment and makes it a plausible extension of the universal minimum religion that can be used in grounding ethics. Prior to the coming of Jesus, religions around the world had mostly been tribal. The resulting ethics from tribal religions elevates someone from within one's community to a more deserving position of benevolence. But the parable of the good Samaritan who shows love to a stranger from Judah breaks down the limit on who counts as one's neighbor.

The two commandments make up a system because unless the authority of God in the first is recognized, the imperative in the second cannot be executed with the religious intentions demanded of it. We can see why Plato, Rousseau, and Locke are concerned about the threat of atheism to the health of the state. But these two commandments, taken as the core of systematized Abrahamic religions, accord with the universal minimum religion. In the minimum religion, we are aware of standing in relation to a Supreme Being to whom we owe our original moral predisposition. The minimum religion is strengthened by the imperative to love God and to love other human beings as ourselves.

For Christians, Jesus's teachings and the writings of the apostles further help to discern principles and practical acts that demonstrate loving God and loving one's neighbor. Similarly, Judaism and Islam supplement these commandments with further scriptural doctrines. But, in contrast to Christianity, we find that more prescriptive rules are found in these two branches of Abrahamism, such that the codified law plays a more significant role in Judaism and Islam than in Christianity. By fulfilling works of the codified law, we get a sense of being on the right track. In Christianity, especially Protestantism, works take a backstage whereas faith is the determining mode of salvation. The religious conscience must determine principles of actions in specific cases and understand the performed works as expressions of gratitude to God.

Systematic Theologies of the Abrahamic Religions

Philosophy and revelation interact in all Abrahamic religions. This is to be expected since revelations are not uttered all at once but are collected as a series and reconnected to a unified religious system. To the Christians, for example, all of the Old Testament is interpreted as pointing to Christ, such that Jewish and Christian readings of prophetic writings in the Old Testament can lead to different interpretations in light of different presuppositional views of Jesus Christ.

If revelations are to be correctly interpreted, and if the desire for knowledge, salvation, and forgiveness of sins are to be met, then a coherent system must be presented to the believer. The God who issues commandments needs to be known. Apart from concrete commandments, we need to know the doctrine of salvation in that religion. What should I do with my sense of guilt? And how does one become a believer? Just as Orphism had initiation rites, these religions must articulate clear paths to membership and doctrines of salvation in the form of visions of the afterlife.

It is fair to say that the Christian branch of Abrahamism has, more than the other two, gone through a tumultuous process of philosophically piecing together the essential doctrines of their faith. Although by the middle of the second century CE the writings constituting the modern New

Testament had been settled, debates on the nature of Christ and the Trinity plagued the Christian faith. After the Reformation, debates on sacraments and the relation of faith to works continued. These debates are animated by the existence of metaphysical possibilities in competing interpretations.

Among the outcomes of these debates are many Christian denominations, although points of consensus exist, such as the principles expressed in the Apostles' Creed of Western Christian churches. It is one of many creeds in which the early Christians sought to coherently state their positions on key issues of their religion. In the Apostles' Creed, we encounter statements that expand the minimum religious beliefs of a Christian toward systematic religion. The creed reciter affirms belief in God who created heaven and earth; belief in Jesus Christ the Son of God; the virgin birth of Jesus; the suffering, death, resurrection, ascension, and the return of Jesus Christ for judgment of the living and the dead; the belief in the Holy Spirit; the belief in the universal church; belief in the fellowship of the believers; belief in the forgiveness of sins; belief in resurrection; and belief in eternal life.

Although these ideas are not elaborated in a single passage of revelation, they are brought together through philosophical reflection. One may question one or all of the asserted beliefs, but it cannot be denied that they are put together without violating obvious principles of logic such as internal contradiction. In more complex questions such as the doctrine of the Trinity and the nature of Christ, it is impossible to conduct these debates without philosophical knowledge. The Apostles' Creed, though it contains all the elements of the Trinity, does not explicitly state belief in the Trinity as a separate doctrine.

We do not easily find analogues of the Apostles' Creed as a condensation of philosophical theology in the other Abrahamic religions. In Judaism, for instance, Maimonides is known to have listed thirteen principles that he deemed to characterize every faithful Jew. A faithful Jew should believe:

1. The existence of God
2. The absolute unity of God
3. The incorporeality of God
4. The eternity of God
5. That God alone is to be worshipped
6. That God communicates to prophets
7. That Moses is the greatest prophet
8. That the Torah was given by God

9. That the Torah is immutable
10. That there is divine providence
11. That there is divine punishment and reward
12. That there will be a Messiah
13. That the dead will be resurrected[15]

As can be seen, these principles are mostly concerned with belief in God and his authorship of revelation. The other two main ideas are divine providence and divine punishment. The future will bring a Messiah and resurrection of the dead. These principles are not universally embraced by other scholars of Judaism. Some have proposed a reduced list of three: belief in God, in creation or revelation, and in providence or retribution.

In Islam, its five pillars offer an idea of the central points: declaration of faith, prayer, almsgiving, fasting, and pilgrimage as one's means permit. It is in the declaration of faith that the person acknowledges the oneness of God and the prophethood of Mohammed. Here again, we are dealing with the products of philosophical reflection on revelation.

C. REASON IS ROOTED IN FAITH, NOT FOLLY

To sum up our discussion so far, we have argued that reason is fundamentally subjective; it justifies past, present, or future action; and the goal of action is determined by faith. Faith builds on revealed religion. That may seem to give rise to a chaotic situation of subjective religious opinions furnishing the goals of actions. But is revealed religion all about revelations and individual opinions? Or is revealed religion in fact a system of philosophy? We can chart a course between the two extremes by considering revealed religion such as the Abrahamic religions to consist of systematic theologies. In these systematic theologies, pure elements of revelation are distinct from the connective processes that confer coherence to the system in a philosophical manner. Complementing these systematic theologies with rituals and doctrines of afterlife brings greater satisfaction to those who are propelled beyond the resources of the universal minimum religion.

What does this mean for reason and rationality? We must abandon the view that faith and reason are contraries or independent of each other. Faith inheres in reason and must be acknowledged as such. But reason cannot be based on a mass of isolated intuitions of faith; a coherence of intuitions is needed at the base. From the inner core of faith, reason builds on contingent

---

15. Birnbaum, *185 CE–1499 CE*, 166.

truths. The origin of these contingent truths has been discussed in part II. Placing faith at the foundation of reason should, however, not be abused by replacing contingent truths in our reasoning with articles of faith. Faith plays the role of axioms at the base of reason but extending the chain from this core must also draw from the library of contingent truths. One may replace a contingent truth with a pure speculation in a transparent way. But it is blasphemous to subtly make a conjectured idea assume the status of divine revelation in a chain of reasoning, far from the faith-based axiomatic core of reason.

When we inquire about the foundation of ethics, we see clearly where the seed of faith is needed. But the actions, or observable motions in the natural world, continue to be caused naturalistically. As discussed previously, Flew distinguishes between movings and motions and describes motions to be physically controlled happenings in the world. Movings are willed happenings in the world.[16] This distinction is apt, and it is like Kant's distinction between laws of nature for the study of natural phenomena and laws of freedom for morality. The latter reveals our innate minimum religion and leads us to God while the systematic religion expands our horizon on questions ultimately connected to ethics and salvation.

In the next chapter, we consider rituals and soteriology, or the doctrine of salvation. This chapter has dealt with the knowledge of God and the seed of duty. It is in religious rituals and soteriology that the final longings of the human soul find their satisfaction and thereby justify the journey beyond minimum religion. Critical religion in the form of atheism recognizes the role of rituals and therefore fails to fully satisfy the yearnings of human beings without reverting to religious rituals and language.

---

16. Flew and Varghese, *There Is a God*, 63.

CHAPTER 9

Rituals and Doctrines of Afterlife Are Central to Systematic Religion

SYSTEMATIC RELIGIONS MEET THE existential needs of human beings through rituals and doctrines of salvation that point to an afterlife. Critical religion (atheists and agnostics) cannot help but be drawn to the ritualistic features of religion. Near-death experiences continue to furnish support for the idea of an afterlife. We see that the world is a metaphysical marketplace where passionate religion, exercised with tolerance, offers hope of universal ethics based on a universal religious conscience—that is, not based on a single, centralized religious body.

In this chapter we want to consider the place of rituals in systematic religion, the atheists' attempt to hold on to the arts and other rituals, and the question of ultimate human salvation. Although the afterlife is rejected by supposed atheists, near-death experiences and visions of the afterlife, such as the mysticism of Emanuel Swedenborg (1688–1772 CE), seem to undermine the dogmatic position on the absence of an afterlife. The doctrine of the afterlife can, and does, impact the ethics of the present life; a minimum religion that serves as the basis for a universal ethics ought to include the idea of an afterlife. We end the chapter by considering the hope of religion, given the theory of reason that reveals subjectivity and a fundamental dependence on faith. We must imagine the sustainable future of mankind as a marketplace of metaphysics, where various systematic religions thrive in competition and mutual understanding. Were such a metaphysical marketplace possible, it would facilitate the reformation of religions toward systems that accord with the universal minimum religion and with the passions that propel people beyond minimum religion.

The journey from the universal minimum religion with which we are all endowed takes us toward a community where we can participate ritualistically. Many predispositions have been used to describe human beings. The innate disposition to suspect that all events have a cause has led to the view of human beings as rational animals. Our affinity for other beings of our kind makes us social animals and our inbuilt legislative and social organizational disposition makes us political animals. The original predisposition to morality makes us moral animals and the attendant cognition of a religious relation in that morality makes us religious animals. But it is in the rituals of systematic religion that we hope to find more substance and meaning to our religious innateness. It is therefore worthwhile to consider rituals in revealed religions and how the absence of these rituals in supposed atheistic circles ultimately return some atheists to religious ideas.

Is there life after death? If yes, how can I be sure I will be able to obtain it? Or does the quality of that life depend on this present life? These are questions that do not escape the skeptics of religion. Seeing how difficult it is to settle the question of the afterlife by experience, cynicism is a possible outcome. But when we consider the various religions of the world, we are struck by the centrality of this question of the afterlife. Western and Eastern religions offer doctrines of salvation. Even religions that are presented as purely nontheistic ethical systems offer a doctrine of the afterlife. As we saw with Rousseau, the question is not just one of personal faith, it affects the core of theoretical and applied ethics. Epicureanism and Stoicism are therefore anomalies on the question of the afterlife.

Atheists and agnostics, disappointed with the absence of a verification procedure for afterlife theories and seeing the competing accounts of the afterlife by various systematic religions, tend to affirm Epicurean nihilism restricting the sphere of existence to this earthly life. We may be tempted to sympathize with these afterlife skeptics when they attack religions that focus solely on the afterlife while despising the earthly life. But if a systematic religion misconstrues, mischaracterizes, or abuses the vision of the afterlife, does this abuse justify a dogmatic rejection of the idea of an afterlife? A poor theory about something cannot serve as proof of the absence of that thing.

Two issues must interest the skeptic about life after death. The one is the growing literature on the near-death experience (NDE). If everything about the human being comes to an end upon death, how can we explain the complexity of these experiences? The second is the convincing mysticism of Swedenborg on the afterlife. Two motivations for the rejection of the doctrine of the afterlife are eternal punishment for some and severe restrictions to the pleasures of the earthly life. But it is possible to interpret NDEs and such visions as offered by Swedenborg to be strong indications of the reality of the afterlife. We can understand atheism and agnosticism as theistic religions with a critical bent but still striving toward a doctrine of salvation like all the other religions. If they remain true to empirical evidence, NDEs should ultimately bring them closer to a doctrine about the afterlife.

Let us then explore the ideas stated above under three sections. The first deals with rituals as an indispensable part of systematic religion. The second considers the doctrines of salvation that can be largely classified as Western and Eastern doctrines. Although funeral rituals belong to the first part, they are best discussed as a prelude to the discussion on the afterlife. The last part considers the hope of religion in a world where tolerant systematic religions passionately sell their metaphysics in a free market of ideas, with one learning from the other and perfecting their own system. In this way, extended systematic religions may dynamically tend toward a universal vision of salvation, where different religions passionately and artistically express a version of a universal truth as an extension of the universal minimum religion.

A. RITUALS AS INDISPENSABLE PART OF SYSTEMATIC RELIGION

We may say that rituals are speech acts or actions carried out with the purpose of elevating a moment in the ordinary course of our busy lives to something special. What is the mind doing when we are busy? It anticipates and accompanies our actions. When these actions are repetitive enough, we can afford a little distraction or spice up the action with a favorite tune. But even when we are not busy, what is our mind doing? It is busy with other thoughts, happily allowing the imagination and memory to suggest more thoughts for further contemplation and enjoyment. But in rituals, we suspend the wonderings of the mind and focus on something of value. In the case of rituals in religion, we participate in a religious experience.

Transcendent rituals are mystical experiences. These can come to us during a ritual, perhaps with the help of the rituals or a spiritual leader. But mystical experiences can also occur outside the framework of rituals. The individual is drawn into an experience of the supranatural. Such experiences are richly profiled by William James in his *Varieties of Religious Experiences*. The mystical goes beyond the rituals of a religion.

The secret and force of religion lie in rituals; we are ritualistic animals, and human beings stand on the bridge between this world of experience and the transcendent world to which religion points. Rituals are repetitive and in this they expose the wrongheadedness of extreme epistemological analysis of religion. Religion is not a course in history or physics, where we are introduced to the facts of the matter, and the next time we meet we carry on with the next set of facts. The intellectual analysis of religion is often aimed at holding up propositions, questioning their truth values, and comparing them with what is often hidden behind the vague idea of rational analysis. Repetition of propositional content for the sake of the understanding alone would appear to be taking one's audience for fools. But this is not the case for rituals. Repetition is at the core of rituals; repetition is at the core of the arts; we cannot imagine a world where we are bombarded with new experiences all the time. This idea is grasped by music composers who skillfully merge new material with repetitive elements to attain a degree of pleasantness that would be destroyed by an avalanche of new material. Good music thrives on creative repetition.

For religious rituals to have meaning to those who practice them, they need to believe the essence of the religion. Although belief is possible in response to a supranatural encounter with God such as that of Paul the apostle, membership in religious communities is preceded by discourse that considers the existential questions pushing people beyond minimum religion. The truth of these discourses may come alive for the one to be initiated through the experience of rituals, such as communal singing.

Let us take the case of the Christian religion, especially in a generic Protestant form of it. We should consider the rituals associated with admission, prayer, homily, singing, and burial of the dead. We are not seeking a comprehensive account of these. Rather, we seek a pointer to the way in which the cares that set the minimum religionist on a journey are taken seriously, and addressed in a way that may satisfy these seekers. Rituals have a community and personal dimension to them. Such acts as prayers can be carried out in private or in fellowship with others. Because of the centrality of community in systematic religion, the need for fellowship is met in a systematic manner. We thus have the three Abrahamic religions with such local worship days as Friday for the Muslims, Saturday for Jews and some Christian sects, and Sunday for most of the Christians. In this arrangement, the social and religious dimensions of the human being come together.

Membership Through Conversion

We may follow Kant's thinking here where, in his *Religion*, he considers the situation of someone outside a religious community to be in the ethical state of nature.[1] He observes that human beings reciprocally corrupt one

---

1. Kant, *Religion*, 104–37.

another's moral disposition, the good will of each of them notwithstanding. They lack a uniting principle. The ethical community presents itself as the people under God's sovereignty, bound by ethical laws of revealed religion. The principles regulating this community, which we can call a church, are derived from historical revelation. The seeker of systematic religion must therefore come into a community, but this community is not regulated by coercive laws as in the civil situation; it is governed by the laws of freedom, conforming to the revealed religion.

We can agree with Kant's view regarding the nature of the community and its regulation based on revealed religion and conscience. The religious community is therefore not a civil situation where coercion, such as could lead to deprivation of one's freedom, can be practiced. But for the community to cohere and realize their ethical mission, a member should know what to expect and should commit to abide by these shared values. From this perspective, the situation of the Christian church from the time of Emperor Constantine to the Reformation has always been a problematic one. The Catholic Church, where it has significant influence or a majority, seeks a union—explicit or implicit—between the church and the state. Were this situation to be allowed, then coercive laws of the state would be applied to matters of conscience within the church. But inability to abide by the precepts of the religious community can lead to mutual separation between a member and the community.

So, how can one become a member of a systematic religion? We must distinguish between the condition of the universal minimum religion and the ethical state of nature to which Kant refers. Just as Locke's view of the state of nature differs from Hobbes's very pessimistic view, we can say that the state of minimum religion is inefficient and unsatisfactory, but it is not one of total irreligion. One's religious views just happen to be vague and overshadowed by doubts, questions, and the force of the evil propensity trying to undermine the deep-seated moral predisposition.

The historical evolution of membership in the religious community within Abrahamism is such that one starts out with the chosen family of Abraham. All those born into the family are automatically members. This principle applies to Jews even today. There are rituals one must follow as a child growing up within the tradition. Nonetheless, there are gentiles today who are converted to Judaism. But for Christianity, we see the membership model change with the preaching and baptizing of John the Baptist. Next, Christ calls his disciples and they willingly follow him; others come to him asking to be allowed to be his followers. In the aftermath of the death of Christ, a standard practice of gaining membership emerges.

One becomes a Christian through an informed decision on the teachings of Jesus Christ, his place as the redeemer of the world, God as the creator and sustainer of the world, and the Holy Spirit as a guide and comforter. With respect to the place of Christ as a redeemer, the seeker of membership comes to acknowledge the operative evil principle within them, their sense of guilt for past wrongs, and their helplessness in knowing and doing the right in future situations. Some Christian denominations baptize infants, drawing a parallel with the covenant of circumcision of male children in Judaism and examples of the gospel coming to a whole family in the apostolic times. But such infant baptism, for it to translate into full church membership, must be followed by a confirmation of baptism in which knowledge of the key teachings is expected. Some denominations express key teachings in catechisms that amount to a systematic theology of that denomination.

Christian communities that emphasize personal conversion and belief in Jesus as a personal savior may differ in their views about baptism. Baptists and other groups from the historical Anabaptist tradition require adult baptism by immersion of those who have professed Christ as their savior, while some Evangelical groups consider the profession of faith as more important.

Those Evangelical Christians who consider personal profession of faith as the more important moment of conversion can be compared to conversion in Islam. In Islam, required for conversion is the conscious profession that there is no God but God and that Mohammed is his prophet.

The admission rituals we find in Western religions can be said to share with Eastern religions the idea of professing faith in a certain set of ideas. In Buddhism, for instance, one must commit to the Five Precepts. These forbid killing, theft, adultery, telling falsehoods, and intoxication. Committing to the ethical principles of the community confers membership on a seeker, establishing a bond of fellowship.

Prayer and the Forgiveness of Sins

Why does prayer matter in this quest for more religion? Perhaps we should start this discussion with some words from an interview given by Karl Popper to Edward Zerin in 1969:

> I don't know whether God exists or not.... When I look at what I call the gift of life, I feel a gratitude which is in tune with some religious ideas of God. However, the moment I even speak of

it, I am embarrassed that I may do something wrong to God in talking about God.²

We find in Popper's words the human desire to express gratitude for the miracle of life and other precious life experiences. This desire to express gratitude is innate, and can, on its own terms, serve as a guide to God and extended religion beyond the universal minimum religion. The last part of this quotation expresses a certain fear that has been expressed even by the prophets of Abrahamism. Standing in the elevated presence of God is terrifying because of his perfection, his holiness. Although not a practicing Jew, Popper shares the same awe in the contemplation of God that is expressed by Jews who refrain from vocalizing God's name in full. We have here an awareness of a desire to express gratitude but also a fear of imperfection before God, if he exists. But prayer can overcome this tension so that we can, with confidence, express gratitude to God and plead for the forgiveness of sins, including such errors as improper words uttered to God. Forgiveness is the only way by which sins can be lifted off our minds, where they otherwise crush us with reminder and condemnation.

Prayer is one of the most important rituals of systematic religions. But what is prayer? If it is a speech act directed toward God, and if it contains a plea for something to be done, how is this justified, given God's attribute of knowing perfectly? These are tough questions that lead to further questions when it is forgotten that what is at stake is a relationship between a finite human being with a limited vocabulary and an infinite perfect God who reveals himself in the hearts of human beings.

In addition to expressing gratitude and seeking pardon for sins, the one who prays brings before God their own desires and pleads for help to have them fulfilled, if these fall within the broad confines of the will of God. This third point is often mistaken and attacked by skeptics of religion and even others within the religion, where material things received from God are taken for signs of spirituality. But against this frame of thinking, Kant's admonition is a fitting response:

> We must never regard prayer as a means to getting our own way; if a prayer concerns our corporeal advantage, we ought to say it both with a trust in God's wisdom and with a submission to this wisdom. The greatest utility of prayer is indisputably a moral one, because through prayer both thankfulness and a resignation toward God become effective in us.³

---

2. Zerin, "Karl Popper on God."

3. Kant, *Philosophical Theology*, 155. These notes were transcribed by Kant's students and reflect his ideas expressed in other published works, albeit in the form of

Prayer in the Christian context therefore addresses the need to express gratitude, the need for help in our concrete circumstances, and a resignation to God. This resignation is that which we feel in the state of being forgiven and being guided by God to overcome the power of the evil principle within us as it fights against our moral predisposition.

Those who develop their minimum religion into the skeptical direction of supposed atheism generally view themselves as not in need of help. What they need, they try to work out for themselves and they solicit help from other human beings on the basis of altruism. They may successfully hide the innate desire to offer gratitude to God for the gift of life and other life experiences. Or they may find an outlet for this desire through what they consider to be altruism—the feeling of giving back to the community. It is admitted that engaging in selfless acts of charity can be a source of enormous joy. But how selfless are these acts when one starts from an original position of indebtedness to God and the people he has placed in our lives? Misguided religion, expressed as atheism, is not honest with itself when this innate impulse to express gratitude is not satisfied—it is the proof of another religious attitude locked into our very nature by the Supreme Being.

If the idea of seeking God's help in our affairs is brushed away with self-pride, and if the innate disposition toward gratitude to the Supreme Being is deemed to be accomplished through altruistic acts, it is the problem of the forgiveness of sin that receives the greatest disregard from atheists. It is worth repeating that the problem of hereditary sin is an obstacle to anyone who would disregard the need for forgiveness of sins. Having shown the true nature of reason, one needs values and contingent truths to conduct reason. It must be admitted that we are not born with such reason. Any ethical system that would be built on reason would have to recognize that children are born with undeveloped reason. Jean Piaget's epistemology showed that the reasoning capacities of a child are different at different ages.[4] Society therefore relies on parents to educate and train their children in a manner that makes them good members of the society. In child upbringing, parents often engage in setting safe boundaries that children would happily want to overstep without foreknowledge of the consequences. A certain rebellious spirit comparable to Augustine's pear tree narrative can be discerned in them. If Augustine calls this rebellious attitude sin, and others call it the lack of reason because it's just a child, aren't we talking about the same thing?

It is therefore easy to see that the idea of the evil propensity in us, overcoming our inborn moral predisposition, is real. It actualizes itself in

---

concise philosophical theology.

4. Piaget, "Stages of the Intellectual Development."

acts against others, acts against the self, and in an improper assessment of our place in our innate religious relation with God.

We now see that we can agree on the reasonableness of the three elements of prayer, being the expression of gratitude, a plea for the forgiveness of sins, and a plea for concrete needs to be met. The act of prayer presupposes recognition and adoration of the authority of God. The relation of the Christian to prayer, and God's response, cannot be subject to the same analysis as that of deterministic mechanical science where we deem that the nature of God precludes God altering his eternal will to meet our needs. These points are well known within the religion itself, as reflected in the model prayer given by Jesus and his exhortation about the simplicity of prayer.

These three elements of prayer can be discerned in the Lord's Prayer in the Christian Gospels (Matt 6:9–13; Luke 11:2–4). A general feature of most religious prayers is to establish the addressee and their authority. Although different analyses of the Prayer are offered, we can consider that God's authority is established and worshipped in all statements before the expression of the concrete need, "Give us this day our daily bread." These prior statements equally express gratitude to God. The plea for the forgiveness of sins is conjoined with a commitment to also forgive others. The plea to be spared from temptation and to be delivered from evil is also an expression of need.

If it is more straightforward to express gratitude to God and recognize his authority in heaven and on earth, it is more challenging to deal with one's sinful nature and to present needs to God. The prayer is therefore a medium where the believer wrestles with insecurity and doubt. But even in such circumstances, the ritual of prayer fulfills a function of strengthening the relation between the believer and God. Thus, we hear prayers such as the publican's "God, be merciful to me a sinner!" (Luke 18:13) or "Lord, teach us to pray" (Luke 11:1) or "Lord, I believe; help my unbelief!" (Mark 9:24). We see that the uncertainty that accompanies any metaphysical question abounds in the believer's life as expressed in prayers, but uncertainty and doubt are anchored in a relationship where the authority, holiness, and saving power of God are acknowledged.

This view of prayer can be applied to all Abrahamic religions. Addressing the One God is the default opening act of Abrahamic prayers. It is only after the death of Christ that the name of Jesus features prominently in Christian prayers. And it is only after the death of Mohammed that the prophet's name gains a central stage in Muslim piety. The use of the names of Jesus Christ and Mohammed can be interpreted as expressions of gratitude for divine revelation; for Christians Christ is the ultimate revelation, and for Muslims Mohammed is the great prophet after Jesus who brought them

Rituals and Doctrines of Afterlife Are Central to Systematic Religion 171

the word of God. But a variety of prayers in all three Abrahamic religions can be found in the Psalms (called Tehillim among Jews and Zabur among Muslims); they all recognize these songs or prayers as inspired by God.

It is not only in Abrahamism that prayers are a central ritual; the Eastern religions also value and practice prayers, even if the exact definition differs. When we inquire whether Buddhists pray, the desire to deny any theistic instinct in Buddhism may cause people to say there are varieties of Buddhism and some pray while others simply invoke the Buddha as a historical figure. But one who has understood the existential need to express gratitude and seek guidance would recognize that we are dealing with prayer in such cases. It is the idea of the forgiveness of sins that is most clearly articulated in Abrahamism, reaching its centrality in Christian practice as it relates to the death of Christ on the cross and the unmerited grace of God.

Those critical minimum religionists who evolve into self-described atheists may say that they do not pray. If this were true, they would be suppressing an innate impulse to express gratitude and seek guidance in conduct. Historically, Epicureans are viewed as the source of their inspiration, and among Epicureans, Lucretius strikes us as the most militant atheist who goes beyond Epicurus to denounce the gods. But we are surprised by the moving prayer to Venus with which he opens his poem *On the Nature of Things*:

> Life-stirring Venus, Mother of Aeneas and of Rome,
> Pleasure of men and gods, you make all things beneath the dome
> Of sliding constellations teem,
> . . . .
>   I invite
> You Goddess, stand beside me, be my partner as I write
> *The Nature of Things*, . . .[5]

It is only after the twenty-second line, after heaping praises and extolling the virtues of the goddess of love, that Lucretius pleads for Venus to stand by him as he writes *The Nature of Things*, in which he declares the indifference or nonexistence of the gods!

We thus see that the ritual of prayer, more than a ritual as part of immediate religious experience, conveys key ideas about human beings' innate gratitude and the need to express it, while also acknowledging the limitations of the human being before the Supreme Being or deity.

Perhaps we should say something about the religious sermon. It is also an important ritual whose goal is the upbuilding of the religious community through the exposition and interpretation of sacred texts. These expositions

---

5. Lucretius, *Nature of Things* 1.1–3, 23–25.

and interpretations are accompanied by practical application to the problems of the day. In Christianity where the Holy Spirit is acknowledged as a person of the Trinity, this Spirit helps in the interpretation of the Scriptures by inspiring the preacher and the hearers. The sermon takes a central place in Protestant worship, since the Scriptures are viewed as the proper source of authority for personal piety. In an interesting study reported in December 2019 by the Pew Research Center, a computational analysis of online sermons was carried out. This study showed that sermons vary in length and content among Christian churches, with the average Catholic sermon being the shortest at fourteen minutes and black Protestant Churches as the longest at fifty-four minutes. Mainline Protestant Churches had average sermon durations of twenty-five minutes in contrast to thirty-nine minutes for Evangelical Protestant Churches.[6] Herein, one sees differences in emphasis of one ritual that may be related ultimately to doctrines on personal piety. The point is that the set of rituals and their relative importance in each systematic religion may constitute distinguishing features and offer compelling reasons for a person to choose one religion over another, depending on what they consider most important.

In pursuit of this discussion, let us first consider music as part of religious rituals before we comment on the way critical minimum religion (atheism or its polite form, humanism) deals with the fact that these rituals being discussed point to some innate desires of the human being.

Religion and Art

Artistic expression of religious ideas is a key part of religious rituals. Art involves the creative use of the imagination to get at reality about the world and the human condition. More than simple assertions of propositions, art plays an important role in communicating an idea or the suggestion of an idea to other human beings. The imagination of the creator and the imagination of the perceiver both participate in elevating that which is imagined to a communication about an aspect of reality. Whereas the imagination of the one who creates may require time and training, the perceiver who grasps a layer of reality in that imagination does so almost instantaneously. The aesthetic force of the artwork strikes the person immediately. For this reason, art is important to religious practice.

In the kingdom of the arts, music occupies a special place. It is interesting to note that some of the nineteenth-century thinkers who reflected much on the role of music in human existence are those who considered

---

6. Pew Research Center, *Digital Pulpit*.

themselves far from orthodox religion where the most expansive use of music was to be found. Schopenhauer, in section fifty-two of his *World as Will and Presentation*, says of music:

> Just for this reason, music has a much more powerful and penetrating effect than any of the other arts, for the others speak only of shadows, whereas music speaks of the essence of things.[7]

One may wonder about the meaning of *essence* and *shadow* here, but the main idea being suggested is that whatever the arts try to communicate, music realizes that communication objective better than the other arts. This is a curious situation because in the acquisition of knowledge about the world, sight plays a central role. But this knowledge is mostly facts in the form of propositions. But when it comes to artistic imagination guiding us to knowledge of certain truths about the human condition in the world, it is sound perception that appears to bring us much farther, as Schopenhauer recognized.

The essence to which music points is not just the true nature of something that may be inconsequential to human existence. One can know the true nature of a certain tropical tree, but we could also do without such precise knowledge, especially if we do not live in the tropics. Nietzsche, however, suggests in his *Twilight of Idols* that music is essential to the lives of human beings. He says:

> What trifles constitute happiness! The sound of a bagpipe. Without music life would be a mistake. The German imagines even God as a songster.[8]

Many would agree with this assessment. Music gets at the essence of our existence, and without music life would be unbearable.

Recognizing the relation of art music to religion, the composer and philosopher Richard Wagner engages with this topic in his essay *Religion and Art*. The essay opens with a quote from Friedrich Schiller:

> In the Christian religion I find an intrinsic disposition to the Highest and the Noblest, and its various manifestations in life appear to me so vapid and repugnant simply because they have missed expression of that Highest.[9]

According to Schiller, the truths of Christianity are deficient in expression. It is for this reason that Wagner sees the role of art as that of redeeming

---

7. Schopenhauer, *World as Will*, 147.
8. Nietzsche, *Twilight of Idols*, 6.
9. Wagner, *Religion and Art*, 212.

religion when it begins to lose its ideals. But it is not just any art that can rescue religion from becoming artificial or empty, it is musical art:

> Strictly speaking, the only art that fully corresponds with the Christian belief is music; even as the only music which, now at least, we can place on the same footing as the other arts, is an exclusive product of Christianity.[10]

We find here a claim to which we can assent: music is the art that is most suited to the expression of Christian truths. We can extend this to other religions. While Wagner restricts himself to Western art music and points out the historical role of the Christian church in its development, we can equally find that, in other cultures such as African and Eastern cultures, religion is a driving force for the development of musical expression.

These opinions of the nineteenth-century thinkers point to the importance of music in human life, and Wagner recounts a dark history of mankind that stands in need of salvation. According to him, that salvation can come from the fusion of religion and music. True religion, to Wagner, has its basis in recognition of the frailty of this world, consequently exhorting human beings to free themselves from that frailty. Unfortunately, Wagner's biased diagnosis of the crisis of the nineteenth century led to the misuse of the sacredness he sees in his music by the Nazis. Although performance of his music is accompanied by a certain religious devotion, it does not seem to have changed the dark course of history he sees in the world prior to his artistic creations. Perhaps the praise of music and its relation to religion are overly optimistic. Are they lacking something about human nature? The atheists who view art as important while judging religion as dispensable do not seem to see the fusion that Wagner celebrates in his essay.

The relation of music to religion and morality is not one of necessity; it depends on the concrete realization of that unity. To those whose first concern is morality or religion, the use of music as a companion ritual must be approached with care. This admonition almost rises to a censorial attitude toward religious music. In this, the role of music is spelled out as serving a larger religious purpose. Plato and Augustine are good examples of this careful treatment of music in morality and religion.

The use of music in Plato's hypothetical city is scrutinized in his *Republic*. Certain harmonies and rhythms are to be avoided, despite the recognition of the valuable role of music to the soul. He says:

> Rhythm and harmonies have the greatest influence on the soul; they penetrate into its inmost regions and there hold fast. If the

---

10. Wagner, *Religion and Art*, 223.

soul is rightly trained, they bring grace. If not, they bring the contrary. One who is properly educated in these matters would most quickly perceive and deplore the absence or perversion of beauty in art or nature.[11]

The listener is therefore understood not just as an untrained perceiver of music; they must also be able to identify how the harmonies and rhythm accord or fail to accord with the harmony of the soul. Plato does not positively recommend harmonic instruments.

As for Augustine, he recalls a personal experience of the power of music in his *Confessions*:

> How did I weep in Thy Hymns and Canticles, touched to the quick by the voices of thy sweet-attuned Church! The voices flowed into mine ears, and the Truth distilled into my heart, whence the affections of my devotion overflowed, and tears ran down, and happy was I therein.[12]

This emotional recollection of how he was moved to devotion by the truth and voices of music is not an automatic approval of all music for worship. Augustine wrestles with the relative value of melodies and text, finding approval in the value of the text being projected by the melodies. He is less sympathetic to beautiful melodies alone. Thus, he admits:

> Thus, I fluctuate between pleasure and wholesomeness, inclined the rather . . . to approve of the usage of singing in Church. . . . Yet when it befalls me to be more moved with the voice than the words sung, I confess to have sinned penally, and then had rather not hear music.[13]

We sense a kind of indecision because the same text can be set to different melodies, but it achieves a greater expressive force in one melody than in the others. A unity of melody and the words sung is therefore realized in good devotional music.

One may say that the concern about music and morality has a history from Plato, through Augustine, and onto the modern church. The emphasis on understanding the message embedded in music can be said to be elevated in Protestant traditions. A sense of this can be found in Rousseau's views on language and music, but in Rousseau, melody is understood to already relate to the use of text. The main point we find in this discussion

---

11. Plato, *Republic* 3.399e.
12. Augustine, *Confessions* 9.6.14.
13. Augustine, *Confessions* 10.33.50.

is that the universal appeal of music is recognized. While thinkers such as Wagner see music as giving life to noble ideas of a religion, those concerned with the morality in music are more likely to be prescriptive in the type of music that should accompany the religious experience of worship, prayer, or moral instruction.

Atheists' Regret: Rituals to Rescue

Philosophical or critical religion that evolves to atheism is mostly focused on epistemological issues, and the way in which religion is implicated in, or not able to give an answer to, the problem of evil. Rigorously pursued as a way of life, supposed atheism soon comes to realize that human beings have other existential needs that the attempted atheistic mode of life cannot satisfy. They may also come to see how complex the problem of evil is, or how the epistemological status of religious knowledge is not completely void of reasonableness. The one thing that seems to trigger this reconsideration is the role of rituals in human flourishing. Most of these missing rituals are historically linked to religious expression.

We thus come to the view that the atheist is a minimum religionist who maintains a critical attitude toward all systematic religions, but they also express a desire to incorporate rituals into their lifestyle. We must see this interest in rituals as an indication of a move beyond the universal minimum religion. We find examples of this approach in Auguste Comte, Alain de Botton, and Ronald Dworkin. Auguste Comte proposed a so-called Religion of Humanity, Alain de Botton pleads for a religion for atheists, and Ronald Dworkin more generally advocates for a religion without God. The motivations for these recommendations are signs of the existential impulses that push us to go beyond our innate universal minimum religion. Let us consider them briefly.

Auguste Comte and the Religion for Humanity

Positivist to the core, Auguste Comte soon realized that empirical science cannot satisfy all the longings of human beings. There was, and there always will be, a place for religious dogma and rituals. Finding the Catholic Church too rigid to adjust its teachings to accord with insights from modern science, Comte set out to design a secular Catholicism he called Religion of Humanity.

We find Comte meticulously designing a hierarchical system, seeing himself as the high priest of the new religion, and even producing a positivist catechism for the new religion. Famous scientists and men of letters are to be venerated as saints in this new religion. Comte is not only seeking an ethical system; he seeks a system with rituals and veneration for the saints of positivism. His system is viewed with ridicule by those who reject theistic religion because the longing for the rejected theistic religion is all too obvious. The man who played a role in founding sociology and promoting positivism realizes that there is a dimension of life that is occupied by the indispensable rituals of religion. Viewed from the perspective of systematic religion, we can only advise Comte and his followers to shop around for systematic religions that are more compatible with positivism as applied to stable causes. Other sociologists from the Anglo-Protestant world didn't have to reinvent Protestant religion without God, as Comte tries to reinvent Catholicism in the form of Religion for Humanity. Protestantism naturally affords variety and freedom in the search for a systematic religion that resonates with the longings of minimum religionists.

Alain de Botton and Religion for Atheists

Alain de Botton is the modern-day Auguste Comte with respect to his view of creating a religion for atheists. Key rituals are to be chosen to mirror those of theistic religions, albeit without committing to theism. He opens his book with a candid account of his upbringing in a secular Jewish family where his parents strongly enforced atheistic beliefs.[14] One can contrast his secular upbringing with that of Anthony Flew, who recounts in *There Is a God* that he grew up as the son of a Methodist minister but had the freedom to declare unbelief at fifteen, and returned to a belief in God in his seventies. Intolerance has no restriction in terms of doctrinaire upbringing of children; one can find intolerance in supposed atheistic homes and freedom of choice in theistic homes, or the other way round.

Alain de Botton describes his encounter with sacred music and how this softened his views on religion. He now exhorts people to recognize in religious rituals resources to build community, express kindness, teach one another, enjoy the arts, and express other human longings. He recommends all these while warning us to stay away from the concept of God. It does not occur to de Botton that the music of Bach that he refers to has its origin in theism. Its most expressive performance occurs in a context where there is a belief in God. If Wagner demands of his music to be listened to with religious devotion, Bach's music pulls one toward the message of Christianity. That message is void if the authority of God and the redemptive work of

---

14. De Botton, *Religion for Atheists*, 13–14.

Christ is rejected. At best, we see in this recommendation a critical religion in the form of atheism coming to terms with the emptiness of the metaphysics it offers to the world. Yet, it is not humble enough to see the truth in the doctrines of the systematic religions that produce the artistic rituals to which atheism is attracted.

Ronald Dworkin and the Idea of Religion Without God

In his book *Religion Without God*, Ronald Dworkin offers an expansive definition of religion, whose intention is to include the atheist in this basic human activity. In essence, it might be said that his definition accords with our view of every human being as a member of a universal minimum religion. But his definition differs in asserting that religion is possible without the concept of God. This is an incoherent declaration of the limitations of atheism. Unlike Comte, a positivist to the core, Dworkin is a critic of legal positivism; he believes, quite rightly, that law is grounded in morality. But he does not go far enough to see that the abstract principles used to set rules of human behavior are derived from the innate moral predisposition of all human beings. This innate moral predisposition, we have argued, is intricately bound up with the sense of being in relation with a transcendent force, a Supreme Being. Other existential and epistemological observations bring Dworkin to assert innate religiosity of human beings, but alas, he must make room for atheism by claiming that religion is possible without God.

Religion is not possible without God. Rituals assume their highest meaning within a religious context. Given the universal minimum religion underlying these impulses toward rituals and meaning, one must wonder why the notion of God scares the supposed atheist, even if God's attributes remain only vaguely known. Why does the atheist go to such lengths to conceive of a justification for imagining the unimaginable or the absurd—religion without God? The attempt by atheists to redefine religion without God solicits far less sympathy than the attitude of the German skeptics Schopenhauer, Nietzsche, and Wagner, who turned favorably to Eastern or world religions in their critique of Christendom.

We are moved to see rituals as playing a vital role in systematic religions and human life. These rituals entice followers of critical religion—that is, atheists—to reconsider their attitude to the broader dimensions of life that are under the influence of religion. These supposed atheists seek a redefinition of the concept of religion by advocating a religion without God. By this they simply reject the systematic theologies of revealed or other speculative religions, but they recognize the importance of religious rituals.

One more class of rituals merits our special attention. Burial rituals take us directly to doctrines of salvation and thus we address this in the next section.

B. SOTERIOLOGY OR DOCTRINES OF SALVATION AND FUNERAL RITUALS

> Death therefore, the most awful of evils, is nothing to us, seeing that when we are, death is not come, and, when death is come, we are not.[15]

If Epicurus has captured the truth about death in these words, we must ask ourselves why we bury the dead. We must repeat with desperation Kant's question about what we may hope about the future state of affairs.

In this section, we first examine and reject the Epicurean vision and the incoherence of any funeral practices associated with such a vision. It is hard to imagine a solid inferential argument in support of afterlife beliefs. We must rely on the innateness of that intuition and the failure of the Epicurean nihilist vision to meet the needs of human beings who ask what they may hope for beyond this earthly life.

What grounds are there for us to believe in the Epicurean view that death is nothing to us? That beyond death, no part of our existence persists? In Epicurus's *Letter*, the quote above is surrounded by a discussion of the fear of death. The doctrine is thus offered as a solution to the problem of the fear of death. According to Epicurus:

1. To experience pain or pleasure we must be sentient, but death ends sentience.
2. The fear of death presents terror to human beings and robs them of the pleasure of the present life. Thus, making death nothing, takes away that fear.
3. Yet, it is incoherent that some view death as the greatest evil, while others view it as the escape from the evils of this life.

Neutralizing death gives value to this present life. Taken together as a system, these arguments should neither console nor convince us; the proposed solution is an easy way out of a problem that continues to plague mankind.

We cannot, on the strength of evidence from NDEs, conclude that there is no sentience beyond death. Although the physicalists try to undermine

---

15. Epicurus, *Letter to Menoeceus*, 87–88.

the mounting evidence gathered from those who experience an NDE, the growing amount of research in this area only exposes the biased militantness of physicalists as being contrary to the methods of science; they seek a dogmatism on this question.

We have reason to believe that there may be life beyond death. If there is life beyond death, the prudential nature of human beings would demand that rather than only fear or dismiss death, one should consider how to live this life in a way that anticipates the next life. It turns out that most religions advocate for a moral life here on earth. Even if the picture of what is moral varies, it seems that the situation is not one of destructive terror that distracts from the present life.

The modern world is indeed more complex and requires a lot more prudence than in ancient Greece; human beings are accustomed to living prudentially, thinking ahead about their retirement. Extending this prudence to cover the afterlife is not too much of a headache to modern human beings, compared to the tranquil life of ancient Greece without the sorts of insurances and social securities of modern life.

Finally, while many generally terrify people with afterlife predictions, those who present that life as a relief from the present evil cannot be dismissed, especially if they are actively engaged in the present life. Take Christians, Muslims, or Sikhs who advocate for a moral life here and hope for a better afterlife. They offer a soothing vision of life after death. Muslims and Christians point to the mercy of God as operative in the final judgment. Rather than terrify people, this account of God's mercy offers meaning in suffering and points to a welcoming future beyond death.

Nihilism combats such hopeful visions of the afterlife. In book 3 of Lucretius's *Nature of Things*, a more involved defense of nihilist mortality is given. He bases his arguments on the "revelations of the god-like mind" of Epicurus.[16] A materialistic account of mind and body is offered, and, on this basis, it is argued that cessation of life of the body translates to cessation of consciousness. The unreasonableness of this argument can be best demonstrated by an analogy.

Suppose a computer is in London and connected to the internet in such a manner that it can be remotely accessed. Suppose now that we have news that an enemy is going to enter the building and destroy the computer in a couple of hours. They seek to destroy sensitive evidential information stored within that computer. Someone sitting far away in New York downloads all the information from that computer through the internet, and hours later the computer is destroyed. The enemy is happy to have destroyed

---

16. Lucretius, *Nature of Things*, 3.13.

all information that ever was stored on that computer. But a few days later, a new computer is bought and the data from the old computer is reinstalled in that new computer. This new computer now has the same information as the old. Won't we laugh at the enemy when in court they project confidence about a false account, emboldened by their belief that the critical evidence stored in the old computer has been destroyed?

There is something about this computer analogy that can be related to the human soul. We can imagine that in the course of one's life a personal history is written, including one's religious outlook and salvation. At death, the physical body is like the computer that is destroyed. But as we increasingly hear from NDEs, one's immaterial self detaches from the physical body. That detached self can view from afar what is being done on the physical frame in a clinically dead state.[17] A review of one's life also tends to be played out in these accounts. This we may liken to the download of information from the computer.

The British philosopher A. J. Ayer, a self-described atheist, had an NDE in which he saw bright red light that he considered to be responsible for governing the world. He recounts the events he experienced, but he is careful to assuage the fears of his fellow humanists with the following words:

> My recent experiences have slightly weakened my conviction that my genuine death, which is due fairly soon, will be the end of me, though I continue to hope that it will be. They have not weakened my conviction that there is no god.[18]

It seems that we should either maintain an open mind regarding the possibility of an afterlife or explore the doctrines offered by several systematic religions, admitting that they point to some transcendent truth that bears on our present lives. But admittedly, the plausibility of an afterlife is problematic to those whose minimum religion has evolved to dogmatic atheism.

If death is final, why do we bury the dead with such rituals and care? Burial of the dead is a central religious ritual that correlates with visions of life after death. It seems that the belief in the possibility of life after death is innate. This idea finds some support through the work of Misailidi and Kornilaki, where they study the attitude of children regarding death.[19] They find that children have innate ideas about the continuation of mental states beyond death. A control study confirms that these ideas are not developed

---

17. Greyson, "Getting Comfortable"; Facco and Agrillo, "Near-Death Experiences."
18. Ayer, "What I Saw."
19. Misailidi and Kornilaki, "Development of Afterlife Beliefs."

through environmental influences from the parents. It seems then that the nihilist mortality offered by Epicurus and Lucretius is the product of faulty speculation without evidential constraints. It is also motivated by a desire to escape the fear of death through a cheap trick. It tries to relieve us of the fear of death by positing the axiomatic finality of death.

We now have reason to reject the false consolation about death offered to us by Epicurus. We find two reasons for this. First, an afterlife may be possible. Second, the people we leave behind are not indifferent to our ceasing to live, even if the whole community has learned to anticipate our death.

If Epicurus is right, then his followers must commit to funeral practices that correlate with the espoused nihilism. But in this area, there is general resistance to follow the Epicurean doctrine to where it leads. We find that nonreligious people opt for funerals with customized rituals that still suggest deeper meaning to life than is supported by the nihilist mortality. Just like Comte and de Botton advocate for religious rituals for the living, special care is being taken to bury those who distance themselves from systematic religion. The post of a nonreligious funeral celebrant is a new profession that seeks to fill the existential need for customized meaningful funeral rituals.[20]

If we follow these prompting practices, we must reject the Epicurean account of death as the ultimate end. The opposite of this account must be a suspicion that there could be life after death. If this is true, then it fundamentally affects the way we live this present life, and the way we bury our dead relatives and friends.

Looking at funeral rituals around the world, we can see that there is a religious element to them, and these rituals signify a belief in an afterlife. The actual practices undertaken to express these beliefs may vary, but they indicate that humans devote special attention to the burial of their dead.

Funeral practices are generally either inhumation or cremation. We can generalize that Western religions (Abrahamism and folk religions) are more tilted toward inhumation, while Eastern religions (Hinduism, Buddhism, Shintoism, Confucianism, Sikhism, etc.) have historically practiced a mixture of inhumation and cremation. The cremation can be indoor or outdoor. We may further relate the practice of inhumation to a belief in the completion of one life and the transition to the next. Cremation seems to be related to the idea of a cycle of rebirths and ultimate liberation of a purified life from the physical frame to eternal bliss.

---

20. Wojtkowiak et al., "Emerging Ritual Practices."

Inhumation and the Linearity of Life

The intuitions surrounding inhumation seem to be wedded to a linear history of human life. The soul takes on a human body and runs its course in this life. When the individual dies, they move to the next world where life continues. Every human being has only one chance to prepare themselves for the life after death. When we consider the destiny of these lives in the world beyond, we can distinguish between an ancestral plane of existence and a dichotomous path to eternal bliss or condemnation.

The ancestral plane of existence appears to be very old. It spans the globe from the Americas through Africa to the East. Along with the dead were buried items that were supposed to be of help to the deceased in the next world. Apart from material things, in some cultures when a powerful man died, some of his wives and slaves were inhumanely slaughtered and buried with him as escorts to the next world. Here we can see the absence of a coherent doctrine about the value of each life, and the distasteful, unjust picture of a slave being a slave in this life and in the next. But in more general terms, it is believed that ancestors have an influence on the living. Although a clear doctrine of the role of God in the afterlife is not painted, it is imagined that the ancestral line goes all the way up to the creator of the universe, the transcendent force, the Supreme Being.

The Abrahamic religions of the Western world belong to this linear interpretation of life. Christians and Muslims believe in two planes of existence beyond this life: the one is paradise for those who pass the last judgment, and the other is a place of doom for those who fail to do the will of God or benefit from God's mercy.

For Christians, different views on what happens after death are held. The Westminster Catechism, for instance, offers the Protestant view. According to this view, upon death the soul separates from the body with the righteous going to heaven and the unrighteous to hell. Protestants deny the existence of a temporary place where neutral souls are purified unto righteousness before going to heaven. This view is held in Catholicism and aligns with some Greek and Eastern visions of the afterlife. On the judgment day, the dead shall be raised and united with their souls. The living shall be transformed and shall take one of two destinations.

Muslims hold that the dead are in an intermediate state awaiting the great resurrection and last judgment, after which the righteous shall go to heaven and the unrighteous to hell. In Judaism, the doctrine of the afterlife is not systematically held. But the Jewish Scriptures and Talmud clearly suggest the immortality of the soul and possibility of resurrection. In the Christian New Testament, the Sadducees, a Jewish group, deny resurrection of the dead while another group, the Pharisees, uphold the doctrine of resurrection. The position of the Sadducees is more complex. One reading may make it closer to the belief in an ancestral plane of existence, where the dead reunite; in 4 Macc 13:17 (RSV), a reunion with famous ancestors upon death is suggested:

> For if we so die, Abraham and Isaac and Jacob will welcome us,
> and all the fathers will praise us.

Cremation and the Cycle of Rebirth

Most Eastern religions hold an account of an afterlife consisting of a cycle of rebirths. The individual advances toward perfection and liberation from the cycle of rebirth to attain a state of eternal bliss. Since it is the soul that is implicated in rebirth, it can then be understood why such religions do not place as much weight on the preservation of the physical body of the dead as the Egyptians did. Cremation therefore is common, but this does not exclude inhumation. This mixed behavior suggests that the body is not the most important aspect in the understanding of the afterlife.[21]

It would often be suggested that Confucianism and Buddhism are ethical systems, rather than religions. This argument does not hold up when one considers the funeral practices and the related vision of afterlife. Confucianism, though an Eastern religion, seems to be closer to the Western religions in terms of ancestral worship and greater practice of inhumation than in other Eastern religions. One lives a moral life and joins the ancestors. The earthly life is to be lived with a pious reflection on the approval of the ancestors. In Buddhism, one's life here leads to a new life after death, embedded in a cycle of rebirths. Rebirth is not a celebratory fact because life on earth is painful and not satisfactory. But one can advance morally until total salvation and release into the state of nirvana, a state of soteriological liberation. One is not only reborn as a human being but rebirth as an animal is possible. These starkly contrasting soteriological doctrines and understanding of the self, this life, and the afterlife explain the mutual criticisms between these two Eastern religions. They also highlight some of the dangers in speculations about the afterlife. It can affect the way we live our present lives, with some being more concerned with the afterlife, neglecting

---

21. Many of the ideas discussed on Eastern religions are articulated with influence drawn from *World Religions: Eastern Traditions* by Willard G. Oxtoby and Roy C. Amore.

this life, and others being more concerned with this life, with little regard to the afterlife.

We may wonder which of the two approaches to the afterlife strikes us as more plausible, the historically linear or the cyclical. If we take NDEs to be suggestive of what happens in the next life, given the general accordance of various features in such experiences across religions, we may see the reasonableness of the historically linear account. There is also a sense in which, if the liberation of life follows from this life, within the system of cycles of rebirth, it can equally be treated as historically linear.

The doctrine of the resurrection contrasted with the liberated soul either going toward heaven or hell poses two problems. The first one concerns the state of the soul of the dead while they await resurrection and judgment. The second one concerns the pervasion of prophecies about the last judgment. Many Christian sects have often offered end-time predictions whose failure not only weakens their faith but also makes the Christian system vulnerable to criticism from other systems. Political views are equally shaped by expectation of the judgment day. What if this cosmic event, the last judgment, is not as central to the doctrine of the afterlife? This seems to be the suggestion by Emanuel Swedenborg, whose visions lead to the understanding that transition into heaven and hell take place immediately after the death of each individual.[22] If this is true, then the Westminster doctrine about life after death is largely correct, except for the resurrection at a later date.

According to Swedenborg, when someone dies, that person is in a complete human form but without the physical body; they enjoy every sense, memory, thought, and affection they had in the world.[23] One's nature in the afterlife is determined by the life one lived; a dominant love remains and is preserved in eternity. It is this love that determines our choices toward the path of heaven or hell. Heavenly love is loving what is good, honest, and fair because it is good, honest, and fair—that is, doing something because of that love. In contrast, materialistic love is loving what is good, honest, and fair but for our own purposes, such as to gain prestige, position, and profit; we focus on ourselves, the world, and deceit.[24] Heaven-bound people pass through three stages of outward concerns, inward concerns, and preparation for heaven, whereas hell-bound persons only go through the first two. The divine design is heaven for all, but only some actually accept the divine invitation. There are non-Christians in heaven, admitted on

22. Swedenborg, *Heaven and Hell*, 170–2.
23. Swedenborg, *Heaven and Hell*, 258, 264.
24. Swedenborg, *Heaven and Hell*, 282.

the basis of morality, acknowledgment of the Divine, and an inner life.[25] The gnashing of teeth in hell is only a figurative saying; the love of God shines on all but is transformed into hellfire by those in hell. Hellfire is love of self and the world. In heaven there are children, wise and simple people, and rich and poor folk.

Swedenborg's soteriology is the result of visions and reflective writing about these visions, integrating Biblical passages. Some of his views contradict standard doctrines but he explains this as having been instructed by the angels in his visions on the proper interpretation of the passages. What he says of those who have recently died corroborates NDE accounts:

> I have talked with some just two days after their deaths and told them that now their funerals and burial rites were being performed so that they could be interred; to which they have responded that it was a good thing they had cast off what had served them as a body for their functions in the world, wanting me to say that they are not dead at all. They were just as alive and just as human as ever, having simply crossed over from one world to another.[26]

Swedenborg turned from a scientist to a mystic in his lifetime. His visions have been criticized as not being based on revelation but rather on Neoplatonic sources. Immanuel Kant is reported to have shown interest in his mysteries but never successfully established correspondence with him. The possibility of mysticism such as Swedenborg's is not entirely excluded by Kant. Whatever we may say of Swedenborg, since afterlife presents itself as a real possibility, it must be recognized that Swedenborg's account cuts across religious strife and sets the afterlife on moral grounds and acknowledgment of the Supreme Being or the Divine. It removes the apparent absurdity of waiting for the last judgment and seeing that people, if they are judged, are judged as they die.

To sum up this chapter, we see that world religions point to the possibility of an afterlife, NDEs seem to corroborate these, and the difficulties in the accounts of what happens after death seem to be lessened by the plausibility of the mysticism of Swedenborg. It has been found that those who experience NDEs subsequently undergo significant positive spiritual growth.[27] The strength of evidence in favor of there being some form of afterlife can shift the position of the supposed atheist, such as A. J. Ayer,

---

25. Swedenborg, *Heaven and Hell*, 174.
26. Swedenborg, *Heaven and Hell*, 171.
27. Greyson and Khanna, "Spiritual Transformation."

away from denying the possibility of an afterlife to the plausibility of that afterlife, even if the bearing of an afterlife on the existence of God is denied.

If these clues were sufficient to convince everyone that there is an afterlife and that a Supreme Being ultimately judges human actions, we would have attained the foundation for ethics that Plato and Rousseau advocate by excluding atheism from a political system as a safeguard. But could immortality of a person in the memory of the living also play a role in promoting an ethical life?

Remember Me: Eternity in the Memory of the Living—Hope for the Supposed Atheist?

According to Swedenborg, it is not only good deeds but also acknowledgment of the Divine that lead to heaven. If one is honest with themselves inwardly, not in a public debate designed to exhibit argumentation skills, one would recognize that the concept of a universal minimum religion offers assurance of the existence of a Supreme Being who is holy, benevolent, and just. But suppose one denies possession of the universal minimum religion in favor of atheism, what sort of afterlife without God can persuade them to take this particular life seriously? Can that view lead them ultimately to a correction of their earlier view of God? For if morality is seriously engaged with, irrespective of the starting point, as long as the pretensions of reason are discounted, morality must lead to God as Kant rightly suggests:

> For morality not only shows that we have need of God, but it also teaches us that he is already present in the nature of things and that the order of things leads to him.[28]

Let us suppose that there are two immortalities: that of the soul and that of the memory of a physical existence here on earth. We should normally be more concerned with the destiny of the immortal soul that transitions into the next life. But a consideration of the immortality of one's memory can, to a degree, even a limited degree, contribute to the grounding of an ethical order in which ultimate justice is rendered on the immortal memory of a person.

On this earthly side of life, we can work toward a good and just memory of our lives. There are many dimensions ranging from our actions as they relate to others, through our professional lives, to our family.

With respect to our dealing with other people, we can act in accordance with our conscience and seek forgiveness for our harmful actions.

28. Kant, *Philosophical Theology*, 110.

When a person dies, stories are told of their lives here on earth. Decorum dictates that we focus on the good that they did to us. But the press is not always as generous; they sometimes get brutally honest in their assessment of the deceased life. Thus, Alfred Nobel was shocked to read a mistaken obituary in which he was labeled "The Merchant of Death" on account of the many lives lost in his dynamite business. Seeing that this was how he would be remembered if he died in that condition, he created the Nobel Prize to honor achievements in the sciences.[29] We thus witness the transformation of a life through consideration of how one will be remembered by the living. This is not a summation of Mr. Nobel's life, but it indicates how immortality in the memory of the living can shift one's moral considerations.

In the conduct of one's professional duties, there are moral choices to be made, excellence to be pursued, and courageous reformation of immoral practices. In the accounts of the African slave trade, slaves who showed courage in their suffering are remembered with admiration while wicked slave masters and their progeny are viewed as irredeemably tainted. But even slave masters who later repented of their engagement in the practice strike us as people who redeemed themselves and returned to a path of justice. History seals all actions done in the past. The deeds may be hidden but will one day still be found out. Good actions will be praised and admired and the wicked ones will be judged by the living. As time passes we witness moral progress, and the later generations may be even more critical of earlier lives.

All moral actions that can be judged by later generations bear on the family of the deceased. If it is instinctive for parents to leave their children better off, then since a life lived and ended in death cannot be corrected, there is every motivation for everyone who is a parent or a relative of the younger generation to consider this life in the much larger scale of immortality in the memory of the living. This is not just memory but also history written about past lives. One stands in a position where one can benefit from the lives of one's ancestors or apologize on their behalf, but a moral impetus leads us to consider our own actions in this life because they leave immortal traces that bear on our families.

Of concern here are not just moral actions but also our worldviews. It is a gift to one's family to make it easier for them to grieve one's transition out of this life. The best gift in this sense is to give them the assurance of transitioning into eternal bliss. If one chooses to militantly oppose religion and the possibility of the afterlife, and especially does so in the light of

---

29. Andrews, "Premature Obituary." Historians have not found the alleged obituary, though it is considered to be highly probable. For our purpose here, we can simply consider that the story illustrates the concern people have about how they will be remembered.

increasing evidence to the contrary, this way of looking at the world may trouble relatives who later come to believe in the afterlife and a Supreme Being. The point is that if one is concerned about a positive immortality in the memory of the living, one can still end up choosing to believe in an afterlife and in a god. What is at stake is not winning an argument, but living a life with consideration of the impact of our worldview on our loved ones who may survive us. A blind, militant insistence on the plausibility of atheism and the absence of an afterlife, despite their implausibility, must strike us as an unworthy legacy.

C. TOLERANT RELIGIONS IN A METAPHYSICAL MARKETPLACE

We have now concluded our discussion on religion. There is a universal minimum religion from which many other systematic religions develop. These have certain differences that do not annul the key ideas of the universal minimum religion (moral predisposition, a Supreme Being, struggle with evil and good, etc.). These religions also present different accounts of the afterlife, apart from the critical philosophical religion of atheism. Although these afterlife accounts may differ, they can still motivate and guide morality. NDEs and Swedenborg's mysticism about heaven and hell can help us to make sense of some afterlife doctrines. But ultimately, religion needs to address the problem of violence arising from differences in systematic religions. Philosophers of religion also need to consider not just the contrasting features of religion; they should serve the greater good by identifying the underlying universal minimum religion. They should equally realize the essences to which various religious symbols point, albeit obliquely.

For religions to thrive and mutually excite one another toward sustainable reforms, the society should be viewed as a metaphysical marketplace. Various systematic religions, if they are convinced of their beliefs, cannot help but proselytize. But religion, being a matter of conscience, cannot admit violence as part of this marketplace of religious metaphysics. The art of persuasion, especially persuasion about religious beliefs, may be deemed to be a form of violence against human conscience. But the kind of metaphysical marketing that can remain consistent with tolerance and nonviolence is one that focuses on explication of the key dogmas and rituals of one's systematic religion. One must positively discuss how one's religion covers the universal minimum religion and how that system goes on to satisfy the metaphysical hunger for more knowledge of God, the need for a system of teachings, doctrines of forgiveness and salvation, and rituals that enhance the passion of a religious life. This exercise is helped by a charitable understanding of competing systematic religions.

Protestant Christians are convinced that in a competitive metaphysical marketplace, their version of a systematic religion would appeal to seekers from all backgrounds. If this is borne out in practice, and if this promotes the flourishing of human beings, we can only expect that other religions will crystallize their doctrines and become positively influenced by the system of Protestantism, its scriptural basis, personal piety, and inbuilt freedom.

For further discussion on ethics, we draw from this chapter the plausibility of an afterlife and the existence of a Supreme Being who is a just magistrate, holy, and merciful. These ideas, together with conscience, the great commandments of Abrahamism, and the gracious forgiveness of sins, can serve as raw material for the development of an overtly theistic religious ethical theory.

PART IV

REASON IN ETHICS RESTS on religious principles. This is the case when we analyze current ethical theories based on sentiments and reason. A more overt invocation of limited religious axioms in ethical theorizing would bring unification and explanatory clarity to current moral intuitions. Such connection to religious axioms also bears on applied ethics such as politics and law.

The goal of part III was to establish the universality of a minimum religion and to discuss how this minimum is further developed toward diverse systematic religions without losing the underlying common core. Some of the common ideas that feature across religions are innate moral dispositions in human beings, the propensity of evil, and the belief in the afterlife where virtue is rewarded and vice is punished.

Returning to our concept of reason, part IV now considers reason in the broader context of theoretical ethics, religion, and applied ethics. Chapter 10 discusses current ethical theories, especially the intuitional ethics where one camp holds that morality is derived from reason, whereas the other camp vehemently opposes this, asserting sentiments or moral sense to be the basis of morality. It is argued in this chapter that these ethical theories all find their origin in the sense of the divine, also vaguely called conscience, and are expanded in the significant commandments of Christianity.

In chapter 11, the question is taken up concerning the grounding of ethics by directly embracing religious axioms and expanding them with reason (whose core principle is religious faith). The imperative to love is explored as better suited to reconcile tensions in commonsense moral intuitions.

Chapter 12 considers the implication on politics and law of this new approach to ethics based on religious axioms. Having shown in part III that true atheism is impossible, the fears of Plato and Rousseau regarding atheism in the political and legal spheres are banished. Some problems of political and legal theories then take on a new light, with new possibilities.

CHAPTER 10

Ethics, Based on Sentiments or Reason, Rests on the Religious Conscience

CURRENT ETHICAL THEORIES HAVE their roots in a key religious assumption: the sense of the divine intricately linked to a moral predisposition, an attendant evil propensity notwithstanding. This rootedness in the same religious assumption means that they assert the same fundamental moral principles in different ways. Any reasoning in ethics is therefore connected to a presupposition of faith in a transcendent force, a Supreme Being.

The field of ethics is marked by a proliferation of theories that leads to various classification for useful comparative analysis. One way to classify these theories is to consider the method by which a moral decision is made. In this case, we have reason and emotions or sentiments as the means by which we decide and act. In this distinction, Kant famously stands out as a proponent of using reason to determine what one ought to do. The other camp is considered to base moral actions on one of these interchangeable concepts: emotions, sentiments, passion, and moral sense. There are nuanced conceptual distinctions, but it is useful to treat them here as interchangeable. David Hume is seen as a key representative of this anti-reason camp. But this conceals the origin of his ideas as being in the Scottish and English school of ethics that includes Francis Hutcheson, Adam Smith, the Earl of Shaftesbury, and Bishop Joseph Butler. The idea that emotions and reason are opposed with respect to ethics immediately places us on a judgment throne to decide which of the two should be the rightful basis of moral actions.

There is another classification of ethical theories suggested by Henry Sidgwick.[1] This classification, although Sidgwick suggests that it is based

---

1. Sidgwick, *Methods of Ethics*, 12–14.

on methods, can be viewed as based on the goal or end of a moral action. According to Sidgwick, various ethical theories can be classified as egoistic hedonism, intuitionism, and utilitarian hedonism. In egoistic hedonism, the goal of a moral action is the greatest happiness of the moral agent. Intuitionists aim at fulfilling a duty whereas the utilitarian hedonist aims at the greatest general happiness. But with respect to how these goals are determined, one can distinguish between calculations based on empirical data or intuitive feelings about what works. Here, too, we are called upon to examine the three methods and decide which one should guide our actions because, at first glance, they aim at different goals and use different methods to determine the best course of action to attain those goals. It is not enough for us to say that we can use reason and discern which one is better, since reason is, according to our analysis, wedded to the goals we set noninferentially.

The various methods and goals of moral actions discussed above can strike us as acceptable, but we are unsettled by the fact that we seem to be assenting to irreconcilable principles. In her recent book on conscience, Patricia Churchland draws from neuroscience and articulates a position that is closer to Hume's moral sentiment theory.[2] She argues against ethics based on rigid principles and she is overly optimistic about the prospects of brain science helping us to understand moral philosophy. She only pushes the problem of morality further; she is closer to Hume and Aristotle who are less focused on exact principles of morality.

But can we imagine ethics without principles? Would that be part of philosophy? Philosophy aims at very general theories about the way things are in the world. But this commitment to generality inspires tribal wars along the way, as partial theories of a complex problem establish themselves and contend against competitors. The solution is not to eschew the search for generality; it is to rise to higher grounds from which we can show that the warring tribes are indeed part of the same nation. That is, it must be attempted to show that there is a certain theoretical standpoint from which the competing ideas accord with one vision of reality. That is what we have already argued here with respect to the opposition between rationalism and empiricism, reason and faith, and reason and sentiments. With respect to ethical theories, this task of rationalizing the competing principles has been undertaken by Sidgwick and Derek Parfit. But they have not gone far enough to find the unifying religious axioms at the basis of morality. It is not by watching neurons that moral philosophy will overcome the confusion,

---

2. Churchland, *Conscience*, 67–69.

but certainly by having a more open mind toward the religious roots of morality.

In this chapter, we want to do three things. First, trace morality-by-reason and morality-through-sentiments to their common root, the sense of the divine or conscience. We can then explain reason as invoked by Kant to be more than one emotion subjected to reflection, and emotions invoked by Hume as conscience trained by religion, education, and culture. The second task is to acknowledge Sidgwick's work as headed in the right direction—namely, to show a common thread connecting the different ethical theories. Sidgwick considers that religion could finally reconcile egoistic hedonism with utilitarian hedonism to form a unified perspective, but he incorrectly dismisses it, elevating the utilitarian principle to a higher position. The third task is to sympathize with G. E. Moore in his destruction of the pretensions of the utilitarian edifice. Moore sees the relevance of religion in overcoming the vexations of ethical theorizing and he insightfully observes, "The Christian doctrines of heaven and hell are in this way highly relevant for practical ethics."[3] We discuss why ethics must abandon the unreasonable reflex of rejecting religious axioms as proper departure points for ethical theories.

A. ETHICS BASED ON REASON OR EMOTIONS?

Once the question is asked whether ethics should be based on reason or emotions, it seems that the answer is obvious. Who would reject reason in favor of emotions? This is the orthodox view in society. But if we are further pressed to consider two separate questions, (1) whether ethics should be based on reason or emotions, and (2) whether ethics is based on reason or emotions, we would get more nuanced reactions. With respect to the first, reason is likely to be the answer, and with respect to the second question, we would be told that current actions of human beings, which may not be considered ethical, are indeed based on emotions.

Hume, Moral Sense, and Emotions in Morality

Those who strongly advocate for naturalistic ethics are simply asking us to systematize current human behavior into a normative code. What is, becomes what ought to be. In principle, this is a conservative approach that would perpetuate prevailing norms. But the way in which Hume uses

---

3. Moore, *Principia Ethica*, 115.

emotions is not devoid of the possibility of training these emotions and passions. In fact, it is important to note the manner of speech used by Hume:

> Morals excite passions, and produce or prevent actions. Reason of itself is utterly impotent in this particular. The rules of morality, therefore, are not conclusions of our reason.[4]

This statement reinforces his statement that "reason is, and ought only to be the slave of the passion." But prior to this statement, Hume opines that if morality had no influence on passions and actions, we wouldn't take pains to inculcate it in people. He holds that people are governed by duties and are prevented from certain actions by the thought of it as unjust while being nudged into other actions by the sense of obligation. To Hume, then:

1. Moral education precedes the use of emotions to direct passions and action.
2. The immediate impulse to perform an action arises from a sense of duty, and the determent from some actions is caused by an opinion of injustice related to the action.

What we are dealing with here is conscience, and this conscience can further benefit from moral instruction. But for this instruction to translate to action, the agent must desire the end. What one ought to do Sidgwick considers to be a hypothetical imperative, but we usually do not explicitly say to what end that action ought to be done. A moral maxim is therefore stated as "If you desire X end, then you ought to do Y." But why someone should desire X end is a separate action. We can imagine a separate argument to convince the agent to desire X end:

P1: All (normal) human beings desire X end under this present condition.

P2: You're a (normal) human being.

C1: Therefore, you desire X end.

But sometimes the moral case for desiring a particular end is not conducted in this manner. A conditional statement is issued: "If you were/are a normal human being, you would desire X end." The person is caught in the awkward position of asserting that they are a normal human being and seeing that C1 follows.

The system of conscience or moral sense consists in recognizing situations of the type "If you desire X end, then you ought to do Y" and immediately desiring that X end, followed by doing Y to attain the X end. How

---

4. Hume, *Treatise of Human Nature*, 356.

do people come to desire the end of a moral action? How do they come to combine desiring a moral end and carrying out the moral action? If we look into ourselves, we will find that we have original moral predispositions. We would also discover that these ideas are strengthened by moral instructions in our society. This is the perspective of Hume when he already invokes morals and emotions in the ordering of actions.

The idea of a moral sense in British philosophy has much of its development in the work of Francis Hutcheson. Hutcheson is known to have influenced Hume through correspondence, and Adam Smith, his student and successor as professor of moral philosophy at the University of Glasgow. It is relevant to note that Hutcheson was the son of a Presbyterian minister and thus aware, perhaps informally, of the doctrine of the sense of the divine or the role of conscience by which non-Christians may come to know the dictates of the moral law without knowledge of divine revelation.

To Hutcheson, we can trace not only the idea of moral sense, but benevolence and the utilitarian principle later popularized by Jeremy Bentham. The idea of a moral sense draws analogy from our senses by which we know things about the world. A moral sense enables us to immediately cognize our moral duty in each situation; it is intuitive and universal. This is basically another name for the sense of the divine used by John Calvin as a summary of Paul's teachings on conscience as a guide for pagans. Benevolence, and not self-interest or self-love, should be the determinant of the goodness of a moral action. We must orient ourselves to act such that we can obtain the greatest happiness for the greatest number.

The centrality of benevolence and moral sense in British moral philosophy develops as a reaction to Thomas Hobbes's elevation of self-interest to the guiding principle of human actions. To Hobbes, human beings are concerned with self-preservation; self-interest must therefore guide their actions. It is with Hobbes and the Epicureans in mind that Sidgwick creates a category of ethical theories known as egoistic hedonism. But this ethical position of Hobbes, combined with his empiricism and mechanical philosophy, invigorates moral theorizing in England and Scotland with the result that the Cambridge Platonists and moral-sense Calvinists take up positions that refute or even overcorrect the role of self-interest in morality.

Hutcheson advocates for benevolence as the central determinant of moral goodness of an action. He even offers formulae to calculate the moral worth of an action and how this moral worth is diminished by any considerations of self-interest.[5] Benevolence is determined as the quantity of public good by an agent's actions divided by the abilities of the agent. But an

---

5. Hutcheson, *Inquiry* 2.3.11.

action may proceed such that it produces benefit for both the agent and the public. We can compare the good produced by an agent with self-interest to that produced by another agent with the same abilities but no self-interest and discover whether the self-interest diminishes the benevolence of the agent. According to Hutcheson, since the determinant of moral goodness is benevolence—that is, happiness brought to others by our action—we must seek the greatest happiness for the greatest number.

That the root of Hutcheson's utilitarianism is benevolence can be missed in the later development of utilitarianism by Bentham, Mill, and Sidgwick. The impression one gets is that later utilitarianism seems to impose itself on the moral agent. But the root of this is already found in Hutcheson when he seeks to make immoral any consideration of self-interest in the determination of the goodness of an action. This is still a sign of overreaction to Hobbes's egoistic ethics.

Still operating from the perspective of moral sense and benevolence, Adam Smith begins to see the problem of making self-interest immoral as Hutcheson does. Smith opens his *Theory of Moral Sentiments* with a commitment to benevolence as a universal attitude:

> How selfish soever man may be supposed, there are evidently some principles in his nature, which interest him in the fortunes of others, and render their happiness necessary to him, though he derives nothing from it except the pleasure of seeing it.[6]

This benevolence notwithstanding, it cannot be that all self-interested actions lack approval as Hutcheson states. But in reaction to Mandeville, who sees self-interest present even in virtuous acts of benevolence, Smith admits that proper disinterested virtue and self-interest may amount to moral goodness.

It is not hard to see that the moral philosophy based on moral-sense, benevolence, and minimization of self-interest is related to the sense of the divine in Calvinist thought, or its relation to Rom 2:14–15. These relations are more explicit in the work of Joseph Butler. His sermons interweave Christian ethics with moral philosophy. From his *Fifteen Sermons*, Sermons II and III deal with the natural supremacy of conscience, and XI and XII deal with loving one's neighbor.

But the problem with the moral-sense and benevolence approach is that it seems to underestimate the attendant propensity in human beings to do evil. When sense of the divine is isolated from the evil propensity in human beings, it can lead to Pelagianism. Pelagianism is an often-criticized

---

6. Smith, *Moral Sentiments*, 9.

Christian doctrine that human beings, through exercise of their free will and improvement, can attain moral progress without divine grace. Morality based on moral sense and benevolence, in overreacting to Hobbes, fails to see the evils that Hobbes is addressing with his social contract and political order. It is possible to arrive at an idea of morality starting from self-interest and regulated by a social contract as an element of justice. This must be complemented by the knowledge and love of a Supreme Being of excellent moral character. We shall explore this line of thought in chapter 11.

From this brief discussion, we can see that Hume's idea of basing morality on moral sentiments is anchored in a more extensive tradition of moral-sense philosophy where Hutcheson plays a central role. This moral sense cannot be disentangled from Calvinist Christianity shared by most of the philosophers. It is more clearly discernible in Butler, raised a Presbyterian and ordained in the Church of England. Hume is often presented as a supposed atheist, such that the influence of Calvinism eludes those who study his philosophy. Where Calvinist ideas are found, they are attributed to the influence of some other Calvinist thinker. For instance, Richard Popkin links Hume's theory of belief to the views of the Calvinist Pierre Jurieu.[7] As of the time of writing, the entry on David Hume on the Internet Encyclopedia of Philosophy by James Fieser says of Hume:

> His background was politically Whiggish and religiously Calvinistic. As a child he faithfully attended the local Church of Scotland, pastored by his uncle.[8]

The root of British moral philosophy based on moral sense is therefore Calvin's sense of the divine and the doctrine of conscience in Rom 2:14-15. This is what we gather on sentiments as the basis of morality in Hume's thought. If we pay attention to Hume's and Butler's language, we will notice that the conscience that animates the moral sense is not simply the natural predispositions of human beings. It is that original predisposition nurtured by moral doctrines and reflection. What the British moral-sense theorists fail to do is to produce a theory of the reflection that improves the sensibility of that original moral conscience. Conscience coexists with the inclination to evil and human ignorance—that is, ignorance about the contingent truths that are invoked to serve as the means of executing the duties of conscience. The inclination to evil can be lessened by moral discourses such as sermons, and the ignorance can be reduced by the study of natural and human phenomena, including Holy Scriptures. Such activities produce a

---

7. Popkin, "Hume and Jurieu," 406–17.
8. Fieser, "David Hume," under 1. Life.

reflective conscience, a heightened moral sense, that remains noninferential in the ultimate determination of the will to act. The reflective conscience attains a facility of intuiting moral duties in given circumstances, the duties bearing the mark of a tacit divine imperative.

Kant's Moral Philosophy: From Reason or Moral-Sense Theory?

If it can be admitted that the British moral-sense theory of morality is traceable to the Calvinist sense of the divine and Paul's doctrine of conscience, can the same be said of Kant's moral theory? Doesn't his theory rest on reason? Isn't there a clear contrast between the loose ideas of the moral-sense theory and the rational edifice of Kant's moral philosophy? A simple answer to the first question is yes, Kant's moral philosophy rests on the same foundation as moral sense. So, the answer to the second question is negative: Kant's morality does not rest on reason that is understood to be devoid of conscience.

Three arguments can be used to see that Kant's apparent reason-based moral theory is indeed founded on moral sense, or sense of the divine, or Paul's idea of conscience. These arguments are evidence of influence of British moral-sense theory, his methodological approach to the categorical imperative, and his religious writings that reflect his Pietist acquaintance with ideas of the sense of the divine or Paul's doctrine of conscience as well as New Testament Christian ethics. But the merit of Kant's theoretical approach cannot be denied. His ethical theory rests on an intuition, but he systematically connects this intuition to a general principle that can be used to generate other ethical principles. His genius lies in mirroring the success of universal laws in the study of deterministic natural science as he approaches the laws of the human will in moral situations. The idea of law immediately suggests universality.

Kant and Moral-Sense Philosophers

There is evidence that Kant is not only very conversant with British moral-sense philosophers but is also influenced by them. Among these influences, one can discern Shaftesbury, the originator of the idea of moral sense, and Hutcheson, the more extensive user of that theory. Hume also features in the more critical reception of moral-sense ideas. It seems that Kant uses or rejects the moral philosophy of Hutcheson and others based on varying interpretations of the theory. One of the weaknesses of the moral-sense theory is the lack of precision in the use of associated concepts. This practice reaches a confusing degree in Hume, where morality is spoken of in terms of passions, sentiments, and emotions in addition to the moral sense, conscience, sympathy, benevolence, utility, and moral feeling already found in earlier works. Moral feeling is the least philosophical, according to Kant, and conscience, insofar as it suggests the idea of a judgment of goodness or an inner tribunal, receives approval from Kant.

These attitudes are best illustrated in Kant's *Lectures on Ethics*. These are generally thought to reflect Kant's views and assessment of the ideas of other thinkers. For instance, in part III, "Morality according to Prof. Kant," recorded by Mrongovius in winter 1785, the section on morality has views on moral feelings:

> The principle of moral feeling. This is null and void. . . . All rules derived from feeling are contingent, and valid only for beings that have such feeling.[9]

Later on, he is more conditional:

> One may still grant the moral feeling, if it were a question of the mind's incentives to morality; but not as a principle for the judgment of moral action. It may be the receptivity of our will to be moved by moral laws as incentives.[10]

Yet further on, he concedes on moral feeling, stating that moral feeling is inner reverence for the law. But he then takes a more negative view on sympathy as a principle of morality.

In part II of the *Lectures*, recorded by Georg Collins in winter 1784–1785,[11] Kant discusses ideas common to the British moral-sense movement, but these are dressed in robes that radiate positively—duties to oneself, proper self-esteem, self-love, self-mastery, etc. We can guess from this attitude that Kant elevates commonsense ideas to philosophical concepts, through greater attention to language, even if this does not always succeed in avoiding contradictions. What is important to our discussion is what he has to say about conscience:

> Conscience is an instinct, to direct oneself according to moral laws. It is not a mere faculty, but an instinct, not to pass judgment on, but to direct oneself.[12]

---

9. Kant, *Lectures on Ethics*, 242–43.
10. Kant, *Lectures on Ethics*, 243.
11. Kant, *Lectures on Ethics*, 41–222.
12. Kant, *Lectures on Ethics*, 130.

By this, he is elevating conscience not only to a faculty of judgment but as something that directs one according to moral laws. He goes on:

> Conscience, however, has a driving force, to summon us against our will before the judgment seat, in regard to the lawfulness of our actions.[13]

Two paragraphs later on, he continues:

> The inner tribunal of conscience may aptly be compared with an external court of law. Thus we find within us an accuser, who could not exist, however, if there were not a law; though the latter is no part of the civil positive law, but resides in reason, and is a law that we can in no way corrupt, nor dispute the rights and wrongs of it. Now this moral law underlies humanity as a holy and inviolable law.[14]

We can thus agree that we are dealing with terminological differences here and the skepticism about, or love of, universal principles. Kant and the British moral-sense philosophers share the same admiration for conscience, which they call by different names. Kant is more willing to tie the various ideas together with legal precision. This is so because he is more acutely aware of the nature of human beings as legislating creatures. Ludwig Borowski, Kant's former student, points to the influence of British moral-sense philosophy more directly:

> In the years when I belonged among his students, Hutcheson and Hume were of exceptional worth, the former in subjects of morals, the latter in his deepest philosophical investigations. . . . He [Kant] recommended both of these writers to us for a most careful study.[15]

Conscience, More than Reason, Grounds the Categorical Imperative.

We need to focus on conscience if we desire to see the relation of the categorical imperative to the general ideas of moral-sense theory. Conscience is more closely linked to the sense of the divine and Biblical teaching on the possibility of divinely inspired universal morality.

---

13. Kant, *Lectures on Ethics*, 131.
14. Kant, *Lectures on Ethics*, 130–31.
15. Walschots, "Hutcheson and Kant," 37.

If we applied the idea of a moral imperative stated at the beginning, that an imperative can be seen to consist in the saying "If you desire X end, then you ought to do Y," we must ask how Kant's theory addresses this. It is often said that people take Kant's categorical imperative to mean that we should use this to determine how to act in particular cases, quite contrary to the goal of the imperative.

To see how one may fit Kant's moral theory into the model, we need to recognize the relation of his *Groundwork for the Metaphysics of Morals*, *The Metaphysics of Morals*, and the *Critique of Practical Reason*. These address different problems, according to Kant. It seems then that the moral theory of Kant is "If you desire X end, you ought to use the supreme principle to deduce principles from which to deduce principles to act so that your principles are consistent with the end, X." The first book develops the supreme principle, the categorical imperative:

> Act only in accordance with that maxim through which you can at the same time will that it become universal law.[16]

According to Kant, a pure moral philosophy should be cleansed from contamination by empiricism. The mistake of the British moral-sense philosophers was often to exemplify their operation of conscience and virtue by pointing to external actions that benefit others. They then enquired whether a disinterested third person would qualify those actions as moral. If morality is to be cleansed from empirical contamination, then one must direct one's attention to the will as a determinant of the end of actions.

A good will is the supreme good that one can aim at. The goodness of an action is determined by the goodness of the principles that determine the will to perform that action. Herein enters the concept of duty as the obligation to act in reverence of the supreme moral principle or law. By *obligation* here, we recognize the role of an imperative.

The categorical imperative is developed in the second section of the *Groundwork*, operating on the idea of an imperative. An imperative can be hypothetical or categorical. A hypothetical imperative requires that something be done if something else is desired, the desired thing being an external good or advantage. The categorical imperative demands that the action be done because it is necessary in and of itself. To Kant, if a good will is good in and of itself, and not good as a means to an end, and if this good will is the proper object of morality, then its determining principle must be a categorical imperative. It cannot be a hypothetical one that aims to produce a good will in order to produce a useful end in the world of experience. If we

---

16. Kant, *Groundwork*, 37.

imagine the will as a person, then the aim of morality should be to render good the character of the person called the will. This perspective of the will is important in understanding the central place of the human will in Kant's discussion; it brings us closer to conscience.

Reason, as used by Kant, is vague; it is invoked with the idea of unity of thought and legislation. In other words, it is related to the generation of principles. It seems that reason plays the role of connecting ideas to produce a certain purposiveness, coherence, or law-like generality. Conscience is hardly mentioned in the *Groundwork*, but it appears more clearly in the *Metaphysics of Morals* and corroborates the tone in the *Lectures on Ethics*.

We can convince ourselves about this by looking at three excerpts from the *Metaphysics of Morals*, even if the extensive quotations may seem redundant:

Kant speaks of key presuppositions in the concept of duty:

> There are certain moral endowments such that anyone lacking them could have no duty to acquire them. They are moral feeling, conscience, love of one's neighbor, and respect for oneself (self-esteem). There is no obligation to have these because they lie at the basis of morality, as subjective conditions of receptiveness of the concept of duty, not as objective conditions of morality.[17]

Here we are dealing with intuitions that serve as a basis for the concept of duty. But we may say these are loose sets of intuitions in the same state as they come to Kant from the British Isles, except that they are now adorned with a more respectful nomenclature. We may then say that it is reason that connects them together with the idea of a moral maxim as a universal law. But later in the same section, Kant elevates conscience to practical reason:

> For, conscience is practical reason holding the human's duty before him for his acquittal or condemnation in every case that comes under law. . . . So when it is said that a certain human being has no conscience, what is meant is that he pays no heed to its verdict. . . . An erring conscience is an absurdity.[18]

Even if Kant were to qualify this statement that practical reason is different from pure practical reason and pure reason, and that these last two are the originators of his universal law, we should not be quite convinced that conscience is not playing a greater role in the theory. Or we should not

---

17. Kant, *Metaphysics of Morals*, 159.
18. Kant, *Metaphysics of Morals*, 160–61.

be dissuaded from suggesting that conscience seems interchangeable with reason in Kant's moral theory.

In the "Doctrine of Virtue" in the *Metaphysics*, the legal imagery surrounding conscience is repeated:

> Every human being has a conscience and finds himself observed, threatened, and, in general, in awe (respect coupled with fear) by an internal judge; and this authority watching over the law in him is nothing that he himself (voluntarily) makes, but something incorporated in his being. . . . He can at most, in extreme depravity, bring himself to heed it [conscience] no longer, but he cannot help hearing it.[19]

Kant's use of conscience tilts toward internal judgment as if it refers mostly to past acts. In the "Doctrine of Right," where he discusses the guarantees of an oath, he regrets the promissory nature of an oath and wishes it were assertory, referring to a perfected action. In such a case, Kant thinks that an officer would have to take an oath asserting that they fulfilled their duty as required by law. The officer stands before an external and an internal court of conscience, and the internal court would have more weight. In terms of determining actions, we see that moral feeling, love of neighbor, and self-love, which can be brought together under conscience, are separated by Kant, while conscience ties directly to the idea of a law.

From the foregoing, we can discern that conscience is central to Kant's universal law, even if Kantian scholarship does not elevate it to the same degree as reason.

Kant's Religious Faith as Source of His Moral Theory

If one is not prejudiced against religion, it is not difficult to see Kant's Protestant Christianity as a driving force in his moral theorizing. Even his epistemology seems to be motivated by a Protestant inclination to put reason in its proper, humbler place. This inclination can also be found in Hume and explained by the Protestant unconscious. There is just something too pretentious about reason that the Protestant conscience cannot stand. In Kant's moral philosophy, Protestant impulses show up more starkly.

Two elements of Protestant ethics show up in Kant's moral philosophy. The one is the idea of the sense of the divine, scripturally grounded in Paul's teaching about conscience in Rom 2:14–15. The other is the emphasis on the two commandments of Jesus as higher rule-generating principles, rather

---

19. Kant, *Metaphysics of Morals*, 189.

than an elaborate list of Old Testament laws or codified canon law. One's conscience reaches the highest elevation when it is bound in the word and grace of God. Romans 2:14 states: "For when Gentiles, who do not have the law, by nature do the things in the law, these, although not having the law, are a law to themselves." In the writings of Kant, we feel a pastoral exhortation to meditate on Rom 2:14. His moral philosophy could well be called the sermons of Kant the prophet from Konigsberg. In a sense, they are expositions of the Holy Scriptures with philosophical grace.

It might be argued that we are reading more religion into Kant's philosophy than he actually intends. The truth is that we have instances where Kant equates conscience with reason or shows that the conscience reaches further than reason. There are also instances where Kant links our innate morality with knowledge of God in the sense of a religious relation. Thus, in *Lectures on Philosophical Theology*, he follows the Protestant doctrine that moral theology leads more directly to God and religion than natural theology:

> Such a moral theology not only provides us with a convincing certainty of God's being, but it also has the great advantage that it leads to religion, since it joins the thought of God firmly to our morality, and in this way it even makes better men of us. Our moral faith is a practical postulate, in that anyone who denies it is brought ad adsurdum practicum.[20]

It may be fashionable in Kant's scholarship not to notice the failure of reason as the true grounding of his morality or to overlook Kant's reliance on Protestant ethics to remedy the failure of reason. Some may view Kant as separating morality from religion, but we have a choice to follow the arguments where they lead or pretentiously set modern philosophy against religion in order to give the appearance of independence. It is not unusual to also see theologians misinterpret Kant and provide support for distancing his moral philosophy from the Christian religion in its Protestant form.

From the consideration of the use of conscience in moral theorizing, we must lay aside these distracting views and acknowledge that Kant and the moral-sense theorists are much ideologically closer. They all draw from the same well of Protestant Christian ethics.

---

20. Kant, *Philosophical Theology*, 122.

B. POINTING TO COMMON GROUNDS IN ETHICS: SIDGWICK'S METHODS

Henry Sidgwick attempts to find harmony in the various methods of ethics used in philosophy and common practice. He approaches this from a utilitarian background influenced by Mill and Bentham. But it is often forgotten that Mill and Bentham only further develop the utilitarianism that branches out from Hutcheson's moral-sense philosophy. His focus on benevolence leads Hutcheson to assert what is later popularized by Bentham:

> That Action is best, which procures the greatest Happiness for the greatest Numbers; and that, worst, which, in like manner, occasions Misery.[21]

In addition to utilitarianism, the egoism of Hobbes acted as the system to which the British moral-sense philosophy was reacting. The ethics of self-interest championed by Hobbes is countered by the benevolence that results from such duty that aligns with a moral sense. Hutcheson does not see self-interest as contributing to morality; it is negative when it diminishes benevolence, and at best, it is neutral when it does not diminish the benevolence. The reference for this judgment is the outcome of another person acting with comparable ability but without the contamination of self-interest. Admirably, Sidgwick penetrates the differences between moral-sense philosophy and Kant's deontology to discover that they are both based on moral intuitions. He thus applies the label of *intuitionism* to all the methods wherein morality is judged by actions in conformity with rules or dictates of duty.

The tapestry therefore shows that mankind acts according to moral principles that fall into one of the three categories: egoistic hedonism, intuitionism, or universal hedonism (utilitarianism). It seems that many people would find each of these methods applicable to various situations where moral judgments are to be made. The natural question then is, seeing the importance of ethics, can't there be a unified theory that captures common-sense morality that seems to be improperly classed as opposing principles? One should suspect that it is possible, at least given that universal hedonism comes out of Hutcheson's intuitionism. Sidgwick pursues this in his seminal book.

The central themes of Sidgwick's *Methods* are summarized in the preface to the sixth edition, and we see that he pursues this project not just as an academic exercise but with a desire to identify a system of ethics to which he

---

21. Hutcheson, *Inquiry* 2.3.8.

can adhere. Starting from a utilitarian point of view, Sidgwick wrestles with the antagonism between private and general happiness as the ends of moral actions. Private happiness or self-interest seems to conflict with the sense of duty to promote the general welfare according to utilitarianism. Mill seems to resolve the conflict by suggesting that when duty and self-interest conflict, the problem is resolved by a heroic act that lets duty triumph over self-interest, as moral-sense morality would recommend.

Sidgwick is not convinced by this moral heroism resolution of the conflict between self-interest and duty; he therefore tames his utilitarian pride and investigates intuitionism for a more satisfying fundamental moral intuition. In Kantian ethics, he finds more satisfying the fundamental principle of acting from a maxim that can be willed into a universal law. An idea of justice, of treating similar cases in a similar way, shines through this principle. But does this principle resolve the conflict between self-interest and duty to others? Not really. One can universalize the superiority of self-interest to duty, which would undermine utilitarianism.

In Butler's morality based on conscience, Sidgwick finds support for reasonable self-love without abandoning the utilitarian principle. But since we don't have a principle for discerning when self-love is not only reasonable but also to be privileged over duty, the conflict between self-interest and duty is not entirely resolved. What Sidgwick succeeds in doing, according to him, is to show that utilitarianism can be founded on an intuitional basis, thus bridging the gap between utilitarianism and intuitionalism. But conscience and its intuitions remain too unphilosophical and vague to bridge reasonable self-love and duty. Added to these problems are new issues related to how one should compute utility, and whether these empirical calculations are sufficient grounds for duty.

In the concluding chapter where Sidgwick discusses the mutual relation of the three methods, he rightly sees that if it is admitted that there is a Supreme Being who can reward and punish the actions of a human being, and if duty is commanded, then self-interest and duty can be reconciled. But Sidgwick is not prepared to take this step:

> I cannot fall back on the resource of thinking myself under a moral necessity to regard all my duties as if they were commandments of God, although not entitled to hold speculatively that any such Supreme Being really exists.[22]

Sidgwick is convinced that the utilitarian principle is certain and irrefutable. If it can be shown that commonsense morality and divine sanctions

---

22. Sidgwick, *Methods of Ethics*, 507n3.

are harmonizable with the utilitarian code, then the divine code should be viewed as related to the utilitarian. But he sees no ground for admitting the crucial element of God rewarding and punishing those who may prefer self-interest where God commands duty. His main problem is admitting a noninferential element, even though he has acknowledged the need for a key intuition. Admitting the intuition of morality being related to God appears to him as an act of philosophical despair. But in reality, what is operative in his thinking is an active desire not to follow the argument where it leads. If we do not hide behind the deceptive concept of objective reason or the infinite regress of empirical evidence, we must be prepared to admit a noninferential intuition—that is, an axiom that grounds a more extensive system of ideas in a way that is better than a system without the axiom. This is the practice that recommends itself but is resisted because of prior commitment to resistance against religion.

There are two problems with Sidgwick's system. The first is the obvious one that the utilitarian principle is not certain and irrefutable as he claims. Moore does a good job of showing this. The second is the harmony he sees as possible between intuitionism in general and utilitarianism. The way to do this is to trace utilitarianism back to moral-sense philosophy and show this to be grounded in the same theistic conscience as Kant does. It is through the theistic conscience, where Moore rightly recognizes the way Christians use motivation and means of moral actions.[23] The intuitionism of Kant is entirely concerned with the will, motivation, and moral principles, not the consequences of moral actions.

Even a vague mention of consequences needs to be clarified, because it is argued that, even in the Kantian system, to motivate an action one must have the consequences in mind. That means the Kantian does consider consequences. It seems that it depends where the consequences end. To the utilitarian, we proceed from motivation through the utilitarian principle to the action that maximizes general happiness. Our analysis of consequences then focuses on the outcome. But since Kant is more concerned about the goodness of the will, the sequence is to will (self-legislate) according to maxims, then act, and then return to the court of conscience, where the agent stands as a double personality in the court—the agent is judge and defendant. The only consequence that matters in the adjudication is whether the goodness of the will is preserved. The judgment focuses on the maxim by which the action was determined, not the action itself. If this action turns out not to have succeeded, the will can still be judged good, provided the maxim by which it was attempted passes the trial of a universal law before

---

23. Moore, *Principia Ethica*, 177–78.

the internal court of conscience. If it passes the trial, then that individual does not emerge from the inner court as a split personality. This is inner justice. Perfection of the will is the ultimate end of morality, and if such perfection was attainable, the goodness of an action would be the maintenance of the perfection in the will.

Kant's universal law ought to be related to the concept of justice. This is what Sidgwick immediately grasped from Kant's imperative: treating similar cases the same way. Viewed this way, we can trace the flow of ideas from Plato's theory of justice, through Kant, to the theory of justice of the neo-Kantian John Rawls. At the core of this connection is the inner justice of conscience, where the connection to the Supreme Being and religion are inescapable. Thus, Sidgwick accomplishes a great job of seeking the harmony of ethical theories, but he does not complete the task because of his willful decision not to follow the argument into the realm of religiously grounded ethics.

C. AGAINST UTILITARIANISM: G. E. MOORE ON THE NATURALISTIC FALLACY AND THE OPEN QUESTION ARGUMENT

The attempts by Sidgwick to put utilitarianism on a scientific basis are undermined by G. E. Moore's penetrating analysis of the claim that pleasure is the good at which our moral actions should aim.

Kant's deontology and utilitarianism are considered rationalistic ethical theories. They offer principles and arguments. But having shown that reason rests on an axiom of faith, and that Kant's system is supported by a theory of conscience, we need to read Kant with an open mind, taking his theology seriously. Kant's system is not threatened by an admission that reason rests on faith in a fundamental way. But the rationality of utilitarianism is undermined by Moore's analytic philosophy. Sidgwick rejects a religious axiom in his ethics because he sees the utilitarian principle to be certain and irrefutable. He obviously thinks it is rational—one can give reasons for all the principles that are involved.

Moore tackles the key idea of utilitarianism that pleasure is good through a logical argument about an inherent open question engendered by the utilitarian principle:

> OQ1: If a certain property, P, is analytically equivalent to good, then the question "Is P the same as good?" is a trivial question.
>
> OQ2: The question "Is P the same as good?" is not a trivial question.

C1: P is not analytically equivalent to good.

From utilitarianism, P is pleasure. The argument means that the question whether pleasure is the same as good is not a trivial question. The concept of pleasure is not analytically contained in the concept good. We can be confronted with a situation where we have pleasure, but we cannot say whether we have the thing we call good.

Moore's argument points to a more general problem in analysis. In "X is Y," X is the analysandum and Y is the analysans. If the analysans is self-evidently contained in the analysandum, then the analysis is correct but uninformative. It just displays our mastery of synonyms and definitions. But if the analysans is not contained in the analysandum, then the analysis is not necessarily correct. This has come to be called Moore's paradox. The matter must be decided contingently. Consider the statement "John is an American." How can we know this statement is correct if this information is not supplied to us by experience? Most often what is intended through such expressions is not "X is Y," but rather "P properties of X are the same as P properties of Y," where X and Y may each have more properties than the P properties singled out for comparison. To make that statement, we are looking at both X and Y from a certain theoretical perspective.

Moore's paradox does not mean that the assertion "X is Y" may not be interesting or true but it cannot be true analytically. Faced with this paradox, we are presented with two things that can stand in a relation of coherence or causality. X causes Y or X and Y cohere to give the appearance of Z. We are using *coherence* here as a theory of truth. Moore's ethical analysis points to the concept of good as a simple concept. It is basic but it is also important in ethics. If it is basic, as it is indeed, then we can inquire how it stands in relation to other basic or composite concepts of ethics. If ethics asks what one ought to do or what actions are right, we must find a substantive theory. If we arrive at the idea that acting in accordance with the obligation of a good will constitutes the good, and that this goodness is judged through the maxims used for the action, then determination of what is good is a problem of truth. We have embraced in this work the coherence theory of truth.

In seeking an ethical theory, we cannot be trapped by Moore's paradox, but we should embrace the coherence of will, action, and a principle of willing certain actions and disallowing other actions. The ethical theory can admit of intuitions and other analytic or contingent truths. It turns out that the most coherent theory must reconcile acting from interest and acting from a sense of duty. A religious axiom presents itself and should not be simply dismissed.

The relevance of a religious doctrine about duty and self-love is not only seen by Sidgwick as a possible solution, Moore says something similar in *Principia Ethica*. He thinks that if metaphysics could tell us that we are immortal, and that our actions in this life will have consequences in the next life, then such information would bear on our sense of duty. According to him:

> The Christian doctrines of heaven and hell are in this way highly relevant to practical ethics.[24]

Moore is right to bring back ethics to the realm of intuitionism and to expose the fallacy inherent in a supposed rational utilitarianism that is deemed to be certain and irrefutable. But by focusing on analysis of the good, the progress attained by Kant is lost. Kant brings out a number of concepts that must cohere to produce an ethical theory: we have a good will as an end, we have freedom to act morally or not, we suppose that we have reason that is in reality a faith axiom directing inferences, we cognize the idea of autonomy of the will from the external world of the sense, we require that the moral law be a categorical imperative, and our ethics is duty-based. We cannot state Kant's theory fully without trying to connect these ideas, but when we do, we can only judge them by coherence and by how sensible they appear to us. There is incoherence if reason is admitted as autonomous and central to the theory, but the ideas attain their coherence and unity through admission of religious intuitions. If we take away religion, and attempt a systematic characterization of Kant's moral philosophy, then it falls like a house of cards.

It is undeniable that ethics is important; it concerns us all and should attract our sustained attention. There cannot be progress in this field if we hide behind pretentious reason as an objective tool of moral decision-making, or so long as we ignore the religious axioms that Kant subtly introduces, such as the positing of human dignity as sacred ends in ethical reflections. It seems that we must first recognize the inevitability of noninferential intuitions in ethics. Having done so, we must not resist the role of religion in advancing the search for a coherent relation among human free will, actions, and the good, true, just, and beautiful.

But a religious ethics that aspires to universality must rest on the universal minimum religion, not on the conflicting aspects of systematic religions. It should, nonetheless, only admit such maxims from systematic religion that can be deemed acceptable by all who are not actively opposed to the idea of a Supreme Being. Such maxims must be consistent with the

---

24. Moore, *Principia Ethica*, 115.

universal minimum religion and religious toleration. Such a system cannot pretend to determine with exact precision what human beings should do in each situation. It must admit that it can only deal with maxims and leave the human being in the company of their enlightened conscience as the ultimate arbiter of duty and their defender in the internal court where they stand as a dual personality—as judge and defender in one person. We therefore consider in the next chapter what ethics would look like if it took seriously the subjectivity of reason and the central role of religion. The inherent religion should reconcile self-interest and duty as well as sentiments and reason. Reason must be viewed as admitting of basic noninferential matters of faith, and reflectively connecting contingent truths and sentiments with desired ends.

CHAPTER 11

Ethics Is Based on a Religious Conscience
A Divinely Commanded Duty to Love God, Neighbor, and Self

We have established that reason is fundamentally subjective and dependent on faith when it comes to determining the goal of the actions that reason precedes, accompanies, or explains. Any supposedly objective rationalistic ethics that is vehemently opposed to religion is internally incoherent. For there to be any objectivity in reason, we must speak of the universalizability of the inherent subjectivity.

Ethics should then become a study of how fundamentally subjective and religiously based reason is used to generate principles for such actions that rise to the quality of good and just. The task of sketching such an ethics is made easy by our realization that there is a universal minimum religion that can furnish the basic ideas. This minimum religion can be extended with a few generalizable results from a systematic religion such as Christianity. Such extension furnishes clear principles that can coherently unite to formulate an account of ethics.

An ethical theory that aspires to meet the approval of commonsense and speculative philosophy must steer away from the analysis of concepts such as the good or pleasure, seeing that ethics involves various entities, some of which are irreducible but bound together in a network of mutual support. It is by coherence, a kind of unity of concepts, that an account of ethics can be found to meet with approval of most, if not all, stakeholders in the matter.

In this chapter, we tentatively provide a sketch of such religiously based, subjective, but universalizable ethics. We do so by (1) consolidating the concept of conscience with systematic religion, (2) showing how ethics is possible based on the duty to love as an imperative from a Supreme Being, (3) recognizing guilt, injustice, and evil as opposition to ethical duty, and (4) relating the sketched ethical view to the three methods of ethics identified by Sidgwick.

An ethical theory can either be descriptive or idealistic. As a descriptive theory, it simply explains how people behave in society. If it does so without identifying any regret about the way people do behave, then it is likely to produce a static account that aspires to the rigor of the laws of nature in physics. But if regret is expressed, and if standards of right and wrong are offered, such a descriptive account cannot stop without enquiring into the source of these standards. The standards cannot arise from empiricism. If they arise from a judgment, then a comparison is being made between the state of affairs and a certain standard or ideal situation. We must inquire into the source of that ideal. If we do our job well, we will abductively find religion at the source of these conceptions of the ideal situation.

If an ethical theory takes an idealistic path, providing a vision of the way things ought to be, then we must answer two questions. First, can and will the people embrace this idea as indeed what ought to be? Second, if they embrace that account, can they reorder the rules by which they act to achieve this ideal? If they cannot do this, is it because of a competing force that bears on their will or are they simply incapable of doing that which is required to attain the ideal state of moral conduct? As good as a vision may be and as much as people agree with it, in practice they will have to contend with evil inclinations that seek to frustrate their moral duties.

Tension is bound to arise between what ought to be, in terms of a society where moral duties are fulfilled, and what is in fact the case. In the actual society, we find a hybrid situation where moral duties are mixed with unethical actions that lead to evil, injustice, ugliness, and even hypocrisy. An idealistic ethical theory cannot be overly optimistic if its objective is to bring about the envisioned ideal society. The nature and relation of the current evil inclinations to the moral will must be considered. The idealistic ethical theory should not be elitist if it is to be adopted by the learned and unlearned; it must be accessible to all members of the society. For this reason, we can argue that the weekly moral instruction provided by various places of worship in the form of sermons goes much further in exhorting human beings toward moral lives than all the sophistry of academic moral philosophy of the present century.

A. BASIC ELEMENTS OF RELIGION FOR RELIGIOUSLY GROUNDED ETHICS

We have already seen that conscience plays an important role in the intuitionist ethics of Kant and the British moral-sense philosophers. The underlying concept of conscience was religiously inspired, but it was also vague and not explicit in its theistic commitments. The sketch in this chapter does not claim originality; rather, it follows Kant and moral-sense philosophers closely, at least in spirit. Conscience needs to play a central role in such a religiously grounded ethics. This conscience therefore needs to be made more precise to reveal the underlying theistic commitments and show how principles of duty may arise therefrom.

The universal minimum religion of chapter 7 involved seven intuitions:

1. Standing in relation with a transcendent being
2. Realizing that this relation is to one's benefit and the glory of the transcendent being, the Supreme Being
3. Having a sense that one's life has meaning
4. Feeling a sense of gratitude that imparts a sense of moral duty
5. Having a sense that not all possible actions are moral duties approvable by the Supreme Being
6. Having a sense of affinity with other human beings whom we imagine to also stand in relation with the transcendent being
7. Having a sense of guilt and regret over past actions that were evil—that is, they were not moral duties

These intuitions are the elements of the universal minimum religion whose insufficiency necessarily propels us to seek more fulfilling systematic religion through revelation and reflection. That process produces greater clarity on some of our big questions.

Religiously grounded ethics must not be synonymous with a particular systematic religion, such that the whole systematic theology of that religion becomes a treatise in moral philosophy. As we have seen with the moral-sense theorists and Kant, they make use of religious ideas without explicitly identifying religion as the source of these ideas. They are therefore forced to defend the rather vague concept of reason as the source of their religious intuitions. The system thus constructed falls apart if one can show, as we have done in this work, that their pretentious objective ground called reason is fundamentally subjective and goal-oriented, with the goals receiving their determination from religious intuitions. Further, where a philosopher is explicit in the use of religious material in moral theorizing, such as Butler, we are introduced to the system as a sermon, with other elements that may prove to be vulnerable to criticism by religious detractors. The system of Butler also lacks simplicity and clarity if we consider the force of Kant's categorical imperative and the elaboration of conscience, will, freedom, autonomy, and the infamous reason.

In grounding an ethical account in religion, we must ask ourselves what fundamental insights from the various systematic religions can be viewed as imparting precision to the universal minimum religion? Do these religious insights accomplish this without becoming overly complex and perhaps intolerant of the other systematic religions? We have spoken of Western religions that are mostly Abrahamic, have historical revelations, and have been systematized with the help of classical Greek thought. We also have Eastern religions, some of which are mixed in their commitment to theism but largely tolerant of copractice of religion (Buddhism and Confucianism, for instance). Sikhism, as a monotheistic religion, shares certain features with Abrahamism; its affinity with Islamic practice is hard to ignore. It therefore seems that looking to an Abrahamic religion for additional religious statements can produce agreeable presuppositions that can ground an ethical theory.

The basic elements of religion can be united with the concept of conscience to yield a more sensitive conscience. The universal religious conscience as basis for ethics should have the following as religious elements:

R1: The duty to love: God, your neighbor, and yourself.

R2: Belief in the afterlife: know that there is life after death, the quality of which depends on moral goodness here on earth.

R3: The duty to love as an expression of gratitude, not works: acting as duty demands is an expression of gratitude to the God.

R4: Grace and justice: believe in, and practice, the forgiveness of sins and justice.

These intuitions now capture and make more precise the commitments of the universal minimum religion. They raise the conscience of the minimum religion to a more sensitive conscience. When Christians speak of conscience, they mean it in the sense that there is a basic universal conscience, but that conscience can also be instructed toward greater piety and moral sensitivity. That is, in one sense, conscience is that moral capacity that makes morality possible even for those who have not received the historical revelation of the prophets and Jesus Christ. This is what is explained by Paul in Rom 2:14–15. But elsewhere, Paul has a Christian conscience in mind, a more sensitive one, when he says to Timothy in 1 Tim 1:5:

> Now the purpose of the commandment is love from a pure heart, from a good conscience, and from sincere faith.

The Christian conscience differs from the conscience in Rom 2:15 in that it has been instructed by the teachings of Christ and the prophets on how to properly discern moral duties and develop principles of action.

We can agree that the four religious elements recommend themselves to all, without restriction to Christianity. R1 makes more precise what it means for the conscience to bring about a moral action. A duty is commanded: we ought to love God, our neighbor, and ourselves. This is the core of the moral theory we want to develop. The other three religious elements lend support to R1 by placing it in a teleological order and making necessary grace and justice as harmonizing elements.

Parts of R1 may be accepted without argument—the idea that you should love your neighbor and love yourself. It may be questioned whether loving yourself is as morally good as loving your neighbor. We will come to that when we discuss how an ethical system can emerge from R1. But the imperative to love God may pose problems to those who question his existence. It should be noticed that the existence of God is not listed as a separate religious idea to support R1. This is consistent with our discussion in chapter 7 that morality implies the existence of a Supreme Being because morality is, in a way, a theistic religion. The two things are found in our original moral predisposition, even if vaguely. The idea of God and religion are properly basic and universal, insofar as we, as human beings, are committed to morality—we all belong to the church of the universal minimum religion. The additional command to love your neighbor and to love yourself is hardly problematic. It can thus be accepted by those who may have doubts about the existence of God and universal religion.

The other three supporting elements of religion are reasonable and worthy of being accepted. In support of R2, we have both the universal cultural ideas of an afterlife in systematic religions and the growing evidence from research on near-death experiences. Regarding the latter point, as more research shows cases where a clinically dead patient experiences an NDE and provides a veridical account of what happened while they were clinically dead, only militant physicalism/naturalism, not science, will stand in the way of elevating the possibility of an afterlife into a universally acclaimed empirical fact.

The duty to love in R1 is an imperative external to the moral agent. It is an imperative from God, established through revelation. It has the virtue that we recognize elements of universal minimum religion in it. But R3 reveals this commanded duty as altogether fitting and responding to our inbuilt desire to express gratitude to somebody for what we feel is a gift of life. It would take careful reflection for us to arrive at the conclusion that there is nothing that we own that is legitimately ours. We must welcome the revealed truth on this matter as an enormous guide that protects us from arrogance. Calvin rightly says:

> We are not our own; therefore let us not propose it as our end, to seek what may be expedient for us according to the flesh. We are not our own; therefore let us, as far as possible, forget ourselves and all things that are ours. On the contrary, we are God's; to him, therefore, let us live and die. We are God's; therefore let his wisdom and will preside in all our actions. We are God's; towards him, therefore, as our only legitimate end, let every part of our lives be directed.[1]

If there is one simple thing that needs to be corrected in ethics it is this view of our own independence from the Supreme Being. Once we conceive of this independence, we become resistant to the idea of admitting, as part of our ethical theory, the idea of a command. Even if this command were arrived at speculatively, subject to the constraint that there is a Supreme Being as intimated by our predisposition to the moral law, we should immediately see the duty to fulfill the command as binding on us. If we are not our own but God's, then our moral duty cannot be viewed as voluntary work of which we can boast and demand justice; our duty is only an expression of gratitude while looking forward to the life after death.

According to Swedenborg, as discussed in chapter 9, one's destination in the afterlife is determined by one's dominant love. This revelation seems reasonable. The idea of reward and punishment only helps us to grasp that there are consequences to our actions. From our common experience, one gets a traffic ticket for a violation, such as driving through a stop sign. The state does not actually reward those who observe the stop sign; their reward is the pursuit of their life as ordered by the law without hindrance. The commanded duty develops in us a grateful heart, recognizing God as the one to whom we owe gratitude. This view of duty bears on any conflict we may have between self-interest and duty, where we now see self-interest as also a duty of self-love. This duty to love oneself must sometimes be considered along with duty toward our neighbor to determine a principle of action.

To understand the agreeableness of R4 in this extended content of conscience, we need to look at the doctrines of the Protestant Reformation

---

1. Calvin, *Institutes*, 619.

five *solae*, or key statements of faith. The idea of extending the account of conscience as grounding for ethics is not intended to promote Christianity in the Protestant version. It is rather to show that, of the various systematic religions, the Protestant regard for conscience and the elimination of extensive ecclesiastical authority provides the best channel for exchange of religious insight in the form of personal piety. This exchange can proceed without desiring conversion or erecting an organized world religion that can stand in the way of individual conscience and freedom of the will. Protestantism is a system of personal faith with a healthy sense of the existential role of community life.

The five *solae* that have emerged over time are: *sola Scriptura* that emphasizes Scripture alone over church tradition and authority; *sola fidei* that emphasizes faith alone over works; *sola gratia* that emphasizes salvation by the grace of God alone over salvation by meritorious works; *solus Christus* that points to Jesus the Christ, the ultimate revelation of God, as the author of salvation and not the church as the source of salvation; and *soli Deo gloria* that recommends Glory be given to God alone, and not to heroic figures who are themselves God's creation. These statements establish that God's salvation of mankind is gracious, it is made known by Christ in the Scriptures alone and accepted by faith alone; for this undeserved grace of God, that is salvation and self-revelation, we give to him alone all the glory. What we are painting is a system of minimum earthly authority that brings us directly to God, and to the concept of duty as an expression of gratitude to him. Beyond salvation, we can see our very existence as a gift from God, and we find solace in the thought that God takes an interest in us, individually.

Before God, the human being stands with wonder and consolation. One asks as in Ps 8:3–4:

> When I consider Your heavens, the work of Your fingers,
> The moon and the stars, which You have ordained,
> What is man that You are mindful of him,
> And the son of man that You visit him?

One extols God's perfect knowledge of the human as in Ps 139:13–14:

> For You formed my inward parts;
> You covered me in my mother's womb.
> I will praise You, for I am fearfully and wonderfully made;
> Marvelous are Your works,
> And that my soul knows very well.

The awareness of evil inclinations, past guilt, and doubts can only be managed with divine assistance, for which one pleads as in Ps 139:23–24:

> Search me, O God, and know my heart;
> Try me, and know my anxieties;
> And see if there is any wicked way in me,
> And lead me in the way everlasting.

From these considerations we can perhaps understand the importance accorded to human dignity as an end in Kant's philosophy, the importance of the good will, and the elevation of duty over virtue or good actions.

The Christian system, through the Protestant lens on key issues, thus furnishes us with an extended religion that links directly to a Supreme Being. We observed in chapter 7 that many people now say that they are spiritual but not religious. This is sometimes rather a critique of systematic religion in a strange manner. They set a much higher standard on the true practice of religion and religious ethics than what they see to be the case in systematic religions. Many critics of organized religion are concerned with the problem of evil, the complicity of religion in that part of human suffering that is caused by free will. These critics also decry the inability of systematic religions to contribute to the alleviation of human suffering. A religious approach that centers on God, personal faith, and our duty as expressions of gratitude can remedy some of these problems, and, at least, move those who are spiritual toward a more conscious doctrine of a religious conscience that is committed to R1 through R4.

R4 contains a tension between grace and justice. We are called upon to practice grace toward others; we are asked to forgive those who wrong us and reminded of our duty to love even our enemies. Bishop Butler's Sermons VIII and IX address these obligations toward those whom common sense would suggest we hate. We should not only practice grace but also be able to receive this grace when it is extended toward us by God or other human beings. It is the sickness of the soul sometimes not to come to terms with being forgiven for injuries done to others or for failure in expressing our gratitude to God and his people. Does this idea of grace do away with justice? Absolutely not. While we may conceive of our duty to love as concerned mostly with acting according to principles that bring about certain good actions, we are called upon to seek justice and bear witness against injustice in the society. Our conscience must be troubled if we fail to call an unjust act for what it is, or if we extend grace to our friends but insist on just punishment for similar acts to those far from our kindred circles. Grace and punishment stand in tension and even here, our duty as dispensers of grace and justice must reflect expressions of gratitude and love.

Thus far, we have established the requisite conscience that unites the universal minimum religion with some insights from a systematic religion without the unnecessary burden of ecclesiastical authority. They are well suited for personal faith as a groundwork for personal ethics. If this elevation of conscience is universal, then methodologicalindividualism leads us to anticipate manifestation of these ethical traits in a sociological system. We are in company with Plato who sees the justice of the city as determined by the justice in the souls of the individual citizens. The idea of a religious conscience as the basis of religiously based ethics is not a promise of an ethical society per se; it is only a promise that citizens of a given society will have knowledge of their duty and will be aware of their failure to abide by the obligation of moral duty.

B. ETHICS BASED ON THE TRIANGLE OF DIVINELY COMMANDED LOVE

A religiously based ethics cannot be a recommendation of an elaborate system of commandments on how to act in particular cases—like, for instance, the Ten Commandments. Ethics must recognize the fundamental nature of the human being as a legislating creature, a maker of laws and principles. In natural phenomena, the human being picks out regular patterns and expresses them in quantified generalizations that can enable future predictions.

In physics, then, we seek to understand phenomena, the properties of things involved in the phenomena, and the dispositions responsible for the regularities we see. The legislating mind confronted with human behavior is not just reading laws from social phenomena. Sidgwick opines that the philosopher should not simply tell people what they already think but should tell them how they ought to think.[2] The philosopher must go beyond commonsense observations. But this does not give the philosopher the license, at least in ethics, to produce that which cannot strike a chord with the ordinary person. As much as the moral philosopher approaches the matter with care and speculation, they cannot see themselves as much different from ordinary human beings who are themselves legislating creatures, mindful of the fact that how they actually live is at variance with a certain ideal. If moral philosophers point out the system of laws by which the human will can attain goodness, they must be convinced that they are presenting these ideas to legislating minds that are capable of seeing the advantage therein.

If we combine the natural legislating disposition of human beings and the infinite actions they may be called upon to choose between carrying

---

2. Sidgwick, *Methods of Ethics*, 373.

out or not, we must see with Kant that an ethical theory must be concerned with a method for generating principles by which to adjudicate competing duties. But the more general the method of generating principles, the less helpful the method may appear to the ordinary person. If, then, in addition to a method for generating principles, it is emphasized that the perfection of one's moral will or conscience should be pursued, the ordinary person begins to see more clearly their role as legislator, judge, and defendant in the inner court of conscience on questions of morality.

An ethical theory cannot also claim to do more than it possibly can. Limits are set by the uncertainty in our knowledge of contingent truths, the fallibility of our memory, and our total lack of knowledge about the future, to the extent that we rely heavily on probability and induction. From these defects can arise all sorts of ills that frustrate our judgments. Indeed, it must be the will and the principle by which the will acts that are scrutinized in the court of conscience as moral judgment. It cannot be the acts themselves because ethics should be concerned with the internal operation of the will. But when the will employs principles mixed with faulty input about the conditions at hand or plausible effects of our action, then the failure of good principles to achieve good results will begin to weigh on one's conscience. Neither hypocrisy nor unfounded pride can be promoted in such an ethical theory.

From the picture of a religious conscience above and these considerations, if we seek a supreme principle of ethics, then it should be to act according to a good conscience. But to be more precise than that, we must embrace the command to love as the answer to the moral question "What ought I to do?" We stand under the obligation of a religious conscience to perform the duty of love. But what or whom should we love? The principle must become R1:

> Principle: love God, your neighbor, and yourself as an expression of gratitude

There are three persons involved in this command and our duty is to love them. It poses two difficulties. The first difficulty is how to determine the proportion of our duty to these three persons, especially in a hypothetical case of competing duties of love and human limitations. The second difficulty is to understand what is meant here by love.

How Much Love to Each of the Three Persons?

With respect to the difficulty of loving three different persons—God, your neighbor, and yourself—we need to have in view a triangle of love. The moral agent occupies one vertex, the second is occupied by the rest of humanity as one's neighbor, and the third vertex is occupied by God. The principle requires us to perform the duty of love to all three so that we appear to be moving away from ourselves toward God and the rest of humanity. It is reasonable to view a position at the center of this triangle as the ideal locus of love orientation. But there is another way of looking at the command of loving these three persons: it is reducible to the duty to love the first person—God.

It is presented as the greatest commandment to "love the Lord your God with all your heart, with all your soul, with all your strength, and with all your mind" (Luke 10:27). There is a sense in which, reflecting on this commandment, one sees that any attempt to fulfill it automatically leads to loving one's neighbor and loving oneself in the right way. The intuitive understanding is that we agree with Hobbes—self-interest and self-love are our main business when we act. That means we arrive at God from an attempt at rational self-interest. This requires that we understand ourselves and know precisely what is in our interest. If we reflect on the degree of our self-knowledge, we will conclude that the self is opaque to us. We need a mirror by means of which we can peer into ourselves. To a greater extent, God is the mirror through which we discover ourselves as we seek him, pray to him, and try to understand his will concerning us. To a lesser extent, our neighbors, as human beings endowed with dignity and the image of God, are also a mirror by means of which we can understand ourselves. The discovery of ourselves through these mirrors is promoted by taking seriously our duty of love.

The indication that we may indirectly express our love to God through loving others is found in the teachings of Jesus. After citing some examples of situations of need, Christ tells his disciples:

> And the King will answer and say to them, "Assuredly, I say to you, inasmuch as you did it to one of the least of these My brethren, you did it to Me." (Matt 25:40)

We get the sense that we exercise our duty to love God if we love those who come our way and stand in need of love. This is just one aspect of loving God, but here we get the indication that the command "love your neighbor as you love yourself" is an extension of the first commandment. In the Matthew account of the commandments, Christ says that the second commandment is like the first. Whereas the Ten Commandments forbid certain concrete actions, here a positive command to love God is given and made more transparent by commanding us, "Love your neighbor as yourself."

The self is used in the second commandment as a reference; if we know anything about love, it is loving ourselves and loving God. The commandments are issued as answers to questions to those interested in knowing what they ought to do to be saved. Those who pose the question understand that they owe God a duty but do not know which duty. The Jewish tradition has it that there are about 613 commandments, both positive and negative commands. The Hammurabi code is said to have had 282 laws. The multiplicity of laws poses a problem of memory as well as a problem of lack of laws for new, compelling moral challenges. Christ offers the great commandment, a positive command to love God, and a second commandment like the first, to love the neighbor as the self. This is a revolution in morality, away from positive laws to the laws of the heart, soul, and mind. The love of self is not condemned but it is at once demonstrated that love of self cannot be the sole preoccupation of the person who seeks to properly express gratitude to God. The offering of sacrifices being rejected, it stands to reason that in addition to loving God with our heart, soul, strength, and mind, we must be able to see in the needs of others the face of God.

We can therefore say of the question "How much love ought I devote to each of the three persons" that the orienting person is God. We can further recognize that the love of oneself, while not rendered unethical, is made a standard for expressing love for others. A principle of justice is introduced. The proportion cannot be made precise because the purpose is not the generation of a series of positive laws for particular actions. We are left in tension, uncertainty, but with a clear sense of the duty to love God, our neighbor, and ourself.

What Does It Mean to Love?

In the concept of love we see unity of things that would otherwise appear to be contrary: emotion, action, and judgment. In loving, a will or a mind of one person must unite with another object through action. This uniting action can range from thoughts to speech and physical actions in the external world. If the Mosaic laws are clear—"Do not kill"—we cannot claim that we have this clarity in this new great command. Is this disappointing? It must be for a person who seeks a checklist of required moral actions. But while challenging, it is welcomed by the one with a religious conscience. The notion of being a legislator, judge, and defender in the inner court of conscience is not new to the one with a religious conscience. This task brings along with it uncertainty that demands humility and honesty; it also brings anxiety that is tempered and relieved by grace. We are commanded to love with all our capacities, but if doing so should still lead to failure of our actions to achieve a good outcome, the grace of God relieves us of our guilt and inspires us to remain steadfast to the duty of love.

The Russian thinker Vladimir Solovyov interestingly approaches love from a negation of egoism. To him, human love "as the actual abrogation of egoism is the real justification and salvation of individuality."[3]

In this, an idea is suggested that we also find in Kant—namely, humanity ought to be an end in itself; we recognize the absolute worth of the human being. But by seeing things this way, are we negating the humanity of the moral agent from whose perspective duty is contemplated? By no means! In fact, it is through the relation of humanity to humanity that the duty of love can be realized, that the idea of humanity as an end in itself can be cognized.

In what sense then is egoism a problem to the consideration of the duty to love? This is not an easy question, but we must acknowledge that the problem exists, and most writers start out by trying to solve it. In so doing, all further considerations of the self can be declared unethical. Some propose altruism as a counterweight to egoism. There are different views of altruism, ranging from the exclusive consideration of the interests of others to a balanced consideration of the interests of others and one's interests. But suppose we take altruism to be concerned with the exclusive interest in the welfare of others, with no consideration whatsoever for one's interests, then we would have an unnatural and unethical situation according to the view being sketched here. Despite the variation in altruism and egoism, we may consider them to be exclusive interests, such that egoism is an exclusive interest in one's welfare and altruism is an exclusive interest in the welfare of others. Neither of these can be the foundation of an ethical theory because of this unnatural exclusivity.

Love cannot be altruism unless by altruism we mean a balanced concern for our welfare and that of others. But if that is the case, one must look closely at the use of the concept of altruism if it suggests negation of self-interest.

To love is to consider the humanity of others as an end, just like one's own humanity, and then to act in such a way that promotes the flourishing of that humanity as an end. In loving with our God-given capacities, we

---

3. Solovyov, *Meaning of Love*, 41.

discern in the humanity of those before us a state that is at variance with the state of their flourishing and it is our duty to conceive of the most effective methods to act to promote that flourishing. We are called to express divine gratitude by seeing ourselves as jointly creating goodness, beauty, truth, and justice in this world, not by our sheer abilities but by the capacities and resources with which we are first endowed by God.

The exclusivist position according to which an ethical theory should privilege the self or others in directing benefit, is not tenable. The view sketched here requires simultaneous consideration of the three persons to whom the duty to love is owed. The emotions, judgments, and actions that enter each duty of love are tied together by coherence of our utmost expressions of gratitude.

Contrary to the utilitarians who remain vague about the boundaries of the social systems for which maximum utility is to be sought, it is useful to view one's social location as an ethical field of action. This is not restricted geographically as Christian missionaries and other humanitarian workers demonstrate. The presentation of need is viewed as an act of God's grace. This presentation can be as radical as the example of Albert Schweitzer, the missionary physician to Lambarene, Gabon. Having completed a doctoral thesis on the religious philosophy of Kant and working as a theologian, he felt the need to become a medical missionary. This led him to take up medical studies for the purpose. The operation of the duty to love does not require consideration of all the world's problems at once, but it does require a responsiveness to the questions of needs that the imagination and direct acquaintance present to us.

To love is to legislate, to make rules according to which we pursue the creation of goodness, beauty, truth, and justice for humanity. Contrary to the view of the categorical imperative as a cool legislative calculus, we are passionately drawn into the action of loving. Our emotional, reflective, and judging capacities are drawn into action. The idea of loving with the mind points to the study of nature, human nature, and especially religion, if we are to properly express our love and stand in approval before the inner court of conscience. To build morality on love is not to depend on emotivism as a guide. As discussed, all our capacities come to bear on the act of loving, but above all, we are constrained to see our actions primarily as an expression of gratitude to God who "first loved us" (1 John 4:19).

The problem of evil has been cited by many as the reason they choose to doubt the existence of God or to abandon systematic religions. According to the view of the duty to love as an expression of gratitude, and the suffering lot of humanity as human faces of God, they who already stand in a debt of gratitude to God cannot, in arrogance, then insult God for not doing enough. They cannot also see suffering in this life as the finality of human existence. The view that Abrahamists offer to us is to see in our suffering some meaning and never to forget our original position of owing God our gratitude. But this original position of indebtedness to God does not open the door to the argument that God is a tyrant. To this, the words of Kant seem proper:

> God is the only ruler of the world. He governs as a monarch but not as a despot; for he wills to have his commands observed out of love, and not out of servile fear.[4]

Any systematic consideration of our situation in the universe must arrive at the position that we are bound by a duty to love as an expression of our gratitude toward God. There is no worst way to fail in this duty than to accuse God of tyranny and sadism, instead of responding to whatever evil we may perceive in this world by fulfilling our duty to love God, neighbor, and the self.

Imperfect Love that Tends Toward Perfect Love

We have said that exclusive love of the self or exclusive love of others cannot be recommended as an ethical principle. It is also not to be judged plausible that we free ourselves of the love of physical persons and entirely focus on loving God alone. This is an orienting attitude to cure the self of excessive self-love but not an ethical principle, seeing the absence of human persons. We are called upon to consider three persons when we contemplate a duty to love. This is how perfect love should proceed. Having excluded the love of any one person as an exclusive means of determining principles for the duty to love, we must see the plausible imperfect but perfectible variant of focusing on at least two persons in our considerations. The possibilities here are loving only God and oneself; loving only one's neighbor and oneself; loving only one's neighbor and God. These are three separate sides of the moral triangle, at the vertices of which we find God, the self, and the rest of humanity.

It is possible to approach the love of God, neighbor, and the self through initial love of at least two of the three persons but not through the love of only one person. Were the love of God alone practically possible, then such an approach would be conducive to ultimately loving the three persons. It is unimaginable to contemplate the love of God without an element of reasonable self-love.

---

4. Kant, *Philosophical Theology*, 156.

It is often said that loving your neighbor as yourself is the same as the Golden Rule that commands us to do unto others as we would have them do unto us. Others have gone further to argue that Kant's categorical imperative is a restatement of the Golden Rule. The Golden Rule is devoid of the notion of a religious conscience; it is not surrounded by any reference to God or any theory of humanity as an end. If the absolute worth of every human being cannot be protected, with such protection grounded in the relation of all human beings to God, then the Golden Rule cannot rise to a dependable ethical principle. Even the Babylonians understood that religious connection. Hammurabi was deemed to have been chosen by the gods, and these gods gave him the legal code by whose means the well-being of the people could be enhanced. The rule is quoted today quite detached from the underlying religious inspiration.

If there is no higher principle giving life to the Golden Rule, a society is conceivable where, for instance, some are labeled slaves from birth and the idea is generalized that do unto your slave what you would have them do unto you if you were a slave but, thank God, you are not a slave. This logic applies to the idea of the veil of ignorance in John Rawls. An aristocrat already conscious of the protected status of an aristocrat in society has no further impulse to think differently whether they be behind the veil of ignorance or not. They already know their place in society and can only pretend to imagine being the other. The same holds for the poor in society; were they to legislate, they'd do so reflective of their actual place. There are instances of the poor gaining access to political power and repeating the policies that reduced them to poverty. Only by understanding our duty as commanded by God can we go farther. The command to love your neighbor as yourself, because of its connection to a religious conscience, is a far superior principle that should not be confused with the Golden Rule or the veil of ignorance, if these are viewed as nontheistic sanctions. Even if in the Christian Scriptures reference is made to connect the command with the Golden Rule, it tacitly proceeds from the givenness of God as the author of the imperative.

Love of neighbor and the self are deficient of the love of God. The duty of love executed in this manner has two possible directions. It could proceed from a willful desire to reject the existence of God, even though the idea impinges itself on our conscience, or it could proceed without any clear statement on the relation of ethics to God. In the first case, our arrogance would have to grow with our experience in loving others. The result is a troubled soul that is in denial of its religious nature. The long-term manifestation of this arrogance is a drift to egoism, or altruism as another form of egoism. But where the love of self and neighbor is exercised with an open mind, seeing that in reality God's image inheres in the self and in the other, then it cannot be too long before one's duty to love is performed as an expression of gratitude. Any reflection shows that the gratitude is most properly directed toward God. The end result of a conscientious commitment to love oneself and the neighbor is ultimately loving the three persons of God, oneself, and the rest of humanity.

In a similar manner, the love of God and oneself can hardly proceed for long without extending to the love of neighbor. The Christian Scriptures point out the incoherence of this position and recognize that God is more easily approached by extending the love we devote to ourselves to others. It is tempting to define the rest of humanity as one's friends or family members. Such a careful carving out of humanity amounts to a variant of the love of oneself. It can only last if practiced without the attending love of God. Motion along any one side of the moral triangle must pull us to the direction of the third.

In religious circles, the view is often found that the love of God and the love of others is the perfect duty. This is a problem of language and cultural modesty. If we view the duty to love to be an expression of gratitude, and not just the performance of works for which we are owed a reward, then it is hardly the case that we do not also love ourselves as a way of expressing gratitude to God. It is true that the language of good works and reward in heaven are used in religious texts, but the view is unmistakable that we are not our own creation but God's. If by works we mean the analogy of the situation where part of the monthly allowance a parent gives to a child is used to buy a birthday gift for the parent, we must not lose track of the fact that the behavior is that of responsible stewardship over entrusted capacities and resources.

C. GUILT, INJUSTICE, AND EVIL AS OPPOSITION TO ETHICAL DUTY

The answer to the feeling of guilt and inclination to evil is acknowledging the power of God to forgive us and the usefulness of asking others for forgiveness. It is sometimes asked how we come to yield to the evil propensity in total disregard of our conscience naturally pointing us to the moral direction. We can find many reasons for this but one of them is a feeling that there is injustice in the world and we should use our discretion to punish those we find guilty. We can see clearly what ought to be done and see clearly that most people choose to do evil. We choose to do same not because we enjoy it or approve of it; we may do so as punishment for the injustice in the world. It is not unlikely to see bank robbers who see themselves as justice warriors or murderers who glorify themselves as knights of justice. This approach is unlikely to lead to sustainable inner peace or elevate our will toward a perfect will—that is, a clear conscience that legislates rightly, judges justly, and does not stand condemned in the subsequent analyses of our adopted principles. God is the ultimate judge and source of grace.

The sense of guilt and the feeling that the world is full of injustice can tilt the battle between evil inclinations and the predisposition to do good toward the evil side, thereby mocking our religious conscience. The solution to this situation is not obvious, even if the indication is obvious that we ought to yield to God for forgiveness, practice forgiveness ourselves, and stick to the promptings of conscience to obey the duty to love. No matter how good the principles by which we perform the duty to love, we lack perfect knowledge of contingent truths and knowledge of the future. We are dealing with uncertainties even with our most sensitive religious conscience.

The forgiveness of sins and the further cultivation of the religious conscience are things that find their easiest realization within a systematic religion such as Christianity. In his *Varieties of Religious Experiences*, William James presents many examples of the experiences of those who undergo religious conversion. Some of these proceed with a significant transformation of the will of the person. Some relate the experience of being overwhelmed with joy and wishing the welfare of all mankind. Such experiences point to the impossibility of exclusive focus on the self or on others. One necessarily thinks of welfare in this world and in the next and that welfare is a sense of community. As significant as the problem of guilt and evil is, it is only through the duty of love and the grace of a forgiving God, who is also a God of justice, that we can nonetheless aim at the good of humanity.

While the duty to love God, one's neighbor, and oneself is the main ethical principle, it is conceivable that repeated exercise of the principle in similar contexts can lead to an inventory of useful actionable rules. Thinking through the proper nature of the duty to love in each circumstance may be a time-consuming and difficult task. One aspect of the legislating nature of human beings makes use of repetition and patterns to ease the burden of thought. But where such rules emerge from reflection on the duty to love God, one's neighbor, and oneself, their durability depends on the proper moral education of users. They ought to be familiar with the operation of the universal religious conscience. They must see themselves as people who would freely arrive at similar actionable rules if they appealed to their consciences in determining the way they should perform the duty to love in the codified situations. The extended laws in various systematic religions therefore have their merit, if they can be shown to be consistent with the main principle.

The ethical principle here defended is conducive to the freedom of conscience that is consistent with the freedom of other consciences. The principle relies for its force and preservation on this requirement for justice. One brings one's subjective freedom of conscience into objective universal freedom of conscience. This justice and universalizability of subjectivity also justify punishment and grace.

D. RELATION OF THIS RELIGION-BASED ETHICAL VIEW TO OTHERS

In this chapter, we considered the British moral-sense philosophy to be variations on the idea of the sense of the divine and conscience. In essence, this is linked to the universal minimum religion, albeit enriched with implicit Christian doctrines. Moral-sense theory is developed to counter the egoism of Hobbes (perhaps Hobbes's egoism is exaggerated for greater effect to weaken the opposing doctrine of benevolence). Kant's deontology, we argued, rests on the same view of conscience, but involves a more systematic treatment of the subject and greater attention to the presence of evil propensities.

Sidgwick classified the competing theories into egoistic hedonism, intuitionism, and universal hedonism or utilitarianism (which remain the main contrasts today, despite variations here and there). Having shown that intuitionism is reconcilable with utilitarianism, the difficulty of reconciling self-interest with duty was cognized but the religious solution rejected by prejudice. We have embraced this possibility, but we focus on the universal religious conscience as the moral legislator, internal judge, and defendant in a system where the moral principle is the duty to love God, neighbor, and oneself. This principle can also be viewed as a principle of justice to God, one's neighbor, and oneself.

Utilitarianism, because of its focus on outcomes, can be considered as a weaker, externalist ethical theory whose best intentions are realized by the intuitionist system of the religious conscience. Neither egoism nor altruism in their pure form can enjoy universal consent as plausible ethical theories. But in the context of reasonable self-love and love of neighbor, these all cohere with the love of God in the proposed view. The view sketched here is by no means a systematic account of ethics based on the religious conscience. The sketch is, however, sufficient for us to consider the implication of this on some aspects of politics and law. The usefulness of ethical theories must be tested in their applicability to these areas of applied ethics. The next chapter therefore considers this. A philosopher who revels in discrediting religion-based moral theories should not deserve our attention until they extend their passionate originality to coherent visions of politics, law, economics, and the arts. On the contrary, the logic of religion-based moral theories shines forth in the expansive coherence of such theories with theories in these domains of applied moral philosophy.

CHAPTER 12

Religion-Based Ethics and Reason Affect Politics, Economics, and Law

THE IMPACT OF ETHICS and reason on politics and law can be felt in theories such as the state of nature, the form of government, and the conception of punishment.

We started with the vagueness of reason and offered an account that reveals the subjectivity and fundamental connection of reason to faith. Reason is grounded in faith as we saw in part III where religion was explored. We now have a new system of religion that stretches from the universal minimum religion to systematic and skeptical religion. But there is a common theistic basis with an afterlife commitment that allowed us to sketch a religion-based ethical view at the center of which is a religious conscience. If this treatment of reason, universal minimum religion, and ethics based on a religious conscience is coherent, it must bear on problems of political and legal philosophy. Contrary to ill-fated attempts to show that law and politics are separate from morality and religion, it is impossible to consistently make the case for a good political system and legal order while avoiding direct engagement with ethics and religion. It is therefore proper for us to consider the impact on politics and law of a religious conscience that claims universality as well as the impact of reason that is fundamentally subjective and grounded in faith.

Talking about the implication of the views in this book on politics and law can take on a very broad dimension. This would distract from the arc of exploration from reason, through our uncertainty about contingent truths, to religion, and then ethics. We must restrict ourselves to a few examples as indicative of the fact that ethical theories and theories of reason must perturb political, economic, and legal debates.

In this chapter, we intend to consider four ideas that may be impacted by the system of religious conscience as it relates to reason. These are (1) the state of nature, (2) liberal socialism, (3) multiparty constitutional democracy, and (4) punishment. These are just a few of the many problems encountered in politics and law that can be affected by our commitment to an account of reason or ethical theory.

Theories of the state of nature rationalize the existence of the state. Being largely hypothetical, they proceed from a certain supposition of the dominant natures of human beings outside the framework of a state and government. There are competing accounts, ranging from pessimistic views such as Hobbes's, to more optimistic ones such as Locke's, or even romantic accounts such as Rousseau's uncivilized society. If we are positing the existence of a universal minimum religion, a battle within each soul between original moral predisposition and inclination to evil, ethics based on a religious conscience, and reason grounded in faith, then our point of departure would have to consider the external conditions of society that can influence the expression of these human features. We must recognize the primacy of law in the social condition. Law emerges before government, which, most agree, must be constituted by a legal process—a social contract. The emergence of government can occur at different stages of the socialization process.

If we depart from the system that constitutes the religious conscience, we must recognize that what we consider to be our property is something entrusted to us for our benefit and to the glory of God, which glory includes taking care of his creation. That commits us to taking care of the environment in a manner that expresses gratitude. It also commits us to embracing that form of government that best expresses this gratitude to God and caters to the warring factions within each soul. No one person should be trusted boundlessly with the exercise of authority. We must also doubt the arrogance of property hoarding through laws whose ethical bases are questionable. These concerns seem to propel us in the direction of greater sympathy with liberal socialism as a system in which political liberalism and socioeconomic considerations stand in healthy tension. They also propel us in the direction of support for multiparty constitutional democracy, be it a republic or a constitutional monarchy. In these two contexts, a dialectic emerges that constrains the course of human affairs toward moral progress.

Regarding punishment, we ought to be guided by notions of justice that is tempered with grace and aiming at the reformation of an insensitive conscience. Our legislation cannot rely fully on the generation of thousands of positive laws that an ordinary citizen is unlikely to know or remember. It is the formation of the religious conscience that should be privileged.

Punishment must aim at restoring the individual to that state of religious conscience where they understand themselves to be legislating, judging, and defending themselves in the court of conscience as they aim at perfecting a good will—that is, a will whose aim is goodness, beauty, truth, and justice. The reasonableness of capital punishment cannot be successfully upheld. With respect to international morality, the absence of a world government with coercive authority does not absolve nations of crimes against other nations. By reflecting on the key fact that law precedes government, and that law is based on morality, humanity holds enormous power in promoting international morality among nation states.

A. THE STATE OF NATURE AND THE PRIMACY OF LAW

Law is the socialization of the operations of the religious conscience. In conscience, the human being is legislator, judge, and defender in the court of conscience, all three persons in an individual. The individual owes their being to the Supreme Being who is monarch, not despot, and governs the world through moral laws. By means of language, the individual can externalize the operations of their conscience and practice division of labor to meet their many needs.

Even if we start from a single family, we see that parents play a complementary role in meeting the needs of each other. When a child is born, their upbringing consists in learning a language and training of the conscience to avoid certain things while being encouraged to pursue others. As the child becomes wiser and able to process various contingent truths, they begin to appreciate the accordance of parental laws with the legislation of the conscience. Conscience stands to err if fed with the wrong contingent truths and improper anticipation of the future. But when many more children arrive, the ability of the parents is scrutinized with respect to acting justly in their administration of the law and cultivation of children's conscience. Even within a family, we can see tension arising between justice and grace. Punishment to restore justice and grace are questioned for their reasonableness.

Grace and justice differ in that people judge differently when presented with a case where person A injures person B. If we are closer to person A, we are likely to testify of A's good conscience and virtues, demanding clemency on this favorable basis. But if we are closer to person B, we sympathize with their fear of a lawless society where anyone can harm us and get away with it. People closer to B are therefore likely to demand justice in the form of punishment for A. But what punishment is commensurate with the injury is not an easy question to decide. It ranges from a disproportionately large penalty to grace or simple warning. Within a human conscience, a divergence between justice and defense of conscience generates guilt in some but not in others, depending on their decision to regard or disregard the judgment of conscience.

In an unfortunate situation where the father of a family accords more grace and benevolence toward some children than to others, and if this is worsened by the mother doing the same with a different set of children, we have a situation of a civil war within the family. But suppose the children are grown up and that there is enough land to migrate away. The situation can be diffused by children moving away from their parents. Perhaps this can even trigger repentance and family reunion in future.

We thus see that the conscience can lead to a society where a sense of justice exists without an explicit government. It is wrong to think of parents as constituting a government, God being the Supreme Magistrate who governs through conscience and the mutual expression of gratitude to him by human beings. It must then be clear to us that law precedes the formation of a government. In fact, the emergence of a government is an act of law when this is through a social contract. A government emerges through a violation of the moral law, when this government is imposed by a conquering people.

From these observations, we can see that population density, among other factors, can account for the variations in the various accounts of the state of nature in history. The concept of the state of nature is unfortunate; it brings along with it the concept of the law of nature whose main goal is to eclipse the universality of the human conscience and the innate inclination to evil among human beings. We can only agree with Kant when he says that to intimate that someone lacks a conscience is only to say that they have evolved to the point where they yield to their inclinations to evil while completely ignoring the prompting of their conscience. We must also see the hierarchy of morality: the foundation is religion, upon which is built moral philosophy, then comes law, and after law emerges politics and economics. Under law can be understood other customs of a people. If this view is correct, then the foundation of positive law must be wanting, unless we view the positing of laws as a transitive stage that lies between moral philosophy and politics. But the contrary of positive law is not natural law, if we understand this to be accessible to us through objective reason. No, the opposite of positive law is moral law; that is, law that recognizes its foundation to be morality that is based on a universal religious conscience. It is the operation of the religious conscience that is invoked when the idea of the law of nature is invoked by Hobbes and Locke.

How Can Population Density Explain the Variation in Theories of the State of Nature?

Theories of the state of nature vary from a very pessimistic account by Hobbes to optimistic views such as that of Rousseau or more pragmatic positions such as that of Locke. It can be said that Rousseau writes from a Calvinist background with awareness of the central ideas of Rom 2:14–15—the law of conscience. His genius lies in giving dignity to the so-called primitive peoples of the world. In the history of Africa, one can find the peculiar role of those elevated to chiefs in some societies. Their primary role consisted in acting as magistrates, not as overbearing governors with coercive powers. Among the most severe punitive sentences were banishment from the tribe, not necessarily death sentences. But as tribes grew bigger, considerations of war gave way to military organizations. Tribes can go to war for one of three reasons: envy of another tribe endowed with resources (euphemized as self-interest), preemptive attack by a prosperous tribe against a tribe they suspect might attack them in future (paranoia camouflaged as fear), or retributive attack against a tribe that attacked them in the past (vengeance as justice). Resources and pride are therefore usually lurking behind such wars. The same conflicts can arise within a given society. Population densities can be used to describe the relation among theories of nature, if we admit that there is a dynamic progression that starts with the socialization of the religious conscience and ends in the deplorable state of Hobbes's war of all against all.

To see how population density can influence the various phases of the pregovernmental form of society, we can turn to Ibn Khaldun who theorizes on the dynamics of human civilizations in his *Muqaddimah*, using the idea of *asabiyyah*—that is, social solidarity or group feeling. According to Ibn Khaldun, group feeling exists within societies, ranging from nomadic societies to states and large empires. This asabiyyah undergoes changes, such that it is strongest at the beginning, as in nomadic tribes, and declines as the civilization advances and eventually dies out. A typical society marked by asabiyyah may last 120 years or three generations of 40 years each.

One can therefore find in the nomadic phase of asabiyyah such an optimistic outlook of the group as sketched by Rousseau. This is a condition of low population density that corresponds to abundance of land and other resources. The operation of the religious conscience must be such that it is also easy to determine the wrong party in a given dispute at that stage of society. A standing magistrate is not needed; judges may be chosen as the need arises. In the history of the people of Israel, we hear of the period of Judges, who were effectively war leaders with the task of repelling or attacking troublesome remnant tribes among the Israelites or other Israelite tribes in internal conflict. But in the state of nature at the early stage of society, judges serve the role of deciding cases among its members.

This pragmatic solution, however, cannot withstand the strain of rapid population increase in a constrained area of land with limited resources. Inefficiencies therefore arise and lead to a society akin to that described by Locke. However, even at this stage, the concept of common law as the externalization and socialization of the religious conscience is never lost. If these deficiencies are not remedied by the establishment of a functional government, the society can descend into a more chaotic state, marked by injustice, limited resources, and lack of trust in the operation of the consciences of our neighbors. This is the pessimistic situation depicted by Hobbes. A strong government must emerge, but such a government must see its role as the establishment of impersonal constitutions and such laws as can revive the sensitivity of the conscience of each citizen toward greater trust in one another. For there to be relative freedom, the strong government must move in the direction of reducing the powers of any one person lest the leadership falls into the hands of a tyrant.

But a cycle of asabiyyah ends with the birth of another asabiyyah. Historically, Hobbes's theory of the state of nature is shaped by the state of war that marked his generation. Prior to his birth, England had known times of peaceful government. It is therefore possible to go from a state of government to a state of nature and back; but what state of nature we have in mind depends on the prevailing characteristics. Thus, England in the time of Hobbes and France in the post-Revolution era are examples of the transition from a state of government to a state of nature marked by inefficiencies that border on the war of all against all.

If we admit that population density plays a role in the transition from a peaceful state of nature to a brutish state and then to a state of government, we face difficulties in explaining the rise and fall of social solidarity or asabiyyah. This social solidarity within a government is thus a transition from a peaceful state of nature to a peacefully governed state, and then to a chaotic government that gives way to a new empire or dynasty or new form of government. The descent to the brutish state of nature may be caused by a high population density. This is a measure of limited material resources and limited opportunities for amicable settlement of differences by trustworthy volunteer judges.

This descent to chaos can also be occasioned by the ego of those who want to play the role of supreme magistrate or legislators. As the population grows, the desire for fame grows with it; and people, being legislators by nature, desire to see themselves as legislators of their fellow men and women.

Herein lies another density as driving force for change of the social structure—the density of egos in a peaceful state of nature. The inclination to evil in every human being is strong enough to create a brutish state of nature between two siblings or between a parent and a child where, although there is material abundance, there is scarcity of positions of fame. In the biblical account, we see Saul express hatred toward David as possible future king, and we see Absalom rise against his father King David to seize the throne.

If we start from a universal religious conscience, further account for the evil propensity of human beings, their conscience notwithstanding, and furthermore factor in population density and egos, then we can see that the state of nature that is initially peaceful progresses to an inefficient state and finally descends into a brutish state of strife. At any stage of the evolution of the state of nature, it can transition into a state of government. But this is not the ultimate end of the process; a return to a brutish state of nature is possible. This can be occasioned by a high population density if this is accompanied by inefficient bureaucracy or hypercentralization and corruption.

The state of minimum anarchy advocated by Robert Nozick[1] as a libertarian solution is only a cautionary measure against inefficient bureaucracy. But as a sustainable solution, it is untenable because it is based on a faulty reading of the nature of a human being in society. Certainly humanity must be treated as an end in itself. Nozick, in further developing the ideas of Locke and Kant, overlooks the Kantian idea of asocial sociability—human beings are caught in the tension of selfishness and cooperation. This corresponds to the battle in the human soul between the operation of a religious conscience and an evil inclination in all human beings. It guarantees benevolence and justice and equally inclines toward evil and selfishness.

We are thus led to see that the religious conscience regulates a peaceful state of nature, but this state is not void of the inclination to evil and human selfishness. At all stages of the evolution of the state of nature toward a brutish state or a governed state, human beings socialize and externalize the religious conscience into common law. Law emerges before any government; therefore, law posited by an established government is untenable as an account of the true source of law. The one who posits a government as a solution reasons from the religious conscience that is already bound up with the idea of moral law. The originator of government reasons from conscience toward a better vision of the society, away from the brutish state of nature, and perhaps does so under the impulse of nostalgia about the original peaceful state of nature marked by low population density and under the influence of the religious conscience.

---

1. Nozick, *Anarchy, State, and Utopia*, 3–6.

B. THE PLAUSIBILITY OF LIBERAL SOCIALISM

If we build on the religious conscience, further admit of a peaceful state of nature that degenerates into an inefficient or brutish state of nature, and if we embrace the necessity of a government arising through a legal process (social contract), then we must reflect on the features of such a government. These features must be consistent with the nature of human beings, and they must strive toward the universal religious conscience that grounds morality, law, and makes government possible.

The Enlightenment thinkers, many of whom were influenced by the Protestant doctrine of conscience, produced certain elements of a government that are consistent with the nature of human beings. From the sacred nature or inviolable dignity of the individual human being, and their existence as being grounded in the will of a Supreme Being, we arrive at the ideas of the rule of law, government by the consent of the governed (through political representation and laid-down guidelines), certain inseparable human rights, private and public property rights, freedom of association, and freedom of speech. These ideas can be shown to cohere with the fundamental religious conscience that allows for the socialization of that conscience, notwithstanding human inclinations to evil. The religious conscience recognizes God as the Supreme Magistrate and benevolent Monarch. It also places the individual in the position of stewardship over what we see as their private property, talents, and personal labor.

Taxonomy has played an unkind trick on humankind by labeling these attributes of the state that cohere with the religious conscience as republicanism. By adding the economic feature of free markets, governed by an "invisible hand," we obtain the concept of liberalism or capitalism. In this nomenclature, the social dimension of the state and the stewardship relation of human beings to their property are eclipsed by an economic individualism that is not in accordance with the religious conscience.

In reaction to the problems arising from economic liberalism, socialism is proposed and often treated as synonymous to the doctrines of Karl Marx. Marxist socialism identifies a struggle between the working class—the proletariat—and those who own the means of production—the bourgeoise. Through dialectic materialism, a victory of the proletariat over the bourgeoisie is inevitable.

Dialectic materialism posits the centrality of material things to historical evolution; historic events are to be seen as the striving of opposite forces. But this idea of the striving of opposites we already encounter in Greek thought, with Heraclitus suggesting that everything is in flux and harmony arises from the striving of contraries. In this understanding of the dialectic of opposites, we must acknowledge that ideas are as real as material things. The actions of human beings on material things are directed by ideas. The movement of history cannot only be treated by a dialectic of material things; a dialectic of propelling ideas must equally be considered.

Marxist ideology is optimistic regarding the future harmony of a world in which the means of production are in the hands of the proletariat, but it is pessimistic with respect to the bourgeoisie. This fragmentation of humanity is arbitrary and not grounded in truth. The doctrine of the religious conscience that makes society possible acknowledges the universality of an original moral predisposition in all human beings—proletariat or bourgeoisie. But that same conscience, based on its ability to reflect on itself in the inner court, is also acutely aware that in all of us lurks a demon with strong evil inclinations. The Marxist fails to see the nested relation of people in economic systems. One can be both a proletariat and a bourgeoisie. If the religious conscience is empowered within free ethical communities, evil inclinations can be brought under control. But the Marxist, void of any benevolence in their theory, is a supposed atheist. This is a logical route once the mistake is made of subscribing to the supremacy of the material in the motion of history. History is propelled by the will, not the material, even if the determination of the will is influenced by material considerations. The radical empiricist cannot see this motion of history because the sensible world is all they stare at in a closed-minded manner.

A closed-minded, atheistic, nonbenevolent Marxist socialism cannot be reconciled with our conception of reason as being fundamentally grounded in a religious conscience.

But a religious socialism follows from the idea of God as the giver of all things that we possess. Our temporary ownership of property is really a condition of stewardship. But this private property is entrusted to us for our benefit and to the glory of God. As a means of giving glory to God, we can share our property with others in a condition of need. If the political and legal systems around us are in fact externalizations of the religious consciences of the citizens, then we can find it useful to make efficient arrangements to take care of the needs of all in a society, without diminishing our positions as original stewards of the talents and property directly entrusted to us by God through our labor, and further development of our personal talents. The socialist spirit is thus ingrained in the society that has as its basis the universal religious consciences of the citizens.

Such socialism based on universal religion and the rule of law does make the human being truly free to flourish in society. Human beings in that condition can express their individuality in accordance with a religious conscience and maintain an attitude of gratitude toward God. But the protections of human beings in society against tyranny or a slide into the brutish state of nature needs those attributes of society that have been subtly labeled liberalism or capitalistic republicanism. Liberal socialism ought to be viewed as the system that best protects the individual against tyranny and anarchy while creating an economic space where everyone can flourish in their varied expression of gratitude to God. If the rule of law can be taken to be what we call political liberalism, and if economic mobility can be viewed as the religious socialism we advocate, then we must see that they constitute what is called liberal socialism. That liberal socialism, protective of property rights and free exchange of goods and services within regulated bounds, does make human beings truly free. They can flourish, unencumbered by the fear of tyranny, anarchy, or abject poverty.

That the direction for the future is liberal socialism can be indicated by what we see in Protestant northern Europe. What is surprising is that these are mostly constitutional monarchies, not necessarily republican governments. Since the diagnostic material for socialism was obtained from the effects of the industrial revolution in countries such as England, Karl Marx's predictions for socialist revolutions would have been expected to start in England. They didn't start there precisely because the religious conscience was operative in that society, with responsible Christian politicians such as William Gladstone and moderate socialist activists.

The prevailing political leadership must recognize the power of institutions in protecting the welfare of all, especially the vulnerable in society. That political class must listen to the people by whose will, and for whose welfare, they govern. The rich employers and owners of capital, if they have any idea of their relation of stewardship and gratitude, must be moved to care for the welfare of their workers as discovered through open consultative deliberations. The state must allow people to associate freely and permit even workers to associate and start a business in balanced competition with other businesses. A political leader of William Gladstone's character can easily nullify predictions of socialist revolutions by showing that economic liberalism (capitalism) can be brought to embrace the acceptable parts of the mixed solutions proposed by liberal socialism.

With respect to economic liberalism, the idea that this is possible can only arise from a system with a low population density and abundant resources. Human beings are by nature conservative, even if they equally long for a better tomorrow. The conservative part can predominate and thus bring out a conservative economic liberalism in societies such as the USA with a historically low population density. This conservative economic liberalism is at odds with liberal socialism, especially with respect to the regulation of the market and the allocation of public resources to basic and commonly needed goods and services. The asocial sociability of human beings suggested by Kant is better served in the hybrid system of liberal socialism than in either pure economic liberalism or pure socialism. Most liberal systems today admit of socialistic features in areas of large-scale education, health care, and labor organizations. But socialization of economic liberalism is a matter of degree. There is room for improvement toward such a degree that better accords with the nature of human beings in society. We should never lose sight of the fact that human beings are endowed with a minimum religious conscience that grounds the legal, political, and economic organization of a society toward the flourishing of all its members.

Economic liberalism in its capitalistic expression cannot successfully use reason to justify its plausibility. This is so because reason immediately brings us to the religious conscience from which arises the need to treat humanity as an end. It also leads us to recognize the universality of human inclination to evil, if the religious conscience is not ethically socialized in the form of laws and political institutions that regulate economic phenomena. Any conception of reason that rejects its dependence on a religious conscience is veiled sophistry; it cannot be used to justify any other substantive claim or metaphysic.

Socialism that crushes the inviolable dignity of the individual human being can neither be defended by empiricism nor reason. A religiously grounded socialism would cognize the inviolable human dignity in every individual human being. Human nature will rudely correct any fallacious thinking that brings us to imagine a socialism that crushes the individual in the crowd of the social and attempts to practically realize that fantasy. This we have seen with the Marxist socialist systems that have been tried. Nothing founded on faulty human nature can prosper, and we know that it is faulty when it violates the dictates of the religious conscience or the dignity of the individual.

It is in liberal socialism that the virtues of political liberalism unite with the features of socialism because they are compatible with the universal religious conscience.

C. THE REASONABLENESS OF MULTIPARTY CONSTITUTIONAL DEMOCRACY

A multiparty constitutional democracy is the representative system of government that best accords with a society grounded by a religious conscience and conscious of our inherent inclinations to evil. A one-party system is at variance with the religious conscience and human weakness; it necessarily manifests its failure in tyranny, incompetence arising from lack of political competition, and widespread corruption. The constitutional democracy can be a republic or a constitutional monarchy. The accompanying multiparty democratic process shields citizens from oppressive single-mindedness and cronyism. The regulating constitution should be marked by stability and should be drafted consultatively by people of a good religious conscience, foresighted, and rich in knowledge of contingent truths about nature and human nature.

The constitution cannot be seen as an instrument at the disposal of elected officials who can completely overwrite or modify at their own will. Unlimited power in the hands of a few attracts wealth, and the union of disproportionate wealth and power in the hands of a few always produces arrogant tyranny. It is impossible for someone to claim to be more informed and sensitive about the needs of people than the people themselves. A multiparty constitutional democracy therefore recommends itself as the path to the flourishing of a community that externalizes the religious conscience of its citizens while limiting the undesirable effects of the evil inclinations of an oppressive majority or a wealthy and powerful few. This arrangement of society enables that, through the general will of the people, good always triumphs over evil, even if by a slim margin. The precondition for this triumph of the general will is transparent elections, preceded by free and informative debates, and conducted in accordance with preestablished rules by the constitution and laws established in accordance with that constitution. But in cases where a mistake is made, the people retain a nonbloody constitutional path to dispose of any tyrannical band that comes to power.

We arrive at these ideas when we consider some relevant questions and the givenness of the religious conscience as the axiom of any speculation about arrangements of a socially contracted government. We ask ourselves key questions. Who should govern in a society where the religious conscience of individuals has given rise to a system of laws and a government? What type of arrangement should the government have? If no human being can be trusted to be morally perfect and infinitely wise as to know the contingent facts that bear on the welfare of all in the state, then is it wise to set up an absolute monarch? The romantic view of liberating anarchy suggested by the libertarian who opposes the idea of a government is not convincing because our innate asocial sociability points us to the reasonableness of a government. We instinctively grasp that a state of government and its attendant rule of law help us to flourish.

A kind of pessimism can be discerned in the conversations of learned folks regarding the ability of citizens to determine what is good for themselves. If it is true that people cannot be trusted to determine what is good for themselves, then democracy may not be the best way to determine who should govern or what we ought to do. But such an argument does not hold sway if we assert the existence of a universal religious conscience and the dignity with which every human life ought to be treated as an end in itself. It is true that our knowledge may differ on the contingent truths that are needed to chart a course of action from a given circumstance to a moral goal. But guaranteeing the freedom of association and the freedom of speech can remedy these gradients in knowledge to the extent that evil inclinations and ignorance about contingent truths do not overcome the right judgment of the good and informed conscience on the matters that are subjected to a vote.

Is the recommended constitutional democracy consistent with any form of socialism? Friedrich Hayek, in his *Road to Serfdom*, asserts that socialism always leads to totalitarianism and a state of serfdom for the citizens. This is not universally true; it is true mostly of Marxist socialism that purports to be atheistic and is illogically optimistic about the morality of the liberated proletariat. Anyone acquainted with the religious conscience would know that the oppressor and the oppressed have deep within their being dangerous inclinations to evil, even if the degrees of these inclinations vary. A society marked by such a realistic conception of the human conscience will always tend toward liberal socialism with an unmistakable religious foundation. Even if Protestant northern Europe cannot be classified as liberal socialist, the socialist degree in the arrangement of political and economic life is noticeable. This is protected by a multiparty constitutionalism that can be monarchical or republican. The answer is therefore affirmative that constitutional democracy and realistic variants of socialism can, or should, coexist.

That the constitutional democracy should be multiparty in nature is hardly to be questioned. To impose consensus through a one-party system is to stifle the driving forces for development and extirpate the spirit of freedom. Most African states after independence, attracted to Marxist socialist centralization, adopted one-party systems that often degenerated into corruption and authoritarianism. But in the 1990s, forced to recognize the need for multiparty politics, some of these African states have gone the opposite direction. It is not unusual to find a state with hundreds of mushroom political parties that are created and promoted by a dominant ruling party as a means of frustrating any constructively competitive opposition. It seems therefore that a multiparty constitutional democracy is best served by a system with a few strong political parties, perhaps two to six. While this arrangement may not eliminate all the inefficiencies that may come with multiple political positions on an issue, people are best served by these contrasting possibilities. The ensuing dialectics align with the idea of a religious conscience that remains aware of the internal conflict with evil inclinations and our fragmentary knowledge of contingent truths.

Even in such a multiparty constitutional democracy, disenchantment of the population is possible. This comes about when citizens feel that their votes do not matter and they have no real part to play in the government of their affairs. This disenchantment can be minimized by a federal system of government, where power is devolved and authority is shared between the federal government and the local governments. The danger in this arrangement is strife between the local and federal government that can lead to inaction. But where this strife exists, it can only spur reforms toward greater mutual understanding and efficiency.

We see that most Marxist socialist systems fail to realize political systems with these features. The reason for this is that their reasoning is fallacious because they are not based on a clear understanding of the religious conscience. They do not have the right understanding of universal human nature, yet they are too optimistic about the goodness of the oppressed in society and their ability to govern by consensus after the defeat of the bourgeoisie. We cannot claim to arrive at organizations of society using objective reason, when such reason does not admit the universal religious conscience as a noninferential point of departure. In addition to this, we must admit the battle between good dispositions and evil inclinations, and our fallible knowledge of contingent truths about nature and human nature.

The conflict between the universal religious conscience and the natural human inclination to evil resolves in favor of a flourishing society when that society is governed as a multiparty constitutional democracy. False optimism about human nature or pretentious elitism and belief in objective reason can lead to tyrannical forms of government with coercive mechanisms for manufacturing consent. This state is not conducive to human flourishing.

In general, today it is less controversial to assert that a multiparty constitutional democracy is to be preferred over elitist alternatives that are built on the assumption that the masses are less intelligent in political matters. The nineteenth and early twentieth centuries witnessed resistance to constitutional democracy, especially in predominantly Catholic Europe. Gustave Le Bon's famous work *The Crowd: A Study of the Popular Mind* should be read from this perspective of skepticism about the fruitful externalization of individuals' consciences. The context of Le Bon's observation is Catholic France, where radical revolutions were attempted by the masses and resisted by the aristocracy with the Catholic Church's support. The demerits of radical revolutions, such as arising from the French Revolution, are more carefully analyzed by Edmund Burke in his *Reflections on the Revolution in France*, without diminishing the achievements and merits of parliamentary government. But in France, the radical impulses of the people, combined with and further promoted by the resistance to change by reactionary elitism and the Roman Catholic Church, lead to the conclusion offered by Le Bon. To him, crowds are necessarily less moral and less intelligent. This view wrongly suggests that a parliamentary government arising from democratic processes is an attempt to normalize that crowd psychology with its attendant lesser moral status and intelligence.[2]

The pessimistic conclusion reached by Le Bon can be avoided. This involves emphasizing the role of constitutions in any democratic externalization of the consciences of human beings. It also involves a fundamental commitment to the freedom of speech, making any outrageous speech an argument that can be refuted in free debate. If we understand all human beings to be endowed with a minimum religious conscience, we can approach any outrageous or radical revolutionary claim with the goal of separating the seed of the good and the just in it from the associated contaminating bad, unjust, and awful. A potentially violent crowd can lose its radicalism if the inherent element of justice and goodness in their grievances can be separated and channeled toward a more pragmatic resolution or dialectical synthesis. One may argue that it is this kind of political dialectics that has shaped predominantly Protestant northern Europe and Protestant North America. From this perspective, the merits of multiparty constitutional democracy as a mechanism of responsible dialectical organization of a community's politics are hard to refute.

D. PUNISHMENT

The idea of punishment is implicit in the idea of law. Starting from a religious conscience and the idea that law precedes the state (even if law is later reformed by the state), positive law is shallow and erroneous. We cannot judge the coherence of law and a religious conscience purely from the positing of law by a sovereign who may happen to be a vicious tyrant or mob. The idea of punishment must therefore be approached based on the clear connection between law and morality as expressed in the underlying universal religious conscience.

Our instinctive grasp of the necessity of punishment can be used to partially explain the origin of our evil inclinations. These inclinations may arise from our wrongfully asserted right to punish humanity or specific

2. Le Bon, *Crowd*, 118.

individuals, or from our blowing a justified minimum punishment out of proportion. We can even bring ourselves to a position of desiring to punish God for a perceived wrong toward us or toward mankind. The supposed atheist pronounces judgment on God with respect to the problem of evil from such presumptuous, erroneous, and ungrateful thinking. If our inclination to evil, derived from a perceived right to punish, can be minimized by a right conception of the nature and degree of punishment, how can we come to the correct understanding of punishment? This is a difficult question.

In formulating theories of punishment, our thinking should be constrained and guided by reflection on the relation between the Supreme Being and human beings. God desires that we all have an abundant life here on earth and salvation in the afterlife. But being a just and gracious God who honors the gift of free will bestowed on us, he also punishes in this earthly life to correct us, and in the afterlife to lead us to the path of our dominant passion—namely, rebellion against the moral predisposition. A crime against the prevailing law offsets the motion of the society in a morally approved manner. The readjustment of the course of life in that society requires reassurance about the protective power of the law. The society needs to see the wrongful action as an aberration, and not as a source of fear and unpredictability about one's safety in society. This reassurance is achieved through retribution or rehabilitation or both.

An unbalanced view of human nature, not informed by the religious conscience, may exclusively advocate either for retribution or for rehabilitation. Retributive exclusivism is the case with those who overweight the depravity of human nature and elevate it to a more powerful force than the original human predisposition to morality. This view, claiming to secure justice for the society, generates more fear in those who are conscious of the inner battle between our evil inclination and the good will. It ultimately leads the criminal to despondency that can manifest itself through worser crimes. The advocate for rehabilitation as the sole response to wrongdoing is an optimistic, healthy-minded religionist who is in denial of the reality of inherent evil inclination as a potent force that can render the religious conscience numb or overburdened with guilt. The rehabilitationist cannot persist in their position for a long time, because sooner or later the criminal takes advantage of the society, and a general fear of potential harm descends on all. A concrete manifestation of human evil inclination may suddenly transform the same rehabilitation advocate to an extreme retributionist, with the rehabilitationist feeling betrayed by the criminal.

There is historical evidence that human beings tend to lean heavily toward retribution. If one is to classify attitudes toward clemency, it would turn out that the offended mob is the least gracious, followed by the more humane laws of a society, and followed by the most gracious Supreme Being. The justice and grace of the Supreme Being are perfectly tempered to bring about moral perfection through a combination of grace, correction, and punishment of unrepentant evil doers. Human law attains its more clement position by virtue of the reflections on the emotions that enter legislation within a constitutional democracy. This means that for human law to be viewed as generally more humane than the law of the mob, its rules must be established prior to the occasion where they are applied. In homogeneous communities, it is possible for humane laws to appear even in the state of nature, prior to the constitution of the state. In heterogeneous communities, laws may lack universality, or dominant groups may apply mercy and justice differently, even in a constituted state. Such was the case with African Americans in the days of lynching and other cruel punishments in the USA. Only the Supreme Being has the capacity to be offended by human behavior and yet remain true to his character of a just and gracious magistrate. It cannot be that a legal system depends on the one who has been injured to pronounce justice; they are more likely to approach that particular judgment from the position of maximum, and possibly incommensurate, retribution.

Why are we justified to punish anyone? We presuppose the freedom of the will in punishing the actions of a moral agent. We consider that the agent could have done otherwise but acted in a manner that offsets the harmonious conduct of social life according to moral laws. A curious situation arises when people act based on impulses determined by addiction. There is a sense in which people who suffer addiction lose their free will to a certain extent. They, or others, may be responsible for their first addiction but once in the grip of addiction, such as alcoholism, drugs, etc., their will is partially determined by the biological cravings for the object of their addiction. Their religious conscience is weakened or silenced, and their evil inclinations unite with the uncontrolled passion for a specific action. This situation must be perplexing for those who view punishment purely through the lens of retribution, but it clearly points to the need for the society to take decisive actions aimed at rehabilitation of the criminal. That can mean curtailing the rights of the person to refuse rehabilitation, since their very condition predisposes them to resist any intervention that would restore the sensitivity of their religious conscience. Rehabilitation restores the strength of their will to oblige as duty commands actions of love and justice.

How often are we called upon to punish in a well-constituted society? Crimes and other injuries in a society are supposed to be rare occurrences. We can determine from some data that our societies are structured with this tacit understanding that the good is stronger than the evil in us. Around the world, the police force is generally about or below five police officers to one thousand residents. This number could be higher in authoritarian states. From analysis of the data by World Prison Brief, the average carceral capacity of modern states is about one prison place per one thousand residents, except in the USA where the statistics approach five to six prison places per one thousand residents.[3] These two observations support the fact that a purely retributive punishment theory cannot guarantee the harmony that societies seek. But someone may object to the use of prison and police capacities to inform our reasoning on these matters; they may say that these are empirical observations without any justifying principles. To this skepticism we reply that this situation emerges from the religious conscience that has always guided society. The dialectics of the good conscience and the evil inclinations of the externalized consciences of the population, on average, tends to the good, making crime a rarity.

How should the religious conscience be further cultivated, considering our previous discussion on the extension or systematization of the inherent minimum religion? The answer lies in a proper philosophy of education of youths. The general tenor of Plato in his *Laws* and *Republic* is a rigorous moral upbringing of citizens and a theory of punishment that leans toward rehabilitation, as discussed earlier in the case of the problematic atheist who would normally be denied the right to live in a Platonic society. It has been a common mistake for some anti-Platonists to paint him as an inflexible totalitarian political thinker. For instance, in *The Open Society and Its Enemies*, Karl Popper takes this view against Plato. The open society is not possible if the youths in the society are denied the rigorous moral training that empowers them to wrestle and win the battle between the good-willed religious conscience and the evil inclinations within. Education is central to that cultivation of conscience, but even in education care must be taken because certain evil propensities may be promoted at the detriment of the society. True freedom is when we are free to act in accordance with a good will, whose goodness includes justice to others. In a lesser form, freedom cultivates a conscience that enables recognition and correction of one's conscience's willing, when one mistakenly wills and acts contrary to the good conscience. But a systematic attempt to anesthetize the conscience against the reflective judgment of evil inclinations can only make a supposed freedom become tyranny against any sensitive religious conscience. We have said that true atheism is impossible but if we observe our institutions of learning, a pattern would be discerned where such incoherent metaphysics is propounded with dogmatic fervor. Plato would not approve of such an

---

3. World Prison Brief, "Prison Population Total."

education of a supposedly free and open society, and he would be deemed an enemy of the open society.

We said that contingent truths are necessary for proper coordination of the goals of the religious conscience with the means of attaining that goal. The system of contingent truths implicated in reason grows exponentially as our societies become more complex, and as the means of action at our disposal become more scientific. To function well as a reasoning being (one who coordinates religious conscience with contingent truths in attaining specific goals), we must acquire a good education. The beauty of education is that it can make us appear as human beings who are two thousand years old or older—we draw on the best insights that history, physics, and sociology have produced. The failure of the pre-university educational system and the costly nature of higher education in the USA can partially explain the unusual high carceral capacity. To these problems can be added the fact that prisons are partly outsourced to businesses whose goal is to make a profit. This is contrary to the system produced by conscience where prison capacity remains at about 0.1 percent around the world and it is often not maxed out, whereas the USA approaches 1 percent.

The punishment of individuals in society must therefore be balanced between retribution and rehabilitation. Retribution tends toward maximum justice to correct the evil course of society arising from a crime. It does so by deterrence of others or same person, and by compensating the injured. Rehabilitation tends toward grace and the view that the conscience can be trained to overcome the inclinations to evil. Where a heterogeneous society exists, a grave danger presents itself when the balance between justice and grace is tilted against one group by a more powerful one. The result is the loss for all. We find complaints about discrepancies between grace and justice as applied to African and European Americans in the USA. As we have seen from the police and carceral capacities, such differences, if systemic and widely known, can plunge the system into anarchy if the discriminated group is sizeable—for instance, at least 1 percent. It can overwhelm the institution charged with punishment.

But if law builds on a religious conscience and its battle with the evil inclination, any society faced with unjust laws cannot endure. The dialectics of asocial sociability, the contraries of good and evil (with slight advantage of the good), will always produce a fairer system in the course of time. The condition for this is the absence of disproportionately deadly weapons and highly organized systems against the smaller units.

We have been talking about punishment of individuals, but what about nations and states? If we look beyond the modern state where human beings stand before the law, we encounter states who may choose to operate in accordance with national evil inclinations rather than the prompting of the moral law. This situation can be said to be the perverse situation of power in the hands of a few who oppress the many within and outside the state. It is a serious problem. The helplessness of the United Nations as an enforcer of good behavior among nations, the emergence of situational alliances around the world, and the differences in the sizes of states, all create conditions for criminal behavior of states against other states. One can only turn to the concept of international morality when we speak of international law or the law of nations.

If we are wedded to the idea of positive law, then it appears that we are totally helpless, given the absence of an international sovereign with legislatively binding authority. But if we follow the implications of the religious conscience, we first admit that there can be no such thing as positive law in a pure sense—that is, the view that law is only law if posited by a sovereign authority. We must also reject the nomenclature of natural law as the opposite of positive law, if by natural law we mean what is common in the Catholic Church's world of ideas. We must speak of moral law or morally grounded law, this being what we previously called the equivalent of Protestant natural law. This law we discover not from natural theology in the Catholic sense, where we follow the general Protestant view that this natural theology is without any binding force on morality. The proper origin of law is the universal religious conscience, and this binds all nations, since nations consist of individuals who are members of the universal minimum religion.

If international law is, in essence, the internationalization of the socialized religious conscience as international morality, then there is a law of nations, even before there is a universal or global government. This is similar to the modern state where we argued that the social contract as an instrument of law precedes the emergence of the modern state. But a universal government is not needed for international morality except as a place where a federation of states meets to deliberate on morality and shame those exhibiting amoral behavior. The existence of such a world federation also accords efficiency to the operation of international morality.

In brief, we see that if we recognize that reason is subjective and fundamentally dependent on faith, then a universal religious conscience offers hope of making that subjective reason become objective. But this requires that we recognize the force of evil inclinations in human beings and the fallibility of their knowledge of those contingent truths that feature in their reasoning about any issue. Given the large populations that make up political systems, efficient and flourishing communities emerge only where the systems are built on the externalization of the prevailing universal religious consciences.

We can now sum up our discussion thus far.

If reason is fallible, then we are called to be humble and honest in our connection of circumstances to goals that we deem morally good, and to connect them through means that we deem are both realistic and good. With this realization comes the dedication to constantly improve our knowledge of contingent matters as well as the desire to further cultivate the religious conscience toward a perfectly good will. The religious nature of our conscience predisposes us to acknowledge our limitations, much more readily than any fallacious rational approach that refuses to acknowledge the dependence of its ratiocination on questionable biases.

Law and politics are central to the organization of society. We ought to apply reason to work out what legal and political models we should use to organize our society. This means coordinating truths of natural, social, and historical sciences with visions of the good, the true, the beautiful, and the just. Here, we have just briefly discussed how this approach reveals that law governs the state of nature, and so, law precedes the organized state by virtue of the minimum religious conscience. Liberal socialism proves to be more in line with the religious conscience, and true freedom and flourishing in a state of government is guaranteed by the dialectics within a multiparty constitutional democracy. In working out theories of punishment, retributive approaches and rehabilitation must be combined to achieve a harmonious society where security and justice depend more on the religious conscience and crimes as rare occurrences than the limited number of police officers or the carceral capacity that modern states can afford.

Bibliography

Akers, Katherine G., et al. "Hippocampal Neurogenesis Regulates Forgetting During Adulthood and Infancy." *Science* 344 (2014) 598–602. https://www.science.org/doi/10.1126/science.1248903.

American Humanist Association. "Humanism and Its Aspirations: Humanist Manifesto III, a Successor to the Humanist Manifesto of 1933." American Humanist Association, 2003. https://americanhumanist.org/what-is-humanism/manifesto3/.

Andrews, Evan. "Did a Premature Obituary Inspire the Nobel Prize?" History, July 23, 2020. https://www.history.com/news/did-a-premature-obituary-inspire-the-nobel-prize.

Aristotle. *Metaphysics*. Translated by W. D. Ross. In *The Basic Works of Aristotle*, edited by Richard McKeon, 689–926. Modern Library Classics. New York: Modern Library, 2001.

———. *Nicomachean Ethics*. Translated by W. D. Ross. In *The Basic Works of Aristotle*, edited by Richard McKeon, 935–1112. Modern Library Classics. New York: Modern Library, 2001.

———. *Physics*. Translated by R. P. Hardie and R. K. Gaye. In *The Basic Works of Aristotle*, edited by Richard McKeon, 218–394. Modern Library Classics. New York: Modern Library, 2001.

Augustine. *The City of God*. Translated by Marcus Dods. In *Augustine*, edited by Mortimer J. Adler et al., 129–623. Great Books of the Western World 18. Chicago: Encyclopaedia Britannica, 1952.

———. *The Confessions*. Translated by Edward Bouverie Pusey. In *Augustine*, edited by Mortimer J. Adler et al., 1–125. Great Books of the Western World 18. Chicago: Encyclopaedia Britannica, 1952.

———. *On Christian Doctrine*. Translated by J. F. Shaw. In *Augustine*, edited by Mortimer J. Adler et al., 624–98. Great Books of the Western World 18. Chicago: Encyclopaedia Britannica, 1952.

Ayer, Alfred Jules. *Language, Truth and Logic*. New York: Dover, 1952.

———. "What I Saw When I Was Dead." *Sunday Telegraph*, Aug. 28, 1988.

Bavinck, Herman. *Philosophy of Revelation: A New Annotated Edition*. Edited by Cory Brock and Nathaniel Gray Sutanto. Peabody, MA: Hendrickson, 2018.

Berkeley, George. "A Treatise Concerning the Principles of Human Knowledge." In *The Empiricists*, 135–215. New York: Anchor, 1974.

Bernecker, Sven. *The Metaphysics of Memory*. Philosophical Studies 111. Springer, 2008.

Birnbaum, David. *185 CE–1499 CE.* Bk. 3 of *Jews, Church & Civilization: An Integrated Historical Timeline.* New York: New Paradigm Matrix, 2012. http://www.jewishhistorytimeline.com/jews-church-civilization/book3/.

Blanshard, Brand. *Reason and Belief.* London: Allen & Unwin, 1974.

Bullinger, Henry. "2-1: The First Sermon: The Laws of Nature and Men." Monergism, last updated Oct. 12, 2017. In *The Decades of Henry Bullinger*, translated by H. I., edited by Thomas Harding (Cambridge: Cambridge University Press, 1849–1852); revised by William H. Gross. https://www.monergism.com/thethreshold/sdg/bullinger/Bullinger%20-%20Decades%20-%20Henry%20Bullinger.pdf.

Burke, Edmund. *Reflections on the Revolution in France, and on the Proceedings in Certain Societies in London Relative to That Event.* Whithorn, UK: Anodos, 2017.

Butler, Joseph. *Fifteen Sermons Preached at Rolls Chapel.* Cambridge, UK: Hilliard and Brown, 1827. https://ccel.org/ccel/butler/sermons/sermons.i.html.

Calvin, John. *Institutes of the Christian Religion.* Vol. 1. Translated by John Allen. Philadelphia: Presbyterian Board of Publication, 1909.

Cartwright, Nancy. "Précis of *Nature's Capacities and Their Measurement*." *Philosophy and Phenomenological Research* 55 (1995) 153–56. https://doi.org/10.2307/2108313.

Chalmers, David J. "What Is Conceptual Engineering and What Should It Be?" *Inquiry* (2020) 1–18. https://doi.org/10.1080/0020174X.2020.1817141.

Churchland, Patricia S. *Conscience: The Origins of Moral Intuition.* New York: Norton, 2019.

Clark, Gordon H., and T. V. Smith, eds. *Readings in Ethics.* 2nd ed. New York: Crofts, 1935.

Comte, Auguste. *Positive Philosophy.* Vol. 1. Translated by Harriet Martineau. Kitchener, Can.: Batoche, 2000.

Damasio, Antonio R. *Descartes' Error: Emotion, Reason, and the Human Brain.* New York: Avon Books, 1994.

Danziger, Shai, et al. "Extraneous Factors in Judicial Decisions." *Proceedings of the National Academy of Sciences* 108 (2011) 6889–92. https://doi.org/10.1073/pnas.1018033108.

De Botton, Alain. *Religion for Atheists: A Non-Believer's Guide to the Uses of Religion.* New York: Vintage Books, 2012.

Dworkin, Ronald. *Religion Without God.* Cambridge: Harvard University Press, 2013.

Epictetus. *The Discourses.* In *Discourses and Selected Writings*, edited and translated by Robert Dobbin, 207–45. London: Penguin Classics, 2008.

———. *Enchiridion.* In *Discourses and Selected Writings*, edited and translated by Robert Dobbin, 1–206. London: Penguin Classics, 2008.

Epicurus. *Letter to Menoeceus.* In *Readings in Ethics*, edited by Gordon H. Clark and T. V. Smith, 87–92. 2nd ed. New York: Crofts, 1935.

Facco, Enrico, and Christian Agrillo. "Near-Death Experiences Between Science and Prejudice." *Frontiers in Human Neuroscience* 6 (2012). https://doi.org/10.3389/fnhum.2012.00209.

Fieser, James. "David Hume (1711–1776)." Internet Encyclopedia of Philosophy. https://iep.utm.edu/hume/.

Flew, Antony, and Roy Abraham Varghese. *There Is a God: How the World's Most Notorious Atheist Changed His Mind.* New York: HarperOne, 2008.

Greyson, Bruce. "Getting Comfortable with Near-Death Experiences. An Overview of Near-Death Experiences." *Missouri Medicine* 110 (2013) 475–81. https://pmc.ncbi.nlm.nih.gov/articles/PMC6179792/.

Greyson, Bruce, and Surbhi Khanna. "Spiritual Transformation After Near-Death Experiences." *Spirituality in Clinical Practice* 1 (2014) 43–55. https://doi.org/10.1037/scp0000010.

Harris, Sam. *The End of Faith: Religion, Terror, and the Future of Reason*. New York: Norton, 2004. Repr., New York: Norton, 2005.

Hayek, Friedrich A. *The Road to Serfdom*. Edited by Bruce Caldwell. Def. ed. Chicago: Chicago University Press, 2007.

Hegel, Georg Wilhelm Friedrich. *The Philosophy of History*. Translated by J. Sibree. Mineola, NY: Dover, 1956.

———. *Reason in History*. Translated by Robert S. Hartman. Hoboken, NJ: Prentice Hall, 1997.

Heisenberg, Werner. *Physics and Philosophy: The Revolution in Modern Science*. World Perspectives 19. New York: Harper & Row, 1958.

Hempel, Carl G. "The Function of General Laws in History." *Journal of Philosophy* 39 (1942) 35–48. https://www.jstor.org/stable/2017635.

———. *Philosophy of Natural Science*. Foundations of Philosophy. Englewood Cliffs, NJ: Prentice-Hall, 1966.

———. "Schlick and Neurath: Foundation vs. Coherence in Scientific Knowledge." In *Selected Philosophical Essays*, edited by Richard Jeffrey, 181–98. Cambridge: Cambridge University Press, 2000.

Hesiod. *Theogony*. Edited and translated by Richard S. Caldwell. Focus Classical Library. Indianapolis: Focus, 1987.

Hirst, William, et al. "A Ten-Year Follow-Up of a Study of Memory for the Attack of September 11, 2001: Flashbulb Memories and Memories for Flashbulb Events." *Journal of Experimental Psychology: General* 144 (2015) 604–23. https://doi.org/10.1037/xge0000055.

Hoffman, Joshua, and Gary S. Rosenkrantz. *Substance: Its Nature and Existence*. London: Routledge, 1997.

Hume, David. *An Enquiry Concerning Human Understanding*. Edited by Eric Steinberg. 2nd ed. Indianapolis: Hackett, 1993.

———. *A Treatise of Human Nature*. New York: Barnes & Noble, 2005.

Hutcheson, Francis. *An Inquiry into the Original of Our Ideas of Beauty and Virtue*. Whithorn, UK: Anodos, 2019.

Iamblichus. *Life of Pythagoras, or Pythagoric Life*. Translated by Thomas Taylor. London: Watkins, 1818.

Ibn Khaldun. *The Muqaddimah: An Introduction to History*. Translated by Franz Rosenthal, edited by N. J. Dawood. Bollingen. Princeton: Princeton University Press, 2005.

James, William. *The Varieties of Religious Experience: A Study in Human Nature*. New York: Barnes & Noble Classics, 2004.

Jaspers, Karl. *The Origin and Goal of History*. Translated by Michael Bullock. New Haven: Yale University Press, 1965.

Jaynes, E. T. *Probability Theory: The Logic of Science*. Edited by G. Larry Bretthorst. Cambridge: Cambridge University Press, 2003.

Kant, Immanuel. *Critique of Judgment*. Translated by Werner S. Pluhar. Indianapolis: Hackett, 1987.
———. *Critique of Practical Reason*. Translated by Lewis White Beck. Indianapolis: Bobbs-Merill, 1978.
———. *Critique of Pure Reason*. Translated by J. M. D. Meiklejohn. New York: Barnes & Noble, 2004.
———. "The End of All Things." In *Perpetual Peace and Other Essays on Politics, History, and Morals*, translated by Ted Humphrey, 93–106. Indianapolis: Hackett, 1983.
———. *Groundwork for the Metaphysics of Morals*. Edited and translated by Alan Wood. Rethinking the Western Tradition. New Haven: Yale University Press, 2002.
———. "Idea for a Universal History with a Cosmopolitan Intent." In *Perpetual Peace and Other Essays on Politics, History, and Morals*, translated by Ted Humphrey, 29–40. Indianapolis: Hackett, 1983.
———. *Lectures on Ethics*. Edited by Peter Heath and J. B. Schneewind, translated by Peter Heath. Cambridge Edition of the Works of Immanuel Kant. Cambridge: Cambridge University Press, 1997.
———. *Lectures on Philosophical Theology*. Translated by Allen W. Wood and Gertrude M. Clark. Ithaca, NY: Cornell University Press, 1978.
———. *The Metaphysics of Morals*. Translated and edited by Mary Gregor. Cambridge Texts in the History of Philosophy. Cambridge: Cambridge University Press, 1996.
———. *Religion Within the Bounds of Bare Reason*. Translated by Werner S. Pluhar. Indianapolis: Hackett, 2009.
———. "Speculative Beginning of Human History." In *Perpetual Peace and Other Essays on Politics, History, and Morals*, translated by Ted Humphrey, 49–60. Indianapolis: Hackett, 1983.
Kierkegaard, Søren. *Journals AA–DD*. Vol. 1 of *Kierkegaard's Journals and Notebooks*, edited by Niels Jørgen Cappelørn et al. Princeton: Princeton University Press, 2007.
———. *Philosophical Fragments*. Translated by David F. Swenson, revised by Howard V. Hong. Princeton: Princeton University Press, 1936. https://www.religion-online.org/book/philosophical-fragments/.
Knight, A. H. J. "Nietzsche and Epicurean Philosophy." *Philosophy* 8 (1933) 431–45. https://www.jstor.org/stable/3746535.
Koons, Robert C., and Timothy H. Pickavance. *Metaphysics: The Fundamentals*. Fundamentals of Philosophy 4. West Sussex, UK: Wiley Blackwell, 2015.
Le Bon, Gustave. *The Crowd: A Study of the Popular Mind*. Loki's Publishing, 2023.
Leibniz, Gottfried Wilhelm. *The Monadology and Other Philosophical Writings*. Translated by Robert Latta. Oxford: Oxford University Press, 1898.
———. *New Essay on Human Understanding: Preface and Book I; Innate Notions*. Translated by Jonathan Bennett. https://www.earlymoderntexts.com/assets/pdfs/leibniz1705book1.pdf.
Lipka, Michael, and Claire Gecewicz. "More Americans Now Say They're Spiritual but Not Religious." Pew Research Center, Sept. 6, 2017. https://www.pewresearch.org/short-reads/2017/09/06/more-americans-now-say-theyre-spiritual-but-not-religious/.
Locke, John. *An Essay Concerning Human Understanding*. Edited by Roger Woolhouse. London: Penguin Classics, 1997.

———. *A Letter Concerning Toleration*. Edited by Mario Montuori. The Hague: Martinus Nijhoff, 1963.

Loux, Michael J., and Thomas M. Crisp. *Metaphysics: A Contemporary Introduction*. 4th ed. Routledge Contemporary Introductions to Philosophy. New York: Routledge, 2017.

Lucretius. *The Nature of Things*. Translated by A. E. Stallings. London: Penguin Classics, 2007.

MacIntyre, Alasdair. *After Virtue: A Study in Moral Theory*. 3rd ed. Notre Dame: University of Notre Dame Press, 2008.

McLaughlin, Wayman Bernard. "The Relation Between Hegel and Kierkegaard." PhD diss., Boston University, 1958. https://hdl.handle.net/2144/6219.

Melanchthon, Philip. "On Law." In *The Loci Communes of Philip Melanchthon*. Translated by Charles Leander Hill, 110–17. Boston: Meador, 1944.

Misailidi, Plousia, and Ekaterina N. Kornilaki. "Development of Afterlife Beliefs in Childhood: Relationship to Parent Beliefs and Testimony." *Merrill-Palmer Quarterly* 61 (2015) 290–318. 10.13110/merrpalmquar1982.61.2.0290.

Moore, G. E. *Principia Ethica*. Mineola, NY: Dover, 2004.

Newbigin, Lesslie. *The Gospel in a Pluralistic Society*. Grand Rapids: Eerdmans, 1989.

Nielsen, Kai. "Historicism." In *The Cambridge Dictionary of Philosophy*, edited by Robert Audi, 386. 2nd ed. Cambridge: Cambridge University Press, 1999.

Nietzsche, Friedrich. "Dem unbekannten Gott." In *Der Wanderer und sein Schatten: Gedichte*, 6. Das Erbe der Vergangenheit 3. Berlin: De Gruyter, 1934. https://doi.org/10.1515/9783111409474-003.

———. "To the Unknown God." Translated by Michael Moynihan. Brute Norse, Aug. 12, 2018. https://www.brutenorse.com/blog/2018/8/12/to-the-unknown-god-by-friedrich-nietzsche.

———. *The Twilight of Idols: Or, How to Philosophise with the Hammer*. Translated by Anthony M. Ludovici. Edinburgh: Foulis, 1911.

Nozick, Robert. *Anarchy, State, and Utopia*. New York: Basic, 2013.

O'Neill, Onora. *Constructions of Reason: Exploration of Kant's Practical Philosophy*. Cambridge: Cambridge University Press, 1989.

Oxtoby, Willard G., and Roy C. Amore, eds. *World Religions: Eastern Traditions*. 3rd ed. Don Mills, Can.: Oxford University Press, 2010.

Pew Research Center. *The Digital Pulpit: A Nationwide Analysis of Online Sermons*. Dec. 16, 2019. https://www.pewresearch.org/religion/2019/12/16/the-digital-pulpit-a-nationwide-analysis-of-online-sermons/.

Piaget, Jean. "The Stages of the Intellectual Development of the Child." *Bulletin of the Menninger Clinic* 26 (1962) 120–28.

Plato. *The Laws*. Translated by Benjamin Jowett. Compass Circle, 2019.

———. *Philebus*. Translated by J. C. B. London: Clarendon, 1975.

———. *The Republic*. Translated by Richard W. Sterling and William C. Scott. New York: Norton, 1996.

———. *Timaeus*. Translated by Benjamin Jowett. https://classics.mit.edu/Plato/timaeus.html.

Popkin, Richard H. "Hume and Jurieu: Possible Calvinist Origins of Hume's Theory of Belief." *Rivista Critica di Storia della Filosofia* 22 (1967) 400–17. https://www.jstor.org/stable/44022188.

Popper, Karl. *The Logic of Scientific Discovery*. London: Routledge, 2002.

———. *The Open Society and Its Enemies.* Vol. 1. London: Routledge, 1945.

Rawls, John. "On My Religion." In *A Brief Inquiry into the Meaning of Sin & Faith*, edited by Thomas Nagel, 259–70. Cambridge: Harvard University Press, 2009.

Reichenbach, Hans. *The Rise of Scientific Philosophy.* Berkeley: University of California Press, 1968.

Rousseau, Jean-Jacques. *On the Social Contract.* In *The Basic Political Writings*, translated and edited by Donald A. Cress, 141–227. Indianapolis: Hackett, 1987.

Russell, Bertrand. *The Analysis of Mind.* Watchmaker, 2010.

———. *A History of Western Philosophy.* New York: Touchstone, 1967.

———. "On Denoting." *Mind* 14 (1905) 479–93. https://www.jstor.org/stable/2248381.

Ryle, Gilbert. *The Concept of Mind.* 60th anniv. ed. New York: Routledge, 2009.

Scanlon, T. M. *What We Owe to Each Other.* Cambridge: Belknap, 2001.

Schacter, Daniel L., and Donna Rose Addis. "Memory and Imagination: Perspectives on Constructive Episodic Simulation." In *The Cambridge Handbook of the Imagination*, edited by Anna Abraham, 111–31. Cambridge: Cambridge University Press, 2020.

Schellenberg, J. L. *Divine Hiddenness and Human Reason.* Cornell Studies in the Philosophy of Religion. Ithaca: Cornell University Press, 1993.

Schopenhauer, Arthur. *The World as Will and Presentation.* Early Modern Texts, 2023. From the translation by Richard E. Aquila (Longman, 2008). Prepared by Jonathan Bennett. https://www.earlymoderntexts.com/assets/pdfs/schopenhauer1818.pdf.

Sidgwick, Henry. *The Methods of Ethics.* 7th ed. Indianapolis: Hackett, 1981.

Smith, Adam. *The Theory of Moral Sentiments.* Digireads.com, 2010.

Solovyov, Vladimir. *The Meaning of Love.* Edited by Thomas R. Beyer Jr. Translated by Jane Marshall, revised by Thomas R. Beyer Jr. Stockbridge, MA: Lindisfarne, 1985.

Steinfels, Peter. "Scandinavian Nonbelievers, Which Is Not to Say Atheists." *New York Times*, Feb. 27, 2009. https://www.nytimes.com/2009/02/28/us/28beliefs.html.

Strawson, P. F. *Analysis and Metaphysics: An Introduction to Philosophy.* Oxford: Oxford University Press, 1992.

Swedenborg, Emanuel. *Heaven and Hell.* Translated by George F. Dole. West Chester, PA: Swedenborg Foundation, 2010.

Taylor, Christopher. "Aristotle on Practical Reason." In *Oxford Handbook of Topics in Philosophy.* Oxford: Oxford Academic, 2014. https://doi.org/10.1093/oxfordhb/9780199935314.013.52.

Van Inwagen, Peter. *Material Beings.* Ithaca, NY: Cornell University Press, 1990.

Wagner, Richard. *Religion and Art.* Translated by W. Ashton Ellis. Lincoln: University of Nebraska Press, 1994.

Walschots, Michael. "Hutcheson and Kant: Moral Sense and Moral Feeling." In *Kant and the Scottish Enlightenment*, edited by Elizabeth Robinson and Chris W. Suprenant, 36–54. Routledge Studies in Eighteenth-Century Philosophy. New York: Routledge, 2017.

Whitehead, Alfred North. *Process and Reality: An Essay in Cosmology.* Edited by David Ray Griffin and Donald W. Sherburne. Corrected ed. New York: Free Press, 1978.

Williams, Bernard. *Morality: An Introduction to Ethics.* Cambridge: Cambridge University Press, 1972.

Wippel, John F. "Aquinas, Saint Thomas." In *The Cambridge Dictionary of Philosophy*, edited by Robert Audi, 36–40. 2nd ed. Cambridge: Cambridge University Press, 1999.

Wittgenstein, Ludwig. *Philosophical Investigations*. Translated by G. E. M. Anscombe et al., edited by P. M. S. Hacker and Joachim Schulte. 4th ed. West Sussex, UK: Wiley Blackwell, 2009.

———. *Tractatus Logico-Philosophicus*. Mineola, NY: Dover, 1922.

Wojtkowiak, Joanna, et al. "Emerging Ritual Practices in Pluralistic Society: A Comparison of Six Non-Religious European Celebrant Training Programmes." *Journal for the Study of Spirituality* 8 (2018) 77–90. https://doi.org/10.1080/20440243.2018.1431287.

World Prison Brief. "Highest to Lowest—Prison Population Total." https://www.prisonstudies.org/highest-to-lowest/prison-population-total?field_region_taxonomy_tid=All.

Zerin, Edward. "Karl Popper on God: The Lost Interview." *Skeptic* 6 (1998) 46–49.

Index

A

Abrahamism, 143–45, 150, 153–60,
    165–66, 168, 170–71, 182–83,
    190, 217, 228
Absolute idealism, 22–23, 25, 90
Afterlife, 136–38, 149–50, 177,
    179–91, 217–19, 234, 249
Against utilitarianism, 210
Agnosticism, 114, 116, 138–39, 164
Amore, Roy C., 184
Antirationalism, 21
Aquinas, Thomas, 13, 116
Aristotle, 5, 7–10, 19, 28–29, 36, 83,
    91, 117, 149, 194
    attribution by, 83
    Ethics, 10
    Metaphysics, 8–9, 28, 36
    Physics, 36
    Theory, 9
Asabiyyah, 238–39
Asocial sociability, 240, 244–45, 252
Assertions, 17, 56, 65–66, 70–71, 78,
    132, 172, 211
Atheism, 113–16, 124, 126–27, 172,
    176, 178, 189, 191, 251
Atomistic materialism, 10
Augustine of Hippo, 5, 13–15, 19, 69,
    136, 150, 155, 169, 174–75
    City of God, 150
    Confessions, 136, 175
Augustinianism, 19
Ayer, A. J., 47–48, 181, 186
    What I Saw, 181

B

Baptism, 167
Bavinck, Herman, 154
    Philosophy of Revelation, 154
Benevolence, 145, 157, 197–99, 201,
    207, 232, 237, 240, 242
Bentham, Jeremy, 197, 263
Bernecker, 102, 107
    Metaphysics of Memory, 102, 107
Blanshard, Brand, 14, 127
    Martin Luther on reason, 14, 127
Botton, Alain de, 176–77, 182
    Religion for Atheists, 176–77
Buddha, Gautama, 145
Buddhism, 145, 150, 167, 171, 182,
    184, 217
Bullinger, Henry, 122
    Laws of Nature and Men, 122
Bureaucracy, 240
Burke, Edmund, 248
Butler, Bishop Joseph, 113, 124, 193,
    198

C

Calvin, John, 14, 115, 122–24, 126,
    136, 197, 199, 219
    Institutes, 122, 136, 219 Calvinism,
    influence of, 199 Capitalism,
    241, 243
Cartwright, Nancy, 51
Categorical imperative, 19–22, 33,
    200, 202–3, 212, 217, 227, 229
Catholic Church, 121, 166, 176,
    247–48, 253

Index

Causal relation, 32, 36, 42, 77–79, 81, 84–86, 94, 143
Cause, causation, 34–38, 46, 48–56, 59, 77, 82–83, 103
Chalmers, David, 73
Christ, Jesus, 24, 125, 135, 154, 158–59, 167, 170, 217
Christ spiritual presence, 23, 90
  Christendom, critique of, 178
  Christian:
  New Testament, 155–57, 183, 200
  Theology, 6–7, 12–14
Christian doctrine, 13–15, 116, 195, 199, 212, 232
Christianity, 19, 25, 121, 154, 205, 214, 218, 220, 231
Chronic depression, 40
Churchland, Patricia, 194
  Conscience, 193–211
City of God, 150
Clark and Smith, 148
  Readings in Ethics, 148
Coherence, 31, 44–45, 48, 52, 56–58, 211–12, 214, 227, 233, 248
Collins, Georg, 201
Composition, 73, 75, 81
Comte, Auguste, 88, 142, 176–77
Concept:
  conceptual analysis, 3–4, 8, 15, 26–27
  conceptual engineering, 73, 98–99
Concept of reason, 3, 5, 7–13, 51, 53, 55, 57–59, 127, 191, 216
Concepts of science, 44
Confucianism, 150, 182, 184, 217
Confucius, 145, 155
Conscience, 193–211
Constitutional democracy, 235, 244–48, 250, 254
Contingent truths, 30, 60–61, 85–87, 95–97, 106, 110–11, 245–47, 252–53
Contractualism, 26
Corruption, 116, 121, 129, 240, 245–46
Cremation, 182, 184
Critical Religion, 140
Critique of Judgment, 21

Critique of Practical Reason, 21, 203
Critique of Pure Reason, 20, 125
The Crowd: A Study of the Popular Mind, 247
Cycle of rebirth, 182, 184
Cynicism, 111, 153, 163

D

Damasio, Antonio, 26
  Descartes' Error, 26
David, King, 240
Death, 6, 12, 40, 114, 149–50, 166, 170–71, 179–86, 188, 217–19, 238
Declarative episodic memory, 99
Democracy, 235, 244–48, 250, 254
Deontology, 207, 210, 232
Descartes, 17, 25–26
Dionysus, 146–47
Discrimination, 85, 91
Divine causation, 82
Divine hiddenness, 116, 119, 126, 133–34
Doctrine of right, 205
Doctrine of virtue, 205
Doctrines of salvation, 113, 143, 158, 162–64, 179
Doubt, 53, 64–65, 69, 89, 97, 134–37, 151, 155, 218, 220, 227, 235
Duty, 19–21, 110, 157, 161, 188, 194, 196–97, 207–32, 250
Dworkin, Ronald, 176, 178

E

Earl of Shaftesbury, 193
Early Christians, 6, 159
Economics, 46, 88, 233–35, 237, 245, 247, 249, 251, 253
Education, 42, 66, 70, 90–91, 148, 195–96, 231, 244, 251–52
Egoism, 207, 226, 229, 232
Egoistic hedonism, 194–95, 197, 207, 232
Electrodynamics, 86
Emergence, 42, 51, 86–88, 143, 145, 235, 237, 253

Emotions, 3, 18, 42–43, 65, 195–97, 201, 227, 250
Empiricism, 10, 15, 17, 26–27, 83, 140, 194, 197, 203, 215, 244
Epictetus, 5, 11
    Enchiridion, 11
Epicurus, 5, 10, 142, 149–50, 171, 179–80, 182
    Letter to Menoeceus, 149, 179
Ethical duty, 215, 230
Ethical theories, 191–97, 210, 232, 234
Ethics, moral philosophy, 8, 121–22, 124, 197–200, 205–6, 212, 215–16, 233, 237
Explanation, 12, 16, 30, 59–60, 67–68, 82, 86, 90–91, 120, 132, 147

F

Faith, 3–5, 7, 13–15, 21–25, 115–17, 119, 125, 127–28, 134–35, 253
Faithful Jew, beliefs of, 159
Fallibility, memory, 106, 223
Fieser, James, 199
    Hume, David, 18, 97, 124, 193, 199
Five pillars in Islam, 160
Flew, Anthony, 83, 152, 161
    There Is a God, 83, 152, 161, 177
Folk psychology, 64
Folk religions, 182
Forgiveness of sins, 158–59, 167–71, 187, 189–90, 217, 230–31
Freedom, 21, 90, 94, 123, 161, 166, 217, 220, 239, 241, 246, 248, 250–51, 254
French Revolution, 4, 247
Funeral rituals, 164, 179, 182

G

Gender, 90–91
Generalization, possibility of, 93
Gladstone, William, 243
God-human, 5
God, Supreme Being, 14, 42, 171, 178, 183, 186–87, 189, 208, 218–19, 221, 241, 249
God-world-human nature, 7, 9

God's existence, 15, 42, 116, 119, 123, 127, 129, 135
Gods of the Greeks, 144
The Gospel in a Pluralistic Society, 154
Gratitude, 117–19, 141, 158, 167–71, 227–28, 230, 235, 237, 242–43
Greyson, 181, 186
    Getting Comfortable, 181
Groundwork for the Metaphysics of Morals, 203
Guilt, 118, 122, 136, 139, 141, 158, 167, 215–16, 220, 226, 230–31, 237, 249

H

Hayek, Friedrich, 246
Healthy-minded, 137, 249
Heaven, 10, 21, 159, 185–87, 189, 195, 212, 220, 230
Heaven and Hell, 185–86, 189, 195, 212
Hegel, Georg Wilhelm Friedrich, 5, 22–25, 31, 90, 94
    Idealism, 7, 22–23, 25, 90
    Lutheran, 23–24, 90, 120–21, 123
    Philosophy, 22, 25, 31
    Philosophy of History, 23, 94
Hell, 183, 185–86, 189, 195, 212
Hellenistic period, 10
Hempel, Carl G., 54, 58, 93 Function of General Laws, 93 Philosophy of Natural Science, 54
Hesiod, 144–45, 152, 155
    Theogony, 143–45, 152, 155
Heterogeneity, 92
Hinduism, 145, 182
Hippo's Confessions, 69
History, 92
The History of Western Philosophy, 140
Hobbes, Thomas, 197
    war, 238
Hoffman, 70, 72
Holy Communion, 23–24, 90
Hotness, 37
Human being:
    legislating creature, 202, 222
    religious creature, 146
    ritualistic creature, 164

Hume, David, 5, 18–19, 21, 36, 50–51, 116, 124, 193–202, 205
  Treatise of Human Nature, 18, 107, 196
Hume, F., 18
  moral sentiment theory, 194
Hutcheson:
  Inquiry, 197, 207
Hutcheson, Francis, 19, 124, 128, 193, 197
  utilitarianism, 198
Hypercentralization, 240

I

Iamblichus, 6–7
  Life of Pythagoras, 6
Idealism, 7, 22–23, 25, 90
Imagination, 31, 58, 61, 95–111, 130, 144, 164, 172–73, 227
Imperfect love, 228
Impressions, 18–19, 31, 35, 45, 57, 59, 64, 98, 103–4, 107
Inclination to evil, 141, 199, 230, 235, 237, 240, 244, 247, 249
Inhumation, 182–84
Injustice, 131, 144, 196, 215, 221, 230–31, 239
Interpretivism, 88–89, 93
Intuitionism, 194, 207–9, 212, 232
Inwagen, Peter Van, 74
Islam, 158, 160, 167
Islam, five pillars in:
  Almsgiving, 160
  Declaration of faith, 160
  Fasting, 160
  Pilgrimage, 160
  Prayer, 160

J

James, William, 113, 137–38, 142, 164, 231
Jasper, Karl, 145–46
  Origin and Goal of History, 146
Jaynes, E. T., 56
  Probability Theory, 56
Jesus's teachings, 158
Jewish faith, 79
Jewish group, 183
John's Gospel, 24
Judaism, 121, 154, 158–60, 166–67, 183
Justice, 8, 42–43, 145, 187–88, 199, 208, 210, 217–22, 240, 248–52, 254

K

Kant, Immanuel, 5, 17–24, 26, 32–33, 39, 45–46, 49–50, 57–58, 226–29, 232, 237, 240, 244
  The End of All Things, 23
  epistemology, 17, 32, 118, 156
  Groundwork, 8, 20, 203–4, 222
  Idea for a Universal History, 23
  Lectures on Ethics, 201–2, 204
  Lectures on Philosophical Theology, 14, 159, 168–69, 187, 206, 228
  Metaphysics of Morals, 203–5
  Moral philosophy, 203, 205–6, 212, 215–16, 233, 237
  Moral-sense theory, 200, 202, 232
  Religion, 205
  Religious faith, 21, 27, 116, 151, 191, 205 *Speculative Beginning of Human History*, 23 Theology, 21
Kant's *Lectures on Ethics*, 201
Kant's *Religion Within the Bounds of Bare Reason*, 20
Khaldun, Ibn, 238
Kierkegaard, Søren, 5, 22, 24–25, 90, 116, 155
Knight, "Nietzsche and Epicurean Philosophy", 150
Knowledge of God, 13, 116, 118–19, 122, 124, 135, 161, 189, 206
Koons, 36, 74

L

Laws, 234–36
  laws of nature, 31, 44–45, 48–49, 53–56, 161, 215
  moral law, 20–21, 201–2, 212, 219, 236–37, 240, 250, 253

natural law, 53, 123, 237, 253
Le Bon, Gustave, 247–48
  The Crowd, 247–48
Leibniz, Gottfried Wilhelm, 5, 15–17, 28, 45, 76, 78
  Monadology, 28, 76
Letter Concerning Toleration, 131
Liberal socialism, 235, 243–44, 246, 254
Liberalism, 235, 241, 243–44
Linearity of life, 183
Locke, John, 15, 131
Logic, 16–17, 19, 54–56, 59, 63, 84, 147, 149, 159, 229, 233
Logical positivism, 44, 47–48, 54, 56, 58
Logistikon, 8, 55
Logos, 55
Love:
  imperfect love, 228
  perfect love, 228
  triangle of commanded love, 222
Lucretius, 5, 12–13, 171, 180, 182
  Nature of Things, 12, 17, 171, 180, 187
Luther, Martin, 14, 127

M

Machiavelli's political science, 90
MacIntyre, Alasdair, 89–90
Magee, Brian, 48
Maimonides, 159
Marxist, 241–42, 244, 246–47
Mechanistic, 12, 20, 36, 38, 50–51, 81, 86–87, 98
  description, 36, 58, 72, 127, 130
  mechanical philosophy, 197
  mechanistic view, 20
Melanchthon, Philip, 123
Memory, 31, 55, 58, 61, 64, 93, 95–111, 157, 164, 185, 187–89, 223, 225
Messiah, 156, 160
Metaphysical marketplace, 162, 189–90

Metaphysics, 8–9, 16, 20, 23, 28, 36, 154, 162, 164, 178, 189, 203–5, 212, 251
Metaphysics of Memory, 102, 107
The Metaphysics of Morals, 203–4
  Methodological individualism, 88, 90, 143, 222 Misailidi and Kornilaki, 181
  Development of Afterlife Beliefs, 181 Mohammed, prophethood of, 160 Moore, G. E., 195, 210
  Principia Ethica, 195, 209, 212
Moore, Michael, 105
Moral feeling, 201, 204–5
Moral sense, 128–29, 132–33, 138, 191, 193, 195–201, 207
Moral-sense theory, 200, 202, 232
Morbid-minded religion, 137
Moses, 153, 159
Multiparty constitutional democracy, 235, 244–48, 254
Muqaddimah, 238
Music, 6, 42, 65, 106, 146–47, 165, 172–77
Muslim, 79, 144, 148, 156, 165, 170–71, 180, 183

N

Natural phenomena, 44–46, 48–50, 52–56, 58–60, 66, 80–86, 130, 161, 222
Nature of a question, 66–67, 78, 85
On the Nature of Things, 171
Near-death experience (NDE), 162–64, 179–81, 185–86, 189, 218
Neighbor, 214
Newbigin, Lesslie, 153–54
Nicomachean Ethics, 9
Nielsen, Kai, 93
  Historicism, 93
Nietzsche, Friedrich, 150, 173, 178
  Twilight of Idols, 173
  To the Unknown God, 150
Nonbelief, between believe and doubt, 132–36
Nozick, Robert, 240
  Anarchy, State, and Utopia, 240

O

Objectivity, 5, 34, 38, 41–42, 58, 129, 214
O'Neill, Onora, 21
The Open Society, 251–52
Orpheus, 146–47
Orphic philosophers, 145
Orphism, 7, 143, 145–48, 151, 154, 158
Oxtoby, Willard G., 184

P

Passions, 3, 5, 18–19, 21, 25–27, 41, 162, 196, 201
  emotions, 3, 18, 196, 201
  sentiments, 201
People's religious beliefs, 91
Perfect love, 228
Persephone, 146
Personal religion, personal faith, 145, 147–48, 163, 220–22
Pew Research Center, 120, 172
Philosophical religion, 114, 139–43, 149–50, 155, 189
Philosophy, 197–216, 221, 227, 232–34, 237, 251
Philosophy, as defined by Pythagoras, 5–7, 140, 142–43
Philosophy of history, 23, 94
Physics, 8–9, 36, 50–51, 81–86, 88, 92, 95, 149, 165, 215, 222, 252
Pickavance, 36, 74
Pictorial language, 98
Pietist Christian, 21, 25
Place of Zeus, 144
Placebo and nocebo effects, 46, 59–60, 78
Plantinga, Alvin, 14
Plato:
  Laws, 131
  Republic, 148, 174–75, 251
  Theory, 18, 41, 58, 210
  Timaeus, 9–10, 144, 148, 155
Platonism, 7, 13, 148
Politics, 8, 11, 130–31, 191, 232–35, 237, 245–49, 251, 253–54
Popkin, Richard H., 199

Hume and Jurieu, 199
Popper, Karl, 84, 90, 167–68, 251
Positivism, 47–48, 88–89, 177–78
Power:
  capacity, 37, 49, 51–52, 59, 103
  potential, 37, 49, 59, 249
Power of music, 175
Prayer, 11, 150, 160, 165, 167–71, 176
Prediction, 50, 65–66, 80–81, 222, 243
Principia Ethica, 195, 209, 212
Probabilism, 41
Probability, 40, 44, 48, 56, 58–59, 73, 91, 223
Problem of reference, 58
Propositions, 16, 55–58, 64–68, 101, 103, 138, 165, 172–73
Protestant, Protestantism, 14–15, 19, 25–26, 89, 190, 205–6, 219–21, 241, 243, 246, 248, 253
Protestant theology, 115
Punishment:
  Capital punishment, 236
  theories, 251
Pythagoras, Pythagoreanism, 5–7, 13, 92, 140, 142–43, 147–48, 154
Pythagoreans, 6–7, 148

Q

Question, 165–66, 210–11

R

Race, 90–91
Radius of rationality, 38–39
Rapid eye movement (REM), 108
Rationalism, 10, 15, 17, 26, 32, 45, 194
Rawls, John, 116, 210, 229
  On My Religion, 116
  Realism, 7
Reason:
  faith and reason, 3, 13–15, 27, 46, 115, 160
  reason and emotions, 193
  theory of, 27, 29, 31, 41–42
Reasonableness, 32–33, 35, 38–42, 153–54, 170, 176, 185, 236, 244–45

Reflections on the Revolution in France, 248 Reformed Protestant Tradition, 14 Reformed Protestantism, 122
Rehabilitation, 249–52, 254
Reichenbach, Hans, 23
Religion:
  critical religion, 139–41, 143, 161–62, 176, 178
  philosophical religion, 114, 139–43, 149–50, 155, 189
  revealed, 3, 13–14, 19, 149, 153–55, 160, 163, 166, 178, 219
  systematic religion, 113–14, 116, 125–27, 129, 132, 137–43
  universal minimum, 113–21, 166, 168, 176, 178, 187, 189, 232, 234–35, 253
Religion and Art, 172–74
Religion for Atheists, 176–77
Religion-based ethics, 234–35, 243, 245, 247, 249, 251, 253
Religion for Humanity, 176–77
Religion Within the Bounds of Bare Reason, 20, 125
Religion Without God (book), 178
Religions:
  eastern religions, 143, 150, 163, 182, 184, 217
  western religions, 143, 154, 184, 217
  World religions, 145, 178, 184, 186
Religious conscience, 21, 156, 158, 162, 209, 211, 213–15, 221–27, 231–54
Religious experience, 128, 137–38, 147, 164, 171, 176, 231
Religiously grounded ethics, 210, 216
Remembered facts, 98, 101
Remembering, 64, 98–102, 108
Rise of Scientific Philosophy, 23, 50
Rituals, 6, 138–43, 147–48, 160–83
Road to Serfdom, 246
Roman Catholic teachings, 15
Rosenkrantz, Gary S., 70, 72
Rousseau, Jean Jacques, 4, 19, 21, 129, 131–33, 157, 163, 175, 187, 191, 235, 238

Russell, Bertrand, 6–7, 22, 47–48, 69, 96, 108, 137, 140, 146, 151
  Analysis of Mind, 96
Ryle, Gilbert, 98
  Concept of Mind, 12, 98

S

Sadducees, 183–84
Salvation, 113–14, 142–43, 146–47, 181, 184, 189, 220, 226, 249
Scanlon, T. M., 26
Schellenberg, J. L., 134–35
  Hiddenness, Divine, 116, 119, 126, 133–34
Schiller, Friedrich, 173
Schopenhauer, Arthur, 173, 178
  World as Will and Presentation, 173
Schweitzer, Albert, 227
Science:
  human sciences, 79
  natural science, 12, 37–38, 44–47, 49–59, 80–89, 91, 93, 200
  social sciences, 47, 53, 80, 87–90, 92, 151
Scriptures, Holy, 199, 206
Sense of the divine, 42, 115–17, 121–29, 193, 195, 197–200, 232
Sensus divinitatis, 115, 117
Sentiments, 120, 157, 203, 205, 207, 209, 211, 213
Sidgwick, Henry, 193–98, 207–10, 212, 215, 222, 232
  Methods of Ethics, 193, 207–8, 215, 222
Sikhism, 182, 217
Sin, sins, 124, 137, 158–59, 167–71, 190, 217, 231
Skepticism, 19, 51, 97, 105, 116, 202, 247, 251
Smith, Adam, 124, 148, 193, 197–98
  Moral Sentiments, 198–99
Sociology, 53, 61, 79, 88–95, 115, 177, 252
Socrates, 8, 24, 55, 113, 140, 147, 155–56
Sola Scriptura, 220

Soli Deo Gloria, 220
Soteriology, 113–14, 122, 161, 186
Soul, Plato's theory of the, 8–10, 18, 41–42, 148
Spirit, 11–12, 23–25, 31, 42, 156, 159, 167, 169, 172, 216, 242, 246
State of nature, 165–66, 234–41, 243, 250, 254
Steinfels, Peter, 120
   Scandinavian Nonbelievers, 120
Stoicism, 5, 10–13, 143, 149–50, 152, 163
Stoics, 10–12, 149–50
Subjective truth, 22
Subjectivity, 5, 17, 24, 31, 53–54, 59–60, 162, 213–14, 232, 234
Substance, 22, 35, 70–73, 76–78, 81, 83, 85, 99, 155, 163
Swedenborg, Emanuel, 162, 185
Syllogism, 55
Systematic religion, 113–14, 120–21, 145–56, 159, 161–73

T

Taxonomy, 36, 55, 70, 74, 241
Taylor, Christopher, 10
   Aristotle on Practical Reason, 10
Teachings of Jesus, 167, 224
Telos, teleology, 20–21, 33–34, 37–38, 50, 106, 128
Temple of Apollo, 117
Test of truth, 56
Theism, 113, 116, 127–28, 131, 142, 148, 177, 217
Theistic monism, 10
Theology, 6–7, 10, 12–14, 121–22, 140, 152, 158–60, 167–69, 216, 228, 253
Theory of Moral Sentiments, 198
Theory of punishment, 131, 251
Theory of truth, 56–58, 67, 111, 211
Thermodynamics, 54, 85
Things:
   a thing-in-itself, 118
   things-in-themselves, 17, 58–59, 109
Thoughts, 60, 63–64, 66, 69–70, 73–74, 77–79, 97–98, 103–4
Timaeus, 9–10, 144, 148, 155

Titans, Titanic, 146
Tolerant religions, 189
Torah, 159–60
True atheism, 113–16, 126, 131, 133, 191, 251
Truth, theories of, 57
Twilight of Idols, 173

U

Universal minimum religion, 113–21, 123–47, 189, 212–19, 234–35, 253
Utilitarianism, 198, 207–12, 232

V

Vague concept of reason, 44–45, 47, 49, 51, 53, 55, 57–59, 127, 216
Varieties of Religious Experience, 137–38, 164, 231

W

Wagner, Richard, 173–74, 176–78
   Religion and Art, 172–74
Walschots, Michael, 202
   Hutcheson and Kant, 202
Will, good will, 22, 166, 203, 211–12, 221, 236, 249, 251, 254
William of Ockham, 14
Williams, Bernard, 33
   Morality, 33
Wippel, John, 14
Wisdom of God, 13
Wittgenstein's Philosophical Investigations, 69
Wojtkowiak, Joanna, 182
   Emerging Ritual Practices, 182
World Prison Brief, 251
   Prison Population Total, 251

Z

Zeno, 5, 10
   of Citium, 10
   Stoicism, 5
Zerin, Edward, 167–68
   Karl Popper on God, 168
Zeus (king of the gods), 11, 144–46

www.ingramcontent.com/pod-product-compliance
Lightning Source LLC
Chambersburg PA
CBHW071243230426
43668CB00011B/1564